The Prenatal Epoch

THE
PRENATAL EPOCH

BY

E. H. BAILEY

Editor of " The British Journal of Astrology "
Fellow of the Astrological Society of America, Inc.

ASTROLOGY CLASSICS
2007

First published in 1916

On the cover: Vera

ISBN   1 933303 24 7

This edition published 2007 by
Astrology Classics

the publication division of
The Astrology Center of America
207 Victory Lane
Bel Air, MD 21014

on the web at
http://www.AstroAmerica.com

CONTENTS.

CONTENTS

INTRODUCTION.

In commencing a book on the subject of the PRENATAL EPOCH—a thesis of immense value to the Astrological student, though misunderstood by many, and attacked and misrepresented by others—it is necessary for me to make several comments and explanations by way of introduction.

First of all, it is my particular wish, for the sake of whatever posterity may read my work, that, by whatever independent or original lines my study of the epoch was taken, it be distinctly understood that, so far as the actual theory is concerned—its discovery, basis, laws, rules of calculation, and its practical value in relation to Natal Astrology—I do not, with the exception of a few minor points, claim any originality whatever. The entire honour and credit for the discovery of the theory and the elaboration of its principles, belongs to the Astrologer and Orientalist—better known to the Astrological world as " Sepharial "—in collaboration with " E. S."—scientist and technicologist and a man of world-wide repute—after some years of patient investigation and research, based upon data supplied by an obstetric surgeon of wide experience, who fully appreciated the importance of accuracy, and was aware of the uses to which such data would be put. Where the reputation, honesty and integrity of such men are involved, the criticisms which have been levelled against them, and which have been emphatically disproved by a practical appeal to facts, can be instantly dismissed and utterly disregarded by all students of the theorem.

So far as I am personally concerned—and I claim to have had more experience with this particular theory than any other living Astrologer, saving only Sepharial himself—what I have to state in these pages is the result of some seventeen years of close study and investigation of its principles, and the application of its rules to many hundreds of horoscopes. Original notes and commentations by way of explaining and elucidating the different points of the theory are added.

My actual study of the epochal theory was a unique one, and commenced some twenty-one years ago, after seeing the first articles on the subject by Sepharial in the *Astrologer's Magazine.* As the complete rules were not given, only those for regular epochs being stated, I made very little headway, continually coming across cases where the rules were apparent failures.   In the winter of 1898, having obtained from the registers of births and deaths in a certain district in England a long and reliable list of the birth data of people who had died, together with the cause of death as certified by the medical man in attendance— a large proportion of these cases being infants, and including a considerable number of twin births and a few triplets where one or all had died—I applied the rules of the epoch, as laid down in the "New Manual of Astrology" by Sepharial, to some 250 of these horoscopes.   My primary object was to find some explanation of the Astrological cause of Infant Mortality, so many horoscopes of children who had died an early death being contradictory and anomalous, and incidentally to test the entire theory of the prenatal epoch as expounded by its discoverer.

My researches were rewarded by some important discoveries, not only in connection with the primary object of my study, but also in connection with the epoch itself. My investigations proved to me that the entire theory was based on a sound and scientific foundation, and that even more than had been actually claimed for it could be not only supported, but actually proved.   Since that time I have had continued experience in rectifying hundreds of horoscopes, and have formulated a series of rules for the calculation of birth times from past events solely by reference to the epoch.   I have, in fact, some of the most remarkable evidence of the absolute truth of the theory which could possibly be known, some of which will be produced in the pages of this book.

Like all great discoveries, the process of time and the opening up of new lines of thought, together with the fact that with all the published rules there were found a certain number of horoscopes which would not conform thereto, have brought about certain important developments and extensions of the theory.   Those of my readers who have followed the elaboration of the theory through the pages of the various Astrological journals will find several variations from the original rules as given in the " New Manual of Astrology."

During the last two years considerable progress has been made in the development of the theory, and several points which had previously been somewhat vague and ill-defined were made the subject of an exhaustive inquiry, and definite conclusions obtained.

The first important development was in connection with the " count " from the moon to the horizon. It had originally been put forward that in the case of " irregular epochs," with the moon above and increasing, or below and decreasing, the " count " was to be made from the moon to the horizon to which it was moving in its diurnal rotation, thus *increasing* the period of gestation by a number of days equal to the moon's distance from such horizon divided by thirteen. This process, however, contradicted one of the prime laws of the epoch, which was to the effect that when the moon was placed as just stated the period of gestation was *less* than the norm.

This contradiction was adjusted in the following manner. The " count " was still to be made to the horizon to which the moon was moving, but in the reverse way. When the moon was increasing and above, it was to be made from the moon to the ascendant and then round under the earth to the descendant, and when decreasing and below, from the moon to the descendant and then round over the earth to the ascendant. In both cases the prime law of the epoch was complied with, but the period of gestation was decreased by a further fourteen days. Likewise, when the moon was increasing and below, or decreasing and above, the same extension of the count was found necessary, in these cases *increasing* the period of gestation by an additional fourteen days.

The credit for this extension of the epochal theory rests entirely with Sepharial, who privately communicated the facts to me in order that I might give them a thorough examination by applying them to numerous horoscopes. This I did, with the result that I was convinced that the original method was altogether incorrect, and that the new method was the right one, and strictly in compliance with the prime laws of the epoch.

A second development, to which attention was drawn in the pages of the *British Journal of Astrology*, was in connection with the several sex degrees. In Sepharial s ' Cosmic Symbolism,'' the table of sex degrees differed from that given in his " New Manual of Astrology," the difference being in the fifth degrees of the common signs, and the twenty-fifth of the cardinal signs. The original arrangement was that of the Sephirothal cadence ; the new one was in accordance with a later discovery of Sepharial, known as the " Law of Polarity."

When my attention was called to this difference I communicated with Sepharial, and, for the purpose of testing this Law of Polarity and the new arrangement of sex degrees, he invited me to supply him with a number of birth data in which the altered sex degrees were involved. The examination of these cases proved conclusively that the new arrangement was vastly superior to the old one, and, after personally testing a number of other horoscopes affected by this re-arrangement, I decided to definitely accept it. Since then I have had no occasion to revert to the former arrangement.

The most important development of the epochal theory was in connection with the determination of sex from the epoch, and in this particular matter I may honestly claim a certain amount of credit. It had originally been put forward that the orb of influence of a sex degree was, roughly speaking, three degrees, and that, when outside this limit, the determining factor of sex was the quadrant held by the moon at the time of the epoch. In the course of my investigations it had been conclusively proved to me that it was quite impossible in a large number of cases to get the moon in the required quadrant at the epoch, and that either some important factor was missing or that the orb of the sex degrees was inadequate.

I communicated my views to Sepharial, who informed me that for some time past he had regarded the orb of the sex degrees as extending half way between each sex point—a distance of $6\frac{3}{7}°$. With this suggestion before me, I put the matter to a final test, and, after examining fifty new horoscopes, I came to the conclusion that, so far as the moon was concerned, Sepharial was quite correct. But I also discovered an equally important point. The ascending degree of the epoch, to be within orbs of a sex degree, had to be within $4\frac{2}{7}$ of the exact sex point, and that when outside of that limit it had no sex influence and was to be considered as negative. Since making this discovery, I have rectified some dozens of horoscopes, and have found no reason to modify or alter this conclusion. The manner in which this discovery is applied to the epoch will be shown in the following pages.

Other developments and elaborations of the laws of the epoch have also been made, and will be duly dealt with in their appropriate place.

In conclusion, I have to state that the whole of my study and investigation of the laws and principles of the epoch have convinced me, beyond the shadow of a doubt, that it is not a " plausible delusion " or " fancy," as prejudiced and shortsighted critics have unsuccessfully tried to label it, but it is a grand, indisputable truth, founded on a strict mathematical and scientific law, a veritable mine of the most valuable information, and an important adjunct to the study of Natal Astrology.

On this point I am fully prepared to stake my whole Astrological reputation, and to stand or fall with it.

E. H. BAILEY.

THE PRENATAL EPOCH.

CHAPTER I.

OBJECTIONS ANSWERED AND REFUTED.

BEFORE commencing to explain the principles of the prenatal epoch, and the application of its laws to Natal Astrology, I think it will be for the benefit of my readers to deal with the various objections which have been brought against the theory. At first I was sorely tempted to disregard these objections, but on second thoughts I decided to deal with them and clear away any misconceptions which may have arisen in the minds of students, and enable them to follow the succeeding chapters clearly and succinctly.

The first public presentation of the prenatal epoch was in the *Astrologer's Magazine*, Vol. I, where the general rules for the calculation of regular epochs were briefly stated. The publication of these rules was the signal for a considerable amount of argument and adverse criticism, and, unfortunately, a great deal of misrepresentation and personal *animus* crept into the discussions, and this has continued up to the present day. It must be stated, however, that—with all their arguments against, and misrepresentations of, the theory—its opponents have never succeeded in demolishing its basis, nor proving it to be unsound or unscientific, but have been signally worsted and defeated in every encounter.

Unfortunately, the opposition to the proper acceptance of the theory arose mainly through the bigoted attitude and prejudice of certain ill-informed astrologers, who could not think for five minutes in a straight line, and who had a more or less superficial knowledge of the science, and still less of the theory in question, and hence were totally incapable of giving a fair and unbiassed opinion thereon. Their objections have repeatedly been proved to be both illogical and groundless, so much so that I have been compelled to state, in the *British Journal of Astrology*, that for the future

I intend to ignore absolutely and completely their belated criticisms. A certain amount of commiseration must be extended to some of these misguided critics, because the subject is a highly technical one, and a considerable amount of medical and obstetric knowledge is necessary to a full and proper understanding of its basis and laws. Their ordinary knowledge of the science was wild and vague, and the deeper mysteries of such a subject as the laws of generation were far beyond their mental powers. Many were the senseless and illogical remarks, such as " delusion," " fancy," " an invention of the devil to bring discredit on the science," etc., etc., hurled against the epoch, but such only served to show the utter ignorance of the theory, as well as the crass stupidity and narrow-mindedness of those who gave vent to these inane expressions.

The chief critic and opponent of the theory was the well-known Astrologer, Raphael, the author of numerous works on the science. His chief objections were levelled against the accepted length of the period of human gestation, one of the primary factors in the calculation of the epoch, and to the fact of the epoch occurring, as it sometimes did in the case of a first child, some few days before the marriage of the parents. Apart from the fact that he repeatedly showed a very bigoted and obtuse attitude when discussing the question, his main contention that he could not accept a prenatal epoch other than conception was not altogether lacking in reason or logic. He has publicly stated that he was never opposed to the idea of a prenatal epoch, but that he refused to accept the basis of the present theory. To use his own words (vide *British Journal of Astrology*, Vol. VII, page 84), " I have never denied that there is a prenatal epoch, but what I say is, that Sepharial's method is not correct."

Now, this objection of Raphael that the epoch should be identical with conception, or at least with either coition or impregnation, is, as stated, not altogether lacking in reason or logic, and is one which, to any ordinary mind, might be taken as containing a considerable amount of truth. But a little reflection will show that some important points were overlooked.

First of all, what are impregnation and conception ? Do these physiological facts take place in an instant ? Are they distinct moments of time, or slow and gradual processes extending over a period of from one to five days, this being the time given by obstetricians "during which, *at any moment*, and from a single coitus, conception may take place." Now, if impregnation and conception are gradual processes, a figure of the heavens cannot be erected for them, and this objection is therefore at once ruled out of court. Further than this, the author of the theory has laid down, as a distinct and authoritative ruling, that the prenatal epoch is not coincident in point of time with either coition, impregnation, or any of the preliminary stages of generation, and, from a study of a number of horoscopes—where the necessary information as to the period of pregnancy, etc., and in some cases the date of marriage have been given—I can confirm this ruling.

On more than one occasion I have had an open discussion with Raphael in the pages of Astrological magazines, but, though I have not succeeded in breaking down the barrier of prejudice which seemed to cloud the mind of my redoubtable opponent, I have never conceded a single point, nor withdrawn from the contention I have always held, viz., that the prenatal epoch—as discovered by Sepharial, and demonstrated by the latter and myself—is the real and true epoch. These discussions, however, have not been barren of results, but have brought to light much evidence of a remarkable nature wholly confirmatory of the basic principles of the epoch. In addition to this, they have elicited the fact that Raphael was imperfectly versed in the working principles of the theory, and his own tacit admission that he had not spent much time in calculating epochs, was a fatal blow to his objections, and deprived him of any legitimate right to be considered a fair and impartial critic of the theory.

Moreover, the general trend of his objections was purely supposititious, merely personal ideas arising from a complete misconception of the entire theory, and more or less only indirectly connected with the actual principles of the epoch. Further than this, the learned Astrologer, in the course of his latest argument on the theory, unconsciously tripped into more than one admission of the chief points of the epochal theory. Still, in spite of this, it has always been my opinion that there has been a certain amount of sincerity in Raphael's attitude, and I am quite willing to admit his objection to accepting an epoch other than conception to be both genuine and reasonable.

The next objection is rather a delicate one, and arises solely from the inability of certain Astrologers to see beyond a certain point. The purely rule-of-thumb methods of Astrology were to them the *ultima thule* of the whole science, and the supposition that at the back of all this was a hidden mystery connected with the why and wherefore of planetary influence was to them a tabooed subject. This is regrettable, but unfortunately there is a spice of prejudice and personal feeling in the matter. This objection has its origin in the fact that the acceptance of the prenatal epoch is the " open door " to certain Theosophical tenets, especially the doctrines of Reincarnation and Karma. But is it so ? There is no disputing the point that to those who study Astrology on esoteric lines the acceptance of the prenatal epoch does most emphatically involve the acceptance of these doctrines. At the same time, it is also indisputable—and on this point I challenge contradiction—that the prenatal epoch can be explained in the light of ordinary accepted scientific and religious beliefs, and need not in any way become mixed up with Theosophy or occult science. I sincerely hope that this statement will be the means of many taking up an impartial study of the theory, and will do away with a large amount of the misconception prevalent with regard to the real truth about the prenatal epoch.

Another objection, and unfortunately the worst, relates to those imaginary cases where the times of birth were altered 40 minutes to make them suit the epoch, and shows the amount of harm done by relying upon incompetent calculators, or rather on those who attempt to calculate epochs without first learning and thoroughly understanding the rules.

Several of these cases were submitted to me for examination, but, on applying the proper rules, I found that no such alteration was required, but that the epoch confirmed the recorded birth-time. Two cases in particular may be here mentioned. The first was one where the time was stated as a few minutes to eleven in the morning, the moon being just above the eastern horizon and decreasing in light. The calculator made the moon's place at birth *rise* at the epoch, and this gave the time as 37 minutes *past* eleven. When the rules were applied correctly the time was found to be twelve minutes before the hour, exactly confirming the recorded time. The second case was similar, the time being given as just before five in the evening, the moon being increasing and above the horizon. The astute calculator made the moon's birthplace *set* at the epoch, and brought the moon to the descendant angle—an utterly erroneous procedure. The time was then stated to be 27 minutes after the hour. The rules properly followed out gave the correct time as nine minutes to the hour, in accordance with the estimate given.

The third objection, quite a new one, is made in the "Combined Introductory Astrology," by Mr. Govind H. Keskar, who states that the prenatal epoch cannot be recommended, as it does not allow for short-period births. Such an astounding statement as this must be met at once with a flat and unqualified contradiction. Seeing that Mr. Keskar admits that he did not begin to study Astrology until 1904, he ought to have known that prior to that date the entire theory had been explained and its connection with short and long period, normal and abnormal births, fully and completely demonstrated.

The question of the whereabouts of the mother at the time of the epoch was brought forward as another objection, and in his Almanac for 1914 Raphael asked the question why prenatal maps were set out for the latitude and longitude of birth, although the parties might be thousands of miles away. This objection was ruled out of court by the fact that it had been distinctly stated, more than twenty years since, that it was absolutely necessary to know the latitude and longitude in which the mother was residing at the time of the epoch. In ordinary practice it is usual to compute the epoch for the same locality as the birth, and it has been shown that, unless there is some considerable distance between the place of residence at birth and epoch, the difference of locality would cause such a minute discrepancy in the birth-time as to be hardly worth troubling about.

Probably the most absurd and illogical objection made against the epoch was that of a well-known Astrologer, a man of more than ordinary abilities. It was, to use his own words: " Whatever moment of the day you may choose, whether it be a birth-time or not, it is always possible to calculate such an epoch as the one under discussion, and it will never alter the time originally chosen more than the amount of an error of observation as regards the original time selected, whether such error was caused by an incorrect watch or clock or in any other manner, and such calculations will allow a fair pecentage of ‘accurate observations to have been made.’ This is a deadly thing for the validity of the epoch in relation to nativities."

This objection is a most egregious one, and without the slightest basis in fact or theory. This gentleman showed that he possessed but a very superficial knowledge of the subject, and was evidently ignorant of the fact that the whole question of the calculation depended upon the sex of the subject, and that the epoch could not be applied to something which was not a birth-time. When my readers come to the chapters detailing the *modus operandi* of the epochal calculations, they will see for themselves the utter fatuousness of the objection put forward, and the amazing ignorance of the formulator of this most absurd contention.

The last objection I will deal with was made privately to me, and was to the effect that, after the horoscope had been corrected by the epoch, Primary directions calculated from such rectified horoscope did not measure to known events in life. This objection I must at once say is utterly groundless. I can bring forward a large number of horoscopes which have been rectified by both Primary directions and the epoch and the times of birth obtained have been found to agree within a very few seconds. In a later chapter I shall deal with this objection by bringing forward some of these cases.

SECTION I.

The Scientific Basis and Laws of the Epoch.

CHAPTER II.

THE ASTRO-PHYSIOLOGICAL BASIS OF THE EPOCH.

IN order to explain the scientific basis of the prenatal epoch, both from an astrological and physiological basis, and to make clear and explicit certain procedure required in its practical application to the horoscope of birth, it is first of all necessary to know what the epoch is, when it occurs, and what relation it bears to the physiological processes of human generation.

Astrologically considered, the prenatal epoch is a certain moment of time, occurring approximately at the commencement of the gestative period—in some cases a few days before, and in others a few days later—when the degree ascending on the eastern horizon, and the longitude of the moon thereat, interchange with the longitude of the moon and the degree ascending at birth, or their respective opposite points.

In other words, there occurs in all cases a certain moment— not coincident *in point of time* with any of the preliminary stages of generation, but occurring approximately at the commencement of the period of gestation, and related to the time of the coitus by a certain mathematical law—when the ascending degree at such time is the place held by the moon at birth, or its opposite point, and the moon at such time is the place of the ascending degree at birth, or its opposite point.

This general law of the epoch shows that the epoch is definitely related to the birth moment by the interchange of certain positions ; in other words, the epoch is related to the birth solely and entirely by lunar tradition, *i.e.* by the passage of the moon's influence from one set of astral conditions to another that is in *horoscopical relations* with it. Every birth is, therefore, directly connected with the epoch, and every authentic natural birth will, within the limits of an error of observation, yield an epoch in accordance with the rules to be hereafter given.

But we must now come to a consideration of the physiological basis of the epoch, and of the mysteries connected with the laws of human generation. I have used certain terms in the preceding paragraphs which require explanation.

The chief stages in the generation of a human being are : (1) The coitus, or act of generation—an important moment, and directly related to the horoscope of birth by a certain well-defined law ; (2) Impregnation, the contact or union of the male fluid (spermatoza) with the female ovum, after which the ovum is immediately sent on its developmental history ; (3) Quickening, or period of viability, the half-way period between impregnation and birth ; and (4) The actual birth of the child.

The period of time from the coitus to the impregnation varies from one to five days, this being the time allowed by obstetricians " during which, at any moment, and from a single coitus, conception may occur." Moreover, the period usually agreed upon by medical authorities is that impregnation can only occur from a coitus which takes place within five days before or after menstruation. This particular period of five days is the extreme length of time the male fluid (spermatoza) is capable of vivifying power, and unless before that period has expired it meets an ovum it then dies. The period from impregnation to birth is one of 273 days, approximately nine calendar months, and equalling ten revolutions of the moon. A lunar revolution —i.e. the return of the moon to the same longitude it previously held—is equal to 27·32 days, and ten similar revolutions are equal to 273 days. The period of quickening occurs at four-and-a-half calendar months, or five revolutions of the moon.

It must, of course, be perfectly understood that these periods relate to normal births, and are the average periods as deduced from obstetric observations. Considerable variations occur, and births take place at seven, eight, and even ten months from conception. All these, however, are fully allowed for in the laws governing the epochal theory, and will be clearly demonstrated in later chapters.

Now this period of 273 days is what is termed the " period of gestation," or pregnancy, and the following extract from " The Modern Physician," edited by Dr. Andrew Wilson, F.R.S.E., F.S.L., &c., will have particular bearing on the question and its relation to the laws of the epochal theory :—

" The normal and natural duration of pregnancy becomes naturally a subject of much importance, because it bears an intimate relation to the period at which the confinement may be expected. A normal pregnancy lasts, as a rule, for 280 days, but great variations occasionally are found, first on the side of pregnancies which may be of shorter duration, and still more on the side of those which extend beyond the period just named.   There is little doubt that allowance must be made for a certain period both below and above the normal duration of pregnancy, seeing that variations may exist here, as in respect of other functions of the human frame."

This extract makes it clear and explicit that medical science confirms the general law of the epoch.   It is. distinctly stated that " allowance must be made for a certain period both below and above the normal period of pregnancy."   The general law of the epoch is that the period of pregnancy will extend on either side of the normal period of 273 days by a certain period dependent upon the distance of the moon from either the eastern or western horizon, according to strict and well defined rules.

The following further quotation from the medical work referred to gives a more definite statement as to the period at which the birth may be expected to occur :—

" The usual way to estimate when labour will occur is that of calculating 280 days from the first day of the last menstrual period of the woman.   But, as regards the actual occurrence of confinement, the rule which probably brings us nearer to the actual date of the confinement is that of counting three months backward from the last day of the last menstrual period, and of adding seven days.   According to this rule, a woman who ceased to menstruate on the 1st of January would fall due to be confined on the 8th of October following.   This rule depends on the fact that probably she will have conceived a few days after menstruation has ceased."

The period usually agreed upon by obstetricians is that impregnation can only take place from a coitus which takes place within five days from the last day of menstruation.

Now, from January 1st to October 8th is a period of 280

days, and, allowing for the stage between the coitus and impregnation, we get the mean normal period of 273 days.

In reference to the statement above that allowance must be made for a certain period both above and below the normal period of pregnancy, the following obstetric statistics will prove confirmatory thereof.

Births occurring in the 36th week, 246 to 252 days, 3%

,,	,,	,,	37th	,,	253 to 259	,, 11%
,,	,,	,,	38th	,,	260 to 266	,, 12%
,,	,,	,,	39th	,,	267 to 273	,, 29%
,,	,,	,,	40th	,,	274 to 280	,, 19%
,,	,,	,,	41st	,,	281 to 287	,, 14%
,,	,,	,,	42nd	,,	288 to 294	,, 9%
,,	,,	,,	43rd	,,	295 to 301	,, 3%

There are a few variations from these figures, such as six and seven months, but they are abnormal, and not of frequent occurrence. Equally, it may be said that there are births over the 43rd week. This point will be dealt with in due course.

The general law of the epoch allows for fourteen days on either side of the normal period of 273 days, or 39 weeks, and the above table shows that 74% of cases do actually take place within that period. Certain variations exist, in which the period is increased or curtailed for a further 14 days, making 28 days on either side of the 273rd day, and, where these variations are concerned with purely normal cases, the whole 100% is covered by these laws.

Hence the remarkable agreement between obstetric laws and the general laws of the epochal theory is a conclusive proof of the validity of the epoch as calculated, and a direct refutation of the various objections made against it.

CHAPTER III.

THE PRACTICAL USES OF THE EPOCH.

THE practical uses of the prenatal epoch in the scientific exposition of Natal Astrology are many and varied, and it is now necessary that I should fully detail and explain these uses before taking any further steps in the elucidation of the theory.

The prenatal epoch was first put forward as a method of rectification of doubtful horoscopes, and its practical value in the correction of all birth-times, as well as of uncertain or approximate times, cannot be too highly estimated. Let it be clearly understood what is meant by " uncertain " and " approximate " birth-times. Statements to the effect that a birth took place " about ten in the morning," or " just as the sun was rising " are frequently heard of. Cases have occurred where a doubt has arisen as to whether the time was fifteen minutes before the hour or fifteen minutes after. Apply the rules of the epoch in such cases and the correct time of birth to the exact second can be obtained. This is an indisputable fact, and has been proved time after time.

The correct moment of birth is an absolute essential, and I make it a hard-and-fast rule that every birth-time, no matter how carefully noted, should be rectified before the horoscope is cast. It is a practice I have rigidly adhered to in my own private study of the theory, and it is also one that I must honestly insist upon if a correct and scientific reading of the horoscope is desired.

Not one in a hundred medical men take more than a casual notice of the birth-moment, while many never look at their watches until the umbilical cord is cut, which may not take place until several minutes after actual birth ; so that it becomes a virtual necessity that all birth-moments should be rectified by this theory, which I have long ago expressed as " the only reliable method of rectification."

The second point of practical utility derived from the epoch is that it determines approximately the actual period of human gestation. The normal period of gestation, as shown in the previous chapter, is one of 273 days, equal to ten lunar revolutions or nine calendar months. The position of the moon in relation to the sun and horizon, as will be explained, increases or decreases this period from one to fourteen days. This, of course, refers to normal cases, and not to short or long-period births. The practical value of this will be shown later in the examples given.

The third point of value is the determination of sex, for a properly calculated epoch, *i.e.* one in exact agreement with the laws, *must* define the sex of the subject. In other words, " sex " is the determining factor in the calculation of all epochs. This point will also be fully explained and illustrated later.

A further proof of the practical value of the epoch is strongly in evidence in the determining of the character and general fortunes from the planetary and zodiacal influences operating in the epochal figure. If we are to accept the occult theory that the prenatal epoch is the descent of the Monad to the Astral plane, then it must show the inherent character of the Ego which is about to reincarnate. It may be here stated that the epoch has more intimate relationship with the Individual than the horoscope of birth, the latter appearing to reflect the personality and its hereditary tendencies and the environment. In other words, the epoch represents the Man about to manifest in the flesh, and the horoscope denotes the actual personal conditions and environment into which he is born.

Another indisputable proof of the value of the epoch in the scientific exposition of Astrology is in connection with the horoscopes of twins. The divergencies of character and fortune in twins are not detectable from the horoscopes of birth, since such would be identical, or but slightly different. Not only in these cases do the epochs illustrate this difference of character and fortune, but they confirm the difference in the time of birth to within the limits of an ordinary error of observation.

A further proof of its invaluable practical use lies in the fact that it illustrates all anomalies in horoscopes, and is the only known means whereby prenatal affections, accidents *in utero,* and physical abnormalities can be ascertained. Children are born with some physical defect, some organ is abnormally developed, or entirely absent. While pregnant the mother suffered from shock, received a blow, or had an injury, and this affected the child in some form or another. The horoscope of birth is inadequate to show the cause of this abnormality, but in the epoch the solution is to be found. Many illustrations of such cases have been given in Astrological magazines, and other interesting cases will be given in a later chapter of this book.

Its value is even more strongly shown in the calculation of directions from the epochal figure. The same rules as those for computing directions from the horoscope can be applied to the figure for the prenatal epoch, and directions will be found not only to agree with the known events of life but frequently filling up blanks occurring in the directions derived from the horoscope. Most particularly is this shown in connection with infant mortality. Death occurs only a few months after birth. There are no directions to indicate the cause or the time thereof. The figure for the prenatal epoch supplies the deficiency. This is, again, a fact which has never been disproved.

In the question of infant mortality the prenatal epoch has a most important and far-reaching influence. Children are born at apparently favourable moments, with little or no affliction to the hyleg, yet their lives are short, perhaps only a few weeks or a few months, or even only two or three days. The horoscope of birth is utterly inadequate to explain these apparent anomalies. Turn to the epoch, and there will be found the master key. The death in infancy is due to the affliction of the moon at the epoch. This is again another point in favour of the validity of the epoch as calculated, and no valid objection can be raised, in a single instance, against the truth of this statement.

The last, but not the least, of the important uses and value of the epoch is that it forms the final and clinching argument in the calculation of doubtful horoscopes. I always have been, and always shall be, a strong opponent of those questionable figures which are more or less based on a few Primary arcs without any reference to the general language of the horoscope, but where an estimated time of birth is checked by reference to the epoch, and directions from the latter found to agree with known events in life, there can be no disputing the accuracy of the horoscope. This view, I know, will not be shared by all, but where a question of principle, coupled with actual experience, is concerned, opinions which are more or less prejudiced must go to the wall.

Summing up the contents of this chapter, the points of value and practical utility of the epoch are as follows :—

(1.) Rectification of approximate horoscopes and confirmation of the times of birth in authentic cases within the limits of an ordinary error of observation.

(2.) It determines approximately the observed period of human gestation, and affords unquestionable proof of the ancient teaching that the moon is the chief controller of human generation.

(3.) It is the only known means of determining the sex of the native.

(4.) It has special relation to the character and fortunes of the individual, in contradistinction to the horoscope of birth which is related to the personality and the present environment.

(5.) It is the key to the divergencies of character and fortune in twins.

(6.) It is particularly illustrative of all anomalies in the horoscope of birth, and the only known means of solving the problems of prenatal affections, accidents *in utero*, and abnormalities of birth.

(7.) It is the key to the anomalies in directional Astrology, and the solution to the present unsatisfactory condition of that branch of the science.

(8.) It is the master key to the subject of infant mortality.

(9.) It is the final and conclusive argument in the calculation of estimated horoscopes.

These are points I shall more particularly deal with, and I am prepared to sustain my views and opinions by a practical appeal to facts in order to prove that the prenatal epoch has in reality a solid basis and foundation in scientific Astrology.

CHAPTER IV.

The Laws of the Prenatal Epoch.

The general law of the prenatal epoch is stated to be due to the philosopher, Hermes Trismegistus. The only evidence to be obtained, however, is that the statement attributed to him, and known as the " Trutine of Hermes," consists of the somewhat vague, and, like many other initial statements of a great natural law, incomplete dictum that " the place of the moon at conception was the ascendant of the birth figure or its opposite point."

Investigations into this statement tended to confirm not only its verity, but also brought to light the fact that it was one half of a very important law, for while the ascendant or descendant of the birth figure was the place of the moon at a certain epoch, the ascendant or its opposite at this epoch was the place of the moon at birth—a remarkable interchange of factors.

Additional investigation settled the point as to when the moon's place and ascendant, or the moon's opposite place and descendant, should interchange, and the main postulate of the epoch was put forward in the following four clearly defined laws :—

(1.) When the moon at birth is increasing in light (*i.e.* going from the new to the full moon) it will be the ascending degree at the epoch, and the moon at the epoch will be the degree ascending at birth.

(2.) When the moon at birth is decreasing in light (*i.e.* going from the full to the new moon) it will be the descending degree at the epoch, and the moon at the epoch will be the degree descending at birth.

(3.) When the moon at birth is (*a*) increasing in light and below the earth, or (*b*) decreasing in light and above the earth, the period of gestation will be longer than the norm.

(4.) When the moon at birth is (*a*) increasing in light and above the earth, or (*b*) decreasing in light and below the earth, the period of gestation will be shorter than the norm.

From these four laws arose what are termed the " Four

Orders of Regular Epochs," each order depending on the position of the moon in regard to the sun and ascendant.

The four orders of epochs are as follows :—

TABLE I.

Order.	Formation.	Period of gestation.
1	☽ above and increasing	273 days − x
2	☽ above and decreasing	273 days + x
3	☽ below and increasing	273 days + x
4	☽ below and decreasing	273 days − x

Before going further, it will be necessary to explain the foregoing laws and to show how the norm, or period of 273 days, is increased or decreased according to the position of the moon in regard to the horizon.

The norm is a period of nine calendar or ten lunar months, equal to 273 days, counted backwards from the date of birth, and it measures to within two or three days of the same day of the month as the day of birth, and the moon on that day is in the same sign and about the same degree as it held at birth. Thus, suppose for example a birth takes place in London on October 29th, 1915, at noon. Nine calendar or ten lunar months counted backwards from this date measure to January 29th, and on that day the moon is in nearly the same position.

The date, which is exactly ten revolutions of the moon prior to the date of birth, is called the " Index Date," and all the subsequent calculations commence from that particular date. It is exactly 273 days before birth.

With regard to the 273 days + or − x, shown in the above table, the normal period of gestation is increased or decreased in accordance with the distance of the moon from either the ascendant or descendant, and the x is a certain number of days equal to this distance in degrees and minutes, divided by 13—the average daily motion of the moon.

In Orders Nos. 1 and 4, the distance of the moon from the horizon last crossed, divided by 13, gives the number of days by which this period is to be curtailed, and in Orders Nos. 2 and 3, the distance of the moon from the horizon to which it is approaching, divided by 13, gives the number of days by which the period is to be increased.

It will now be seen that the controlling factors in the calculation of the prenatal epoch are the sun, moon, and ascendant. The relationship of the two luminaries determines whether the ascendant and moon at birth shall interchange with the moon and ascendant at the epoch, or their respective opposite points, while the moon's position in regard to the sun and ascendant determines the exact period of gestation.

The following diagrams and explanations of the four Orders of Epochs will show this procedure in a clear and concise manner :—

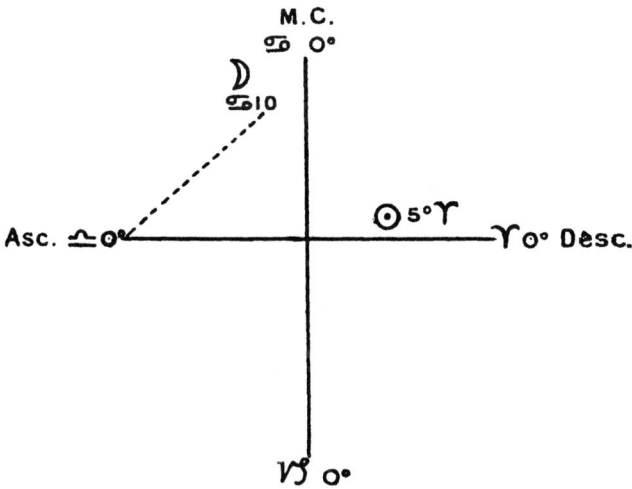

Fig. 1.

ORDER NO. I.—*Moon above the earth, and increasing in light.* By Table I. the period of gestation is 273 days — x.

The above illustration shows the moon in Cancer 10°, above the earth and increasing in light ; it is only just past the square of the sun in Aries 5°, and, therefore, between the new and full. The moon being increasing, the "count" is made to the ascendant; in other words, the longitude of the moon is subtracted from that of the ascendant. The distance from Cancer 10° to Libra 0° is 80°, as shown

by the dotted line, and this, divided by 13—the average
daily motion of the moon—yields 6 and 2 over.   This represents a little more than six days by which the period of
273 days is to be curtailed, so that the epoch will fall six
days *after* the index date, the 273rd day before birth.
It will then be in Libra 0°.

ORDER NO. 2.—*Moon above, and decreasing in light.*
Reference to Table I. will show that the period of gestation
is 273 days + *x*.

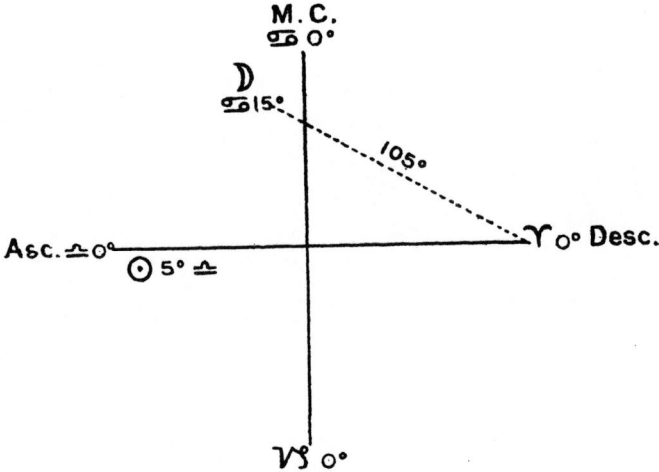

FIG. 2.

In this illustration, the moon is in Cancer 15°, above the
earth, and, as will be seen from the position of the sun,
decreasing in light, *i.e.* being from full to new moon.   As
the moon is decreasing, the " count " is made to the descendant, along the dotted line.   In other words, the longitude
of the descendant is subtracted from that of the moon.
The distance from Aries 0° to Cancer 15° is equal to 105°,
which, divided by 13—the moon's daily motion—gives 8 and
1 over.   This denotes that the normal period of gestation,
273 days, is to be increased by eight days, and that the
epoch will fall eight days *before* the index date.   It will
then be in Aries 0°.

ORDER NO. 3.—*Moon below, and increasing in light.*
Reference to Table I. shows the period of gestation to be
273 days — *x*.

In the diagram below we find the moon below the earth,
in the 25th degree of the sign Capricorn, and as it is going
away from the sun it is increasing in light. The "count"
is, therefore, made from the moon to the ascendant, and
from Libra 0° to Capricorn 25° is a distance of 115°. This
distance, divided by 13—the moon's daily motion—gives
nearly 9 (nine times thirteen being 117), and, therefore, the
normal period of gestation is to be increased by nine days.
The epoch will, therefore, fall nine days *before* the index
date, and it will then be in Libra 0°.

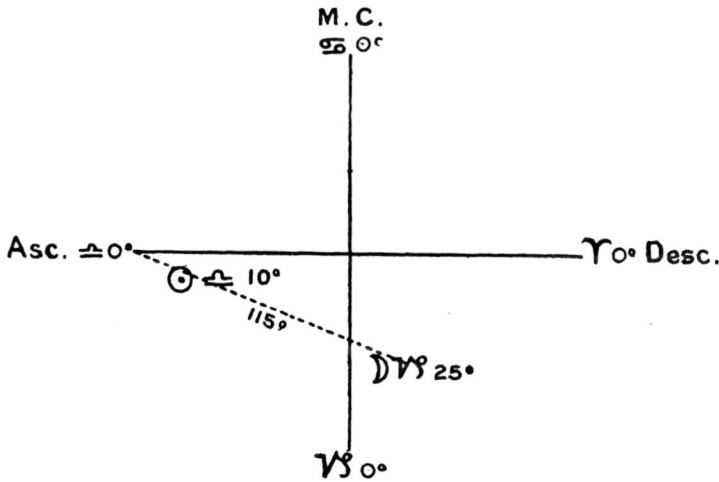

M.C.
♋ 0ᶜ

Asc. ♎ 0° ———————————— ♈ 0° Desc.

☉ ♎ 10°

115°

☽ ♑ 25°

♑ 0°

FIG. 3.

ORDER NO. 4.—*Moon below, and decreasing in light.*
Table I. shows that the period of gestation is 273 days — *x*.

The diagram (Fig. 4) shows the moon in the 7th degree of
the sign Sagittarius, and, from its position in regard to the
sun, decreasing in light. The "count" is, therefore, made
from the moon to the descendant, as shown by the dotted
line, and the distance between the two points, Sagittarius 7°
and Aries 0°, is 113 degrees. This distance, divided by 13—
the average daily motion of the moon—yields nearly 9, and,

therefore, the normal period of gestation is to be decreased by nine days. The epoch will, therefore, fall nine days *after* the index date, and the moon will then be in Aries 0°.

I now come to one of the most important developments of the epochal theory, and the student should very carefully note the following variation in the method of taking the " count." In the illustrations just given, it will be seen that the " count " is taken from the moon to the ascendant when that luminary is increasing in light, and from the

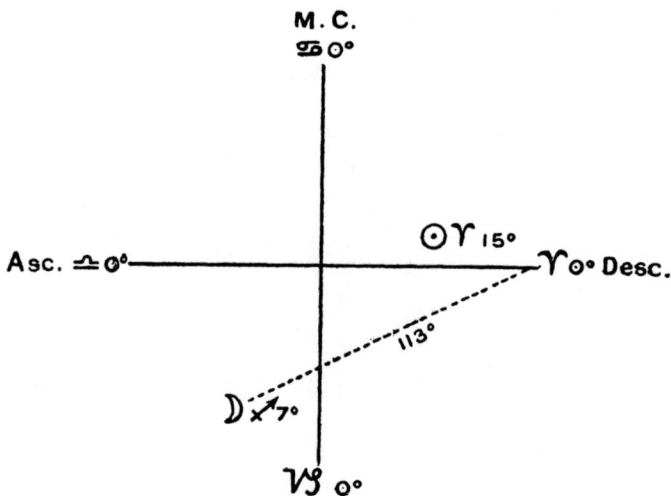

M.C.
♋ 0°

Asc. ♎ 0° —————— ♈ 0° Desc.

⊙ ♈ 15°

113°

☽ ♐ 7°

♑ 0°

FIG. 4.

moon to the descendant when decreasing. This variation consists, not of reversing the " count," but of *continuing it round to the opposite horizon, i.e.* from the moon to the descendant when increasing, and to the ascendant when decreasing, in accordance with the following rules, viz. :—

1.—When the moon is increasing and above, the " count " is taken from the moon to the ascendant, and continued round under the earth to the descendant, curtailing the period of gestation from 1 to 28 days—according to the moon's distance from the descendant, divided by 13.

2.—When the moon is decreasing, and above, the " count " is taken from the moon to the descendant and continued round under the earth to the ascendant, increasing the period of gestation from 1 to 28 days—according to the moon's distance from the ascendant, divided by 13.

3.—When the moon is increasing, and below, the "count" is taken from the moon to the ascendant and continued round over the earth to the descendant, increasing the period of gestation from 1 to 28 days—according to the moon's distance from the descendant, divided by 13.

4.—When the moon is decreasing, and below, the "count" is taken from the moon to the descendant and continued round over the earth to the ascendant, curtailing the period of gestation from 1 to 28 days—according to the moon's distance from the ascendant, divided by 13.

The following four diagrams and explanations, on the same lines as those already given, will show this process quite clearly :—

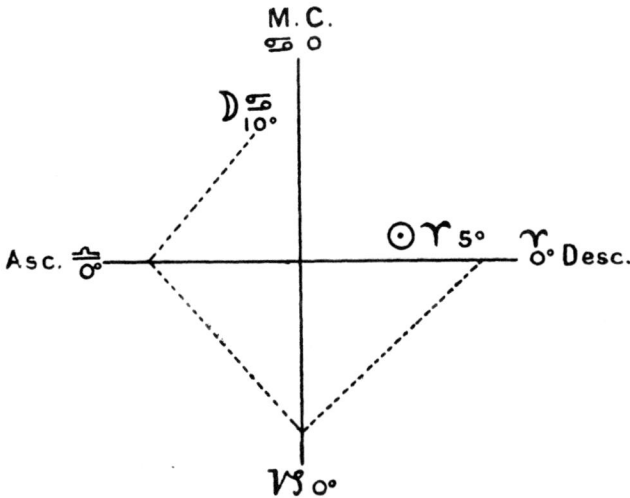

FIG. 5.

ORDER No. 1.—*Moon above the earth, and increasing.*
Table I. shows the period of gestation to be 273 days —*x*.

The above illustration shows the moon in Cancer 10°, above the earth, and increasing in light, being between the new and full moon. In an ordinary regular epoch the "count" would be made from the moon to the ascendant, a distance of 80°, equal to 6 days, by which the period of gestation would be curtailed. By the variation which may be applied to this Order, the "count" is made from the moon to the descendant along the dotted line shown above, and the distance, therefore, becomes: moon to ascendant, 80° *plus* ascendant to descendant, 180° = 260°, which, divided by 13, gives 20 days, by which the period is to be curtailed. The epoch will, therefore, fall 20 days *after* the index date, and will then be in Aries 0°, the descending degree of the horoscope.

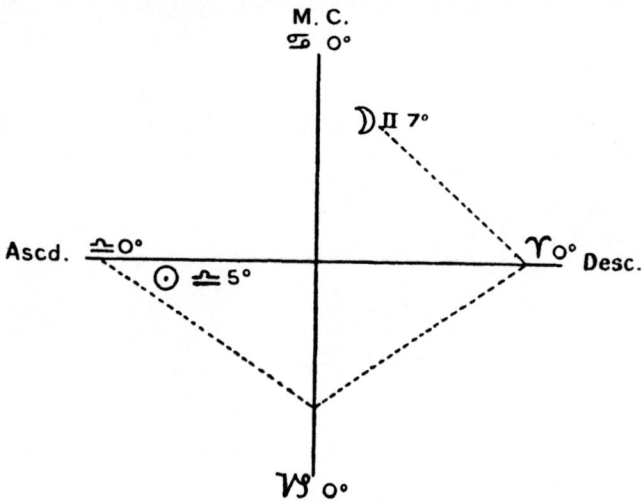

Fig. 6.

ORDER No. 2.—*Moon above the earth, and decreasing in light.* Table I. shows the period of gestation to be 273 days + *x*.

This diagram shows the moon in Gemini 7°, above the earth, and decreasing in light, and, in the ordinary way, the "count" would be made from the moon to the descendant— a distance of 67°, equal to a little over 5 days, by which the normal period is to be increased. The variation is to continue the "count" right round to the ascendant, as shown in the dotted line, giving a further distance of 180°, or 247° in all. This, divided by 13, will give 19 days by which the period of gestation is to be increased, and the epoch will, therefore, fall 19 days before the index date, with the moon in Libra 0°, the ascendant of the horoscope.

ORDER No. 3.—*Moon below the earth, and increasing.*
Table I. shows the period of gestation to be 273 days + *x*.

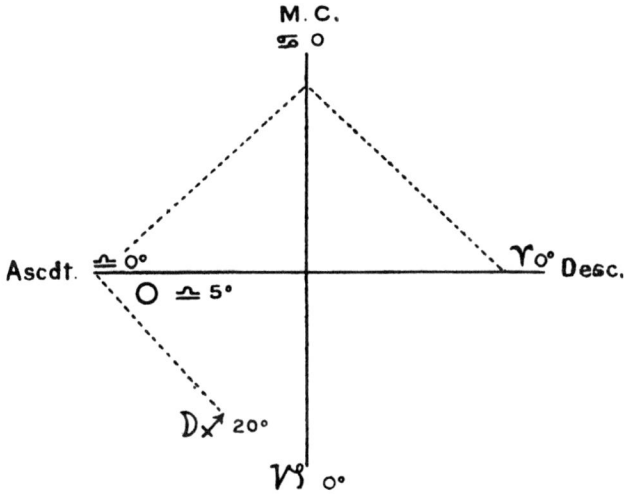

FIG. 7.

In this diagram the moon is placed in Sagittarius 20°—
below the earth, and increasing in light—and in the ordinary
way the "count" would be made from the moon to the
ascendant—a distance of 80°, or nearly 7 days, by which the
period of gestation would be increased. The variation which
may be applied here is to continue the "count" round to
the descendant, along the dotted line, making an addition
of 180°, or 260° in all, equal to 20 days by which the period
is to be increased. The day of the epoch will then fall
20 days earlier than the index date—on the day the moon
is in Aries 0°, the descendant of the horoscope.

ORDER No. 4.—*Moon below the earth, and decreasing.*
Table I. shows the period of gestation to be 273 days—*x*.
　　The diagram (Fig. 8) shows the moon in the seventh degree
of the sign Sagittarius, and decreasing in light, and in the
ordinary way the "count" would be from the moon to
the descendant, as shown in Fig. 4, page 32. The
variation which may be applied to this Order allows the

" count " to be made from the moon to the descendant—a distance of 113°—and round again to the ascendant—a further 180°, making 293° in all, as shown in the dotted line above. This, divided by 13, yields 22½ days by which the period

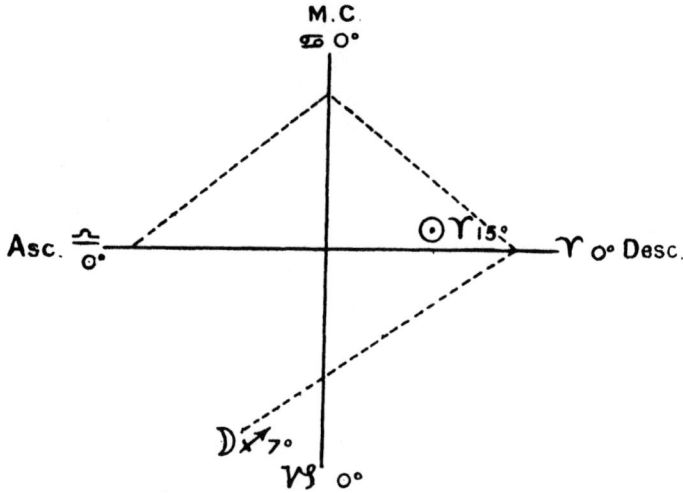

FIG. 8.

is to be curtailed, and the epoch will, therefore, fall 22½ days after the index date, with the moon in Libra 0°, the ascendant of the horoscope.

The cause of this variation will be fully explained later.

CHAPTER V.

The Paramount Law of Sex.

I now come to the explanation of the most important principle of the whole epochal theory—the Law of Sex. It is a strictly unalterable law that the epochal figure must determine the sex of the native, and unless the epoch, as calculated, conforms to this fundamental condition—*i.e.* unless it defines the sex of the subject, in addition to showing a general agreement with the rules—it is not correct.

The author of the epochal theory has more than once stated—and those who have any considerable experience with the subject know full well—that rectification is not always easy to effect, on account of the numerous factors that are employed, and the several conditions which have to be satisfied. It is not merely sufficient to follow the rules for calculation in a blindly mathematical manner. It is only too easy to find a fictitious epoch, which agrees with the time of birth, merely as a time measure. Every epoch must conform to four separate and distinct conditions, viz. :—

(1.) It must confirm the time of birth, within the limits of an ordinary error of observation.

(2.) It must define the sex of the subject, according to certain rules.

(3.) It must show the general character and fortunes of the individual.

(4.) It must furnish directions to accord with the events of life.

Unless, therefore, an epoch conforms strictly to these four conditions, it may be regarded as a fictitious one.

The Law of Sex is primarily based on the Hindu subdivision of the zodiac into 28 asterisms or mansions, each being $12\frac{6}{7}°$ in extent. The four cardinal points are the starting posts for the determination of sex, and these, with their respective sex distinctions, are: Aries 0°, *Female*, Cancer 0°, *Female*; Libra 0°, *Male*; Capricorn 0°, *Male*.

They follow the lines of the segmentation of the cell in animal organisms.

The following diagram will make this clear :—

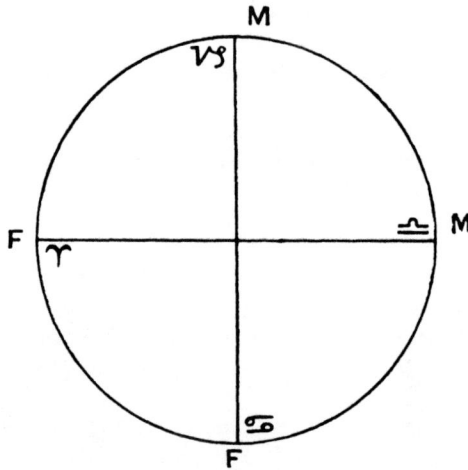

FIG. 9.

A further extension of this division is now to be made by dividing the whole circle of the zodiac into seven equal parts of $51\frac{3}{7}°$, commencing at each point of the quadrant, making the 28 asterisms or divisions. Each point of the zodiac cut by these divisions is alternately male and female, commencing with the sex of the cardinal point from which the division is made.

Starting from Aries 0° (*Female*), the points of the zodiac arrived at and the sex are: Taurus, 21° 26', *Male*; Cancer, 12° 51', *Female*; Virgo, 4° 17', *Male*; Libra, 25° 43', *Female*; Sagittarius, 17° 9', *Male*; and Aquarius 8° 34', *Female*.

Commencing with Libra 0°, the opposite point, and *Male* sex, the points of the zodiac are the same degrees and minutes of the opposite signs to those named in the last paragraph, *with the sex reversed.*

Starting with Cancer 0° (*Female*), the several points are: Leo, 21° 26', *Male*; Libra, 12° 51', *Female*; Sagittarius, 4° 17', *Male*; Capricorn, 25° 43', *Female*; Pisces, 17° 9', *Male*; Taurus, 8° 34', *Female*.

Commencing with Capricorn 0°, the opposite point to Cancer, and *Male*, the points of the zodiac cut by these divisions are the same degrees and minutes of the opposite signs to those named in the last paragraph, *with the sex reversed*.

Collating these in a tabular form in their proper order the following is obtained :—

TABLE II.

Degree	Sign	Sex	Sign	Sex	Sign	Sex	Sign	Sex
0. 0	♈	F.	♋	F.	♎	M.	♑	M.
12.51	♈	M.	♋	F.	♎	F.	♑	M.
25.43	♈	M.	♋	M.	♎	F.	♑	F.
8.34	♉	F.	♌	M.	♏	M.	♒	F.
21.26	♉	M.	♌	M.	♏	F.	♒	F.
4.17	♊	F.	♍	M.	♐	M.	♓	F.
17. 9	♊	F.	♍	F.	♐	M.	♓	M.

It will be seen, therefore, that there are four sets or series of sex degrees, alternately male and female, which have their genesis in the four cardinal points. Each point is separated by $12\frac{6}{7}°$, approximately agreeing with the diurnal motion of the moon, and forming the twenty-eight lunar mansions, or asterisms.

The application of these sex, or " critical " degrees as they are termed, to the theory of the prenatal epoch has now to be considered, and here a further extension of the division must be properly understood. The position of the two prime factors, the moon and ascendant, in relation to these degrees must be noted, but it will hardly ever occur that either of the two factors in any horoscope will occupy the exact degree and minute of any of them ; but so long as they are placed within a certain distance of the exact point they are considered as within orbs of the particular sex degree.

A very important point must now be considered. It is one of the later developments of the epochal theory, and one which I personally discovered. The orb of the sex degrees is not the same for both the moon and ascendant. In the case of the moon the orb is $6\frac{3}{7}°$, or one-half of each asterism.

TABLE III.

Sex.	Limits of		Exact Sex Point.	Limits of	
	Moon's Orb.	Ascendt's Orb.		Ascendt's Orb.	Moon's Orb.
F	—	—	♈ 0. 0	♈ 4.17	♈ 6.26
M	♈ 6.26	♈ 8.34	♈ 12.51	♈ 17. 9	♈ 19.17
M	♈ 19.17	♈ 21.26	♈ 25.43	♉ 0. 0	♉ 2. 9
F	♉ 2. 9	♉ 4.17	♉ 8.34	♉ 12.51	♉ 15. 0
M	♉ 15. 0	♉ 17. 9	♉ 21.26	♉ 25.43	♉ 27.51
F	♉ 27.51	♊ 0. 0	♊ 4.17	♊ 8.34	♊ 10.43
F	♊ 10.43	♊ 12.51	♊ 17. 9	♊ 21.26	♊ 23.34
F	♊ 23 34	♊ 25.43	♋ 0. 0	♋ 4.17	♋ 6.26
F	♋ 6.26	♋ 8.34	♋ 12.51	♋ 17. 9	♋ 19.17
M	♋ 19,17	♋ 21.26	♋ 25.43	♌ 0. 0	♌ 2. 9
M	♌ 2. 9	♌ 4.17	♌ 8.34	♌ 12.51	♌ 15. 0
M	♌ 15. 0	♌ 17. 9	♌ 21.26	♌ 25.43	♌ 27.51
M	♌ 27.51	♍ 0. 0	♍ 4.17	♍ 8.34	♍ 10.43
F	♍ 10.43	♍ 12.51	♍ 17. 9	♍ 21.26	♍ 23.34
M	♍ 23.34	♍ 25.43	♎ 0. 0	♎ 4.17	♎ 6.26
F	♎ 6.26	♎ 8.34	♎ 12.51	♎ 17. 9	♎ 19.17
F	♎ 19.17	♎ 21.26	♎ 25.43	♏ 0. 0	♏ 2. 9
M	♏ 2. 9	♏ 4.17	♏ 8.34	♏ 12.51	♏ 15. 0
F	♏ 15. 0	♏ 17. 9	♏ 21.26	♏ 25.43	♏ 27.51
M	♏ 27.51	♐ 0. 0	♐ 4.17	♐ 8.34	♐ 10.43
M	♐ 10.43	♐ 12.51	♐ 17. 9	♐ 21.26	♐ 23.34
M	♐ 23.34	♐ 25.43	♑ 0. 0	♑ 4.17	♑ 6.26
M	♑ 6.26	♑ 8.34	♑ 12.51	♑ 17. 9	♑ 19.17
F	♑ 19.17	♑ 21.26	♑ 25.43	♒ 0. 0	♒ 2. 9
F	♒ 2. 9	♒ 4.17	♒ 8.34	♒ 12.51	♒ 15. 0
F	♒ 15. 0	♒ 17. 9	♒ 21.26	♒ 25.43	♒ 27.51
F	♒ 27.51	♓ 0. 0	♓ 4.17	♓ 8.34	♓ 10.43
M	♓ 10.43	♓ 12.51	♓ 17. 9	♓ 21.26	♓ 23.34
F	♓ 23.34	♓ 25.43	♓ 30. 0	—	—

EXPLANATION.—Column 4 of the table shows the exact sex point. Cols 3 and 5 show where the influence of the ascendant commences and finishes respectively. Cols. 2 and 6 show where the moon's influence commences and finishes respectively. Col. 1 gives the sex of the area between the longitudes in Cols. 2 and 6.

EXAMPLE.—Ascendant at epoch, Cancer 18° 5′. Moon, Scorpio 15° 24′. Looking down the columns headed "Ascendant's Orb," it will be seen that Cancer 18° 5′ is outside the limits given. It is, therefore, negative. Looking down the columns headed "Moon's Orb," it will be seen that Scorpio 15° commences a male area, and the moon will therefore be in an area of that sex. The same rule applies to all cases.

The ascendant, to be within orbs of a sex degree, must not be distant more than $4\frac{2}{7}°$, or one-third of each asterism.

It will be seen from this that, in whatever position the moon is placed, it will be in either one sex or the other. The ascendant, when within $4\frac{2}{7}°$ of an exact sex point, can be either sex, but when outside that limit it is negative or non-sex. The moon will, therefore, govern a space equal to $12\frac{6}{7}°$, in equal parts of $6\frac{3}{7}°$ on each side of the exact point. The ascendant will govern only $8\frac{4}{7}°$, or equal parts of $4\frac{2}{7}°$ on each side of the exact degree.

It must, however, be remembered that it is the positions of the moon and ascendant in regard to the sex degrees in the epochal figure which determine the sex, and *not* those positions in the horoscope of birth.

Table III. will show at a glance the exact sex degrees, and the orb of influence of both the moon and ascendant in relation to each.

Having obtained all these factors, the final process is to determine the sex of the subject from the epochal figure. This is performed in accordance with the following rules :—

(1.) When the ascendant is negative, as in strict regular and irregular epochs, the sex of the area occupied by the moon will be the sex of the subject.

(2.) When both the moon and ascendant are within their respective orbs of a degree of the same sex, the sex of the subject is the same as the sex of the area so occupied.

(3.) When the moon and ascendant are placed within their respective orbs of degrees of the opposite sex—the moon in a female area, and the ascendant in a male, or *vice versa*—the sex of the subject is determined by the quadrant held by the moon. There will then be two points of one sex, and one of the other, and whichever sex predominates that will be the sex of the subject.

The sex influences of the quadrants of the epochal figure are as follows :—

South-East Quadrant : Meridian to Ascendant .. Male.
North-East Quadrant : Ascendant to Fourth house Female.
North-West Quadrant : 4th house to Descendant Male.
South-West Quadrant : Descendant to Meridian .. Female.

Fig. 10 will show the sex influence of the quadrants at a glance.

This concludes my exposition of the Law of Sex, and completes the first section of this book.   A thorough understanding of the Laws of the Epoch, and of the paramount Law of Sex, as detailed in the last two chapters, is absolutely necessary for the proper calculation of the epoch and the

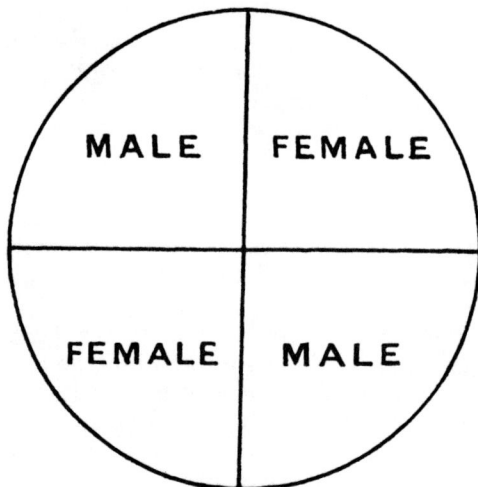

FIG. 10.

subsequent rectification of the time of birth, and no further steps should be taken until these aforesaid laws are thoroughly mastered, or the student will find himself confused in following the rules for rectification to be detailed in the next section.

SECTION II.

The Prenatal Epoch as a Factor in Rectification.

CHAPTER VI.

PRELIMINARY STEPS.

THE theory of the prenatal epoch was first put forward as a method of correcting doubtful horoscopes, and for obtaining the exact and true moment of birth—a matter which had always been a stumbling-block of considerable magnitude in the path of the student. Several methods of rectification were extant, notably one of making events fit exactly with some suitable arc of direction, but it was more than often found that, when the time had been apparently determined by this process, another event would come along which would not measure exactly with the required direction, thus necessitating a further rectification which nullified the former.

The prenatal epoch, however, introduced a further method of correcting the birth-time, by which all these anomalies and obstacles were done away with. Its importance in this particular process is of so great a nature that it stands first and foremost, unequalled and unrivalled, as " the only reliable method of rectification "—a designation which was given to it by myself in the year 1901, as the result of my investigations of some 250 horoscopes during the winters of 1898-99. Its chief point of value and practical utility in connection with Natal Astrology is put forward in Chapter III, in these words : " Rectification of approximate horoscopes, and confirmation of the times of birth in all authentic cases, within the limits of an ordinary error of observation."

The process of rectification is performed in four different ways, and is regulated according to the position of the moon at birth in regard to the sun and ascendant, and consists of the interchange of the longitudes of the ascendant and moon at birth with the moon and ascendant at the epoch, or their respective opposite points. Of these four methods, the first is a regular interchange, and the other three are variations.

When the interchange is equally performed—the ascendant at birth with the moon at the epoch, or its opposite point, and the moon at birth with the ascendant at the epoch, or its opposite point—the epoch is termed *regular*. This regular interchange of the two factors is the main postulate of the epoch, and can only occur under certain definite sex positions of the ascendant and moon, taken in conjunction with the sex of the subject.

Dealing concisely with this matter of interchange it will be seen that in a regular epoch :

1.—*With an increasing moon at birth*
> (*a*) The ascendant at birth becomes the place of the moon at the epoch ;
> (*b*) The moon's place at birth becomes the ascendant at the epoch.

2.—*With a decreasing moon at birth*
> (*a*) The ascendant at birth becomes the opposite point to the moon at the epoch ;
> (*b*) The moon at birth becomes the opposite point to the ascendant at the epoch.

Or, in other words,
> (*a*) The descendant at birth becomes the place of the moon at the epoch ;
> (*b*) The moon's place at birth becomes the descendant at the epoch.

This interchange of the two factors in the four Orders of Regular Epochs is as the Law of the Medes and Persians, which altereth not.

A second class of epoch has now to be considered, wherein this regularity in the interchange of the two factors is not maintained, and these are termed " Irregular Epochs." This irregularity or variation of the main postulate of the epoch applies to each of the four Orders, and consists of either of the following :—

(1.) Taking the " count " from the moon to the ascendant or descendant, according to rule, but reversing the rising or setting of the moon at birth, making its place *set* when increasing and *rise* when decreasing.

(2.) Taking the " count " from the moon to the descendant when increasing, and from the moon to the *ascendant* when decreasing, but making the moon's place rise or set according to rule.

(3.) Taking the " count " from the moon to the *descendant* when increasing, and from the moon to the *ascendant* when decreasing, and reversing the rising or setting of the moon, as in Variation I.

These variations can only occur under certain definite sex conditions of the moon and ascendant, taken in conjunction with the sex of the subject, and the second and third variations include a fair percentage of cases in which the period of gestation is increased or decreased by more than the usual period of fourteen days.

The result of these variations or irregularities produces the following comparisons :—

Variation I.	*Birth.*	*Epoch.*
Moon increasing in light	Ascendant becomes	Moon
	Moon ,,	Descendant
Moon decreasing in light	Descendant ,,	Moon
	Moon ,,	Ascendant
Variation II.		
Moon increasing in light	Descendant becomes	Moon
	Moon ,,	Ascendant
Moon decreasing in light	Ascendant ,,	Moon
	Moon ,,	Descendant
Variation III.		
Moon increasing in light	Descendant becomes	Moon
	Moon ,,	Descendant
Moon decreasing in light	Ascendant ,,	Moon
	Moon ,,	Ascendant

It must be properly understood that this irregularity, or variation from the main postulate of the epoch, is in no sense arbitrary or fortuitous. The variation must be made in order that the epoch conforms to the four prime conditions. It should be borne in mind that in all regular and irregular epochs the moon at birth holds a negative area, and, therefore, its rising or setting does not affect the sex, and the variation in this point is for the purpose of requiring the epoch to confirm the birth-time. In the second and third variations it is the sex of the area held by the ascendant which requires a deviation from the main law. Thus, if the " count " has to be made from the moon to the ascendant, and that point is in an area of the opposite sex to the subject, the " count " must be continued round to the opposite horizon, which will bring it into an area of the required sex. The moon's place may rise according to rule, but it may also be necessary to reverse the process. More detailed information will be given on this point in the next chapter.

A third class of epochs are those which are more strictly designated " Sex Epochs," and the interchange of the two factors is wholly and exclusively controlled by the sex of the areas in which both the moon and ascendant are placed, taken in conjunction with the sex of the subject. Sometimes the interchange will be regular, and in others either of the three irregular methods, while the sex of the quadrant held by the moon at the epoch is brought into use in a very large number of cases. This class also includes the large majority of cases where the period of gestation is increased or decreased by periods longer than the usual fourteen days.

The actual mathematical process of rectification is very simple, and demands only a knowledge of addition and subtraction and simple rule of three. On the other hand, it will be gathered from the statements made in the preceding pages that the whole matter requires careful handling, on account of the varied sex positions in which the two factors can be placed, and of the sex of the subject under rectification. As already stated, more than once, it is only too easy to find a fictitious epoch which agrees with the birth-time merely as a time measure only, and it is in this respect that the student will find his greatest difficulty, more especially in dealing with the third class of epochs. The rules are given, however, in such a manner as to give the greatest assistance in overcoming these difficulties, which are more apparent and superficial than real.

It should be duly noted that these terms " Regular," " Irregular," and " Sex " epochs are merely descriptive and not distinctive. As a matter of fact, all epochs, without exception, are strictly Sex Epochs, for the interchange of the two factors at birth with those at the epoch is controlled absolutely by the sex of the areas in which they are placed, taken in conjunction with the sex of the subject.

CHAPTER VII.

The First Steps in Rectification.

The first steps in the calculation of the prenatal epoch and the subsequent rectification of the time of birth are very important, because the whole process depends entirely on having the essential factors properly computed and correctly described. It is, therefore, necessary to carefully calculate the longitudes of the ascendant and moon at birth, to determine the order of the epoch, to find the index date, and to ascertain the sex positions of the ascendant and moon. The following rules should, therefore, be carefully committed to memory :—

(1.) First compute the longitudes of the ascendant and moon at the given time of birth, and note them down.

(2.) Note whether the moon is above or below the horizon, and whether it is increasing or decreasing in light. This will determine the proper order of epoch, according to Table I (Chapter IV).

(3.) To compute the index date, calculate backwards from the birth-date ten revolutions of the moon, which is equal to nine calendar months. The date so found will be the same date as that of the birth, or within three days, in the ninth month preceding that of the birth.

The simplest plan is to add three months to the date of birth and then refer to the corresponding date in the year preceding. On the date so found, or within three days thereof, the moon will be in the same longitude as at birth. This date is known as the " Index date."

(4.) The final step is to determine the sex position of the ascendant and moon. This can be done by reference to Table III (Chapter V). Be careful to remember that, in the horoscope, the orb of the ascendant is equal to half a sex area or 6° 26′, while that of the moon is one-third of a sex area, or 4° 17′, contrary to the orbs of the two factors at the epoch. This will determine the class of epoch required, according to the following regulations :—

1.—(*a*) Moon increasing, either above or below, and negative—ascendant in same sex as subject; or

(*b*) Moon decreasing, either above or below, and negative—ascendant in opposite sex to subject.

The epoch in the above cases will be either regular or irregular (1st variation).

2.—(*a*) Moon increasing, either above or below, and negative—ascendant in opposite sex to subject; or

(*b*) Moon decreasing, either above or below, and negative—ascendant in same sex as subject.

The epoch in these two cases will never be regular, but always irregular of either the 2nd or 3rd variation.

3.—(*a*) Moon increasing, either above or below—ascendant and moon both in the same sex as subject;

(*b*) Moon decreasing, either above or below—ascendant and moon in opposite sex to subject.

The epochs in these cases will be either regular or the 1st and 2nd variations irregular; they will never be irregular (3rd variation).

4.—(*a*) Moon increasing, either above or below—ascendant same sex as subject, moon opposite sex;

(*b*) Moon decreasing, either above or below—ascendant opposite sex to subject, moon same sex.

The epochs here will be either regular or irregular (1st and 3rd variation); they will never be irregular (2nd variation).

5.—(*a*) Moon increasing, either above or below—ascendant opposite sex to subject, moon same sex;

(*b*) Moon decreasing, either above or below—ascendant same sex as subject, moon opposite sex.

The epochs in these cases will be always either regular or irregular (2nd and 3rd variation); they will never be irregular (1st variation).

6.—(*a*) Moon increasing either above or below—ascendant and moon both in opposite sex to subject;

(*b*) Moon decreasing, either above or below—ascendant and moon both in same sex as subject.

The epochs in these cases will always be irregular, of either of the three variations, but they will never be regular.

It will now be seen how easy it is to find a fictitious epoch which agrees with the birth-time merely as a time measure, and the difficulty which exists in determining which class of

epoch is the one required.   No hard-and-fast rule can be
laid down on this point, and the only plan is to take the
first method given.   In most cases it will be the correct
one, but the real guide in the matter is the sex of the
ascendant at birth.   If the moon is increasing, and the
ascendant is of the same sex as the subject, the epoch
will be regular in the large majority of cases.   If the moon
is decreasing, and the ascendant is in the same sex as the
subject, the epoch will be irregular, always, of the 2nd or
3rd variation, and *vice versa* for the opposite conditions.

An illustration of the preliminary steps to be taken is
now given.

Princess Arthur of Connaught (Duchess of Fife) : Born
May 17th, 1891, at 5 a.m., in London, W. Long. 47s. W.

1.—The birth taking place before noon, the sidereal time
at noon on the previous day is taken, and the time of birth
from that noon added thereto.

	H.	M.	S.
Sid. time, noon, May 16th ..	3	35	39
Time of birth from „ ..	17	0	0
Correction for 17h.		2	48
	20	38	27
Less for W. long.			47
Sid. time at birth	20	37	40

This gives the ascendant 11° 51′ ♊ .
The moon's longitude is 11° 27′ ♍.

2.—The moon being only 90° from the ascendant in the
order of the signs, it will be below the earth.   It is between
the new and the full, and is, therefore, increasing in light.
This shows that the epoch will be of the Third Order.   (*See*
Table I).

3.—Three months added to the birth date will give
August 17th, 1891.   On that date in the previous year the
moon will be in the same longitude as at birth.   Moon on
August 17th, 1890, was in ♍ 14° 27′ at noon.   This latter
date is, therefore, the index date.

4.—Reference to Table III will show that the ascendant
is in a female area, being less than 6° 26′ from the female
point ♊ 17° 9′.   The same table will show the moon to be

more than 4° 17′ from the female point, ♍ 17° 9′. It is, therefore, in a negative area.

The ascendant being of the same sex as the subject, and the moon increasing, the epoch will, therefore, be either regular or irregular (1st variation).

These preliminary steps are required in all cases of normal births.

In the succeeding chapters of this section I am giving, in full detail, the rules for the performance of rectification, according to the four Orders of Epochs, with their several variations, showing all the possible positions in regard to sex in which the two factors, the moon and ascendant at birth, are placed. Illustrations from the horoscopes of notable people, under each of the four Orders of Epochs, will be given, showing the calculations in full, as this will be less confusing than taking cases indiscriminately, and, further, will tend to fix in the minds of students the particular set of rules appertaining to each Order of Epoch.   The student should, therefore, have little difficulty in following the various steps taken, and, with a little study and patience, should soon be able to clearly understand the entire *modus operandi* involved.

CHAPTER VIII.

Rectification by Epochs of the First Order.

ALL the preliminary calculations having been made, according to the rules given in the last chapter, and the several essential factors duly noted, the next step is the actual calculation of the date and time of the epoch, and the rectification of the time of birth.

The essential factors are :

(1) The longitudes of the ascendant and moon.
(2) The order of the epoch.
(3) The index date.
(4) The class of epoch.

The necessary process for each class of epoch is now performed according to the following rules :—

I.—FOR REGULAR EPOCHS ONLY.

Ascendant same sex as subject : Moon negative.

1.—As the moon is increasing in light and above the earth, the " count " is made from the moon to the ascendant, and the exact day of the epoch will be within the fourteen days following the index date, and on the day when the moon crosses the longitude of the ascendant of the horoscope.

2.—Calculate the time on the day of the epoch when the moon's birth longitude rises. This is the time of the epoch. At the same time calculate the longitude of the moon on this particular date and hour. This is the correct ascendant of the horoscope.

3.—Calculate the time on the day of birth when this longitude rises. This is the correct time of birth.

Rules for calculating the time of the rising or setting of particular longitudes are given in the Appendix.

II.—FOR IRREGULAR EPOCHS ONLY.

First Variation.

Ascendant same sex as subject : Moon negative.

1.—As the moon is increasing in light and above the earth, the " count " is made from the moon to the ascendant, and the exact day of the epoch will be within the fourteen

days following the index date, and on the day when the
moon crosses the longitude of the ascendant of the horoscope.

2.—Calculate the time on the day of the epoch when the
moon's birth longitude *sets*. This is the time of the epoch.
Then calculate the longitude of the moon at this particular
date and time. This is the correct *ascendant* of the horoscope.

3.—Calculate the time on the day of birth when this
longitude rises. This is the correct time of birth.

SECOND VARIATION.
Ascendant opposite sex to subject : Moon negative.

1.—As the moon is increasing in light and above the
earth, the " count " is made from the moon to the ascendant
and round under the earth to the descendant. The exact
day of the epoch will be within the twenty-eight days
following the index date, on the day when the moon crosses
the descendant of the horoscope.

2.—Calculate the time on the day of epoch when the
moon's birth longitude *rises*. This is the time of the epoch.
Then calculate the longitude of the moon at this date and
time. This is the exact *descendant* of the horoscope.

3.—Calculate the time on the day of birth when this
longitude sets. This is the correct time of birth.

THIRD VARIATION.
Ascendant opposite sex to subject : Moon negative.

1.—As the moon is increasing in light and above the earth,
the " count " is made from the moon to the ascendant and
continued round under the earth to the descendant. The
exact day of the epoch will be within the twenty-eight days
following the index date, and on the day when the moon
crosses the *descendant* of the horoscope.

2.—Calculate the time on the day of the epoch when
the moon's birth longitude *sets*. This is the time of the
epoch. Then calculate the longitude of the moon at this
particular date and time. This is the correct *descendant*
of the horoscope.

3.—Calculate the time on the day of birth when this
longitude sets. This is the correct time of birth.

In all the epochs derived from the four processes described, the moon's position at such epoch *alone* determines the sex by being placed in an area of the same sex as the subject. The cause of this is due to the moon at birth being negative, and, as the ascendant at the epoch will also be negative, the moon alone will determine the sex.

III.—FOR SEX EPOCHS ONLY.

1.—*Ascendant and Moon both in the same sex as subject.*

1.—Follow the rules for an ordinary regular epoch. The epoch so derived will show the moon and ascendant in areas of the same sex as the subject.

2.—Follow the rules for an irregular epoch (1st variation). The epoch so derived will show the moon in an area of the same sex as the subject, but the ascendant in an area of the opposite sex. The moon must then be placed in a quadrant of the same sex as the subject.

3.—Follow the rules for an irregular epoch (2nd variation). The epoch so derived will show the moon in an area of the opposite sex to the subject, and the ascendant in one of the same sex. The moon must then be in a quadrant of the same sex as the subject.

The third variation of irregular epochs cannot be employed in this case, as it would give both factors in degrees of the opposite sex to the subject at the epoch.

2.—*Ascendant in same sex as subject : Moon opposite sex.*

1.—Follow the rules for an ordinary regular epoch. The epoch so derived shows the moon in the same sex as the subject ; ascendant in opposite sex. The moon has, therefore, to be in a quadrant of the same sex as the subject.

2.—Follow the rules for an irregular epoch (1st variation). The epoch so derived shows the moon and ascendant both in degrees of the same sex as the subject.

3.—Follow the rules for an irregular epoch (3rd variation). The epoch so derived shows the moon in the opposite sex to the subject ; ascendant in same sex. Moon must, therefore, be in quadrant of same sex as subject.

The second variation of irregular epochs cannot be employed in this class, as it would give an epoch showing both factors in areas of opposite sex to the subject.

3.—*Ascendant opposite sex to subject : Moon same sex.*

1.—Follow the rules for a regular epoch. The epoch so obtained shows the moon in the opposite sex to the subject ; ascendant in same sex. Moon must, therefore, be in a quadrant of same sex as subject.

2.—Follow the rules for an irregular epoch (2nd variation). The epoch so derived shows the moon and ascendant both in degrees of the same sex as the subject.

3.—Follow the rules for an irregular epoch (3rd variation). The epoch so derived shows the moon in same sex as the subject ; ascendant in opposite sex. The moon must be in a quadrant of the same sex as subject.

The first variation of irregular epochs cannot be employed in this class, as it would give an epoch showing both factors in areas of the opposite sex.

4.—*Ascendant and Moon both in opposite sex to subject.*

1.—Follow the rules for an irregular epoch (1st variation). The epoch so derived shows the moon in opposite sex to subject ; ascendant in same sex. Moon must, therefore, be in a quadrant of same sex as subject.

2.—Follow the rules for an irregular epoch (2nd variation). The epoch so derived shows the moon in the same sex as the subject ; ascendant in opposite sex. Moon must, therefore, be placed in a quadrant of the same sex as the subject.

3.—Follow the rules for an irregular epoch (3rd variation). The epoch so derived shows both the moon and ascendant in same sex as subject.

The rules for a regular epoch cannot be employed in this class, as the epoch so obtained would show both factors in areas of the opposite sex to the subject.

In the next chapter illustrations will be given from the horoscopes of notable people of the different processes enumerated in this chapter.

CHAPTER IX.

ILLUSTRATIONS OF EPOCHS OF THE FIRST ORDER.

An interesting and instructive point has now been reached, and if students will carefully follow the examples of epochs given in this chapter they will see that the laws governing the calculation of the epoch and the subsequent rectification of the time of birth, as detailed in the previous chapters, are in no wise twisted or distorted to suit each particular case, but are exactly and precisely followed, and they will have no difficulty in applying the same laws and rules to any other cases which may come under their notice.

All the horoscopes chosen for illustration are those of notable people whose birth-times have been given in official bulletins or otherwise reported in the papers. I have taken this course in order to prevent opponents of the theory suggesting that private cases were chosen in order to deceive students as to the alteration in the time of birth effected by the rectification.

(1) Raymond Poincaré, President of the French Republic, was born on August 20th, 1860, at 5 p.m., at Bar-le-duc, France. Lat. 48° 46′ N. ; Long. 5° 11′ E.

The time of birth given is Paris time, the corresponding Greenwich time will, therefore, be 4h. 50m. 38s., and the true local mean time of birth 5h. 11m. 22s. p.m. This data yields :

R.A.M.C.	..	..	..	15h. 8m. 20s.
Ascendant	..	..	..	17° 44′ ♑
Moon	..	..	..	20° 40′ ♎

The moon is above the earth and increasing. The ascendant is in an area of the male sex, being less than 6° 26′ from the male point, ♑ 12° 51′. The moon is in a negative area.

The moon being above and increasing, the " count " is made from the moon to the ascendant, and the period of gestation is curtailed by 7 days. The index date is November 21st, 1859, and the exact day of the epoch *before* noon of November 28th.

	H.	M.	S.
Sid. time, moon's place rising ..	7	53	38
Sid. time, noon, Nov. 27th ..	16	23	29
	15	30	9
Subtract for E. long.		20	44
	15	9	25
Less correction		2	29
	15	6	56

or, November 28th, 1859, at 3h. 6m. 56s. a.m. The longitude of the moon at this time is 16° 59′ ♑, within orbs of a male degree, thus determining the sex.

♑ 16° 59′ rises on the day of the birth with a Sid. time of 15h. 5m. 42s., which is 2m. 38s. less than at the recorded time. The correct time of birth was, therefore :

Paris time ..   .. 4h. 57m. 22s. p.m.
G.M. time ..   .. 4h. 48m. 0s. „
L.M. time ..   .. 5h. 8m. 44s. „

(2) Prince Joachim of Prussia was born on December 17th, 1890, at 8.45 p.m., at Berlin. Lat. 52° 30′ N. Long. 13° 24′ E. Standard time was observed, so that the G.M.T. was 7.45 p.m. and the true L.M.T. 8h. 38m. 36s. p.m. This data gives :

R.A.M.C.   ..   .. 2h. 24m. 27s.
Ascendant   ..   .. 22° 36′ ♌
Moon ..   ..   .. 12° 17′ ♓

The moon is above the earth and increasing, and both factors are placed in male areas. The index date is March 19th, 1890, and the " count " being made from the moon to the ascendant, decreases the period of gestation by nearly 13 days, the epoch falling on April 1st, before noon. The moon's radical place ascends at the epoch.

	H.	M.	S.
Sid. time, moon's place rises ..	17	31	15
Sid time, March 31st	0	35	15
	16	56	0
Subtract for E. long.		53	36
	16	2	24
Less correction		2	38
	15	59	46

This is April 1st, at 3h. 59m. 46s. G.M.T., and the moon is then in 22° 25′ ♌, which is the correct ascendant of the horoscope. The correct time of birth is obtained in the following manner:

		H.	M.	S.
Sid. time, 22° 25′ ♌ rises	..	2	22	59
Sid. time, Dec. 17th, 1890	..	17	44	16
		8	38	43
Subtract for E. long.			53	36
		7	45	7
Less correction			1	16
		7	43	51

This is 7h. 43m. 51s. p.m. G.M.T., or 8h. 37m. 27s. p.m. Berlin mean time—1m. 8s. less than the recorded hour. The epoch shows both factors in male areas, thus confirming the sex.

(3) The Queen of Spain, born 3.45 p.m., October 24th, 1887, Balmoral Castle. Lat. 57° 2′ N.; Long. 3° 12′ W. This data gives:

R.A.M.C.	.. ..	17h. 43m. 6s.
Ascendant	.. ..	16° 13′ ✕ Male
Moon ..	.. ..	11° 32′ ♒ Female

Moon being above and increasing, period will be less than the norm. Ten revolutions of the moon measure to January 24th, 1887, and the epoch will fall before noon on the 27th. The moon increasing at birth, its longitude will rise at:

		H.	M.	S.
		16	51	4
Sid. time, Jan. 26th	.. ..	20	21	51
		20	29	13
Add for W. long.			12	48
		20	42	1
Less acceleration			3	23
		20	38	38

equal to January 27th, 8h. 38m. 38s. a.m.

The longitude of the moon at this time is 12° 41′ ✕, which is the ascendant of the horoscope.

Now as to the correct time of birth :

			H.	M.	S.
12° 41′ ✶ rises at	..	..	17	38	32
Sid. time, Oct. 24th	..	..	14	10	17
			3	28	15
Add for W. long.	..	..		1?	48
			3	41	3
Less acceleration ..	..	..			36
			3	40	27

This shows the birth to have taken place at 3h. 40m. 27s.
p.m., less than five minutes from the recorded time.

The epoch shows a female area rising, and the moon in
a male area, but as the quadrant occupied by the moon
is female so is the sex female.

(4) The Astrologer " Orion," Editor of the Almanac of
that name, was born at Melton Mowbray on October 9th,
1858, at 1.10 p.m. Lat. 52° 47′ N. ; Long. 0° 53′ W.
This data gives :

R.A.M.C.	..	..	14h. 17m. 58s.
Ascendant	..	..	29° 41′ ♐
Moon ..	..	..	15° 14′ ♏

The moon is increasing and above, and the ascendant is
in a male degree. The period of gestation will, therefore,
be less than the norm, the " count " being taken from the
moon to the ascendant.

The index date—10 revolutions of the moon before birth—
falls on January 9th, and the exact day of the epoch is
after the noon of January 12th.

The following calculation determines the epoch :

		H.	M.	S.
Sid. time, moon's place rises ..		10	22	19
„ Jan. 12th, 1858	..	19	26	45
		14	55	34
Add for W. long.			3	32
		14	59	6
Less correction			2	27
		14	56	39

equal to January 13th, 1858, at 2h. 56m. 39s. a.m.

The moon's longitude at this time is 29° 8′ ♐ , which is the ascendant of the horoscope.

		H.	M.	S.
Saggitarius 29° 8′ rises at	..	14	15	24
Sid. time at birth	..	14	17	58
Difference ..	..		2	34

The birth-time is, therefore, 2m. 34s. earlier, or 1h. 7m. 26s. p.m.

The epochal figure shows the moon in a male degree, confirming the sex.

(5) Bramwell Booth, son of the late General Booth, founder of the Salvation Army, was born at Halifax on March 8th, 1856, at 8.30 p.m. local time. G.M.T., 8h. 37m. 28s. Lat. 53° 43′ N. ; Long. 1° 52′ W. This data gives :

R.A.M.C.	..	..	7h. 36m. 54s.	
Ascendant	..	..	16° 35′	♎
Moon ..	..	..	16° 47′	♈

The moon is increasing and above. The ascendant is female, and the moon male.

The tenth revolution of the moon took place on June 9th, 1855, and although the ascendant is female, the " count " is made thereto, and the day of the epoch is June 24th, early morning.

The moon increasing at birth, and male, its place will rise with a sidereal time of :

			H.	M.	S.
			18	25	37
Sid. time, June 23rd	..	..	6	4	21
			12	21	16
Add for W. long.	..	..		7	28
			12	28	44
Correction ..	..	..	..	2	3
			12	26	41

This is equal to June 24th at 0h. 26m. 21s. a.m., at which time the moon is in ♎ 16° 47′, which is the ascendant of the horoscope. This degree rises with a sidereal time of 7h. 38m. 8s., or 1m. 14s. later than at the given time of birth, showing that the correct time is 8h. 31m. 14s. local time, or 8h. 38m. 42s. G.M.T.

The epoch shows a male degree rising, and the moon in a female area, but male quadrant, thus determining the sex to be male.

(6) The late Crown Prince Rudolph of Austria was born at Vienna on August 21st, 1858, at 10.15 p.m. (G.M.T. 9h. 9m. 28s. p.m.).   Lat. 48° 12′ N.   Long. 16° 23′ E. This data gives :

R.A.M.C.	..	..	20h. 14m. 34s.
Ascendant	..	..	0° 6′ ♊
Moon ..	..	..	27° 43′ ♑

The moon is increasing, and above, and both factors are in female areas.   Ten revolutions prior to birth measure to November 21st, 1857.   The ascendant is female, so that the " count " has to be taken from the moon right round the map to the descendant, making the index date before noon on December 14th.   The moon increasing, its place will rise with :

			H.	M.	S.
Sid. time of	..	..	15	38	49
Sid. time, Dec. 13th	..	..	17	28	28
			22	10	21
Subtract for E. long.	..	..	1	5	32
			21	4	49
Correction ..	..	..	..	3	27
			21	1	22

This is December 13th, 21h. 1m. 22s., equal to December 14th, 9h. 1m. 22s. a.m   At this time the moon is in 29° 43′ ♏ which is the descendant of the horoscope.   This degree sets with a sidereal time of 20h. 13m. 24s., or 1m. 10s. earlier than the given time, making the correct birth-time 10h. 13m. 50s. p.m
The epoch shows a female degree rising, but the moon is in a male area and a male quadrant, thus determining the sex to be male.

(7) Prince Henry of Wales was born on March 31st, 1900, at 7.30 a.m. at Sandringham.   Lat. 52° 52′ N.   Long. 0° 32′ E.   This data gives :

R.A.M.C.	20h. 5m.	0s.
Ascendant	3° 29′	♊
Moon	16° 37′	♈

The moon is in a male area, increasing and above, and the ascendant in a female area. The " count " in the ordinary way would be made to the ascendant, but, as that degree is female, it is continued round to the opposite horizon. The index date is June 30th, 1899, and the distance from the moon to the descendant, 227°, decreases the period by 17½ days, making the epoch fall on July 18th.

	H. M. S.
Sid. time, moon's place rising ..	18 26 27
„ „ July 18th, 1899 ..	7 44 19
	10 42 8
Subtract for E. long.	2 8
	10 40 0
Less correction	1 45
	10 38 15

This is July 18th, 1899, at 10h. 38m. 15s. p.m., and the moon's longitude at this time is 2° 0′ ♐, the descendant of the horoscope. This degree sets with a sidereal time of 20h. 0m. 43s., or 4m. 17s. earlier than at the given birth-time, showing the exact moment of birth to be 7h. 25m. 43s. a.m.

The epochal figure shows both factors in degrees of the male sex, thus determining this point.

CHAPTER X.

RECTIFICATION BY EPOCHS OF THE SECOND ORDER.

THE preliminary calculations having been made, according to the rules given in Chapter VII, the process of computing the epoch and rectifying the birth-time, when the epoch is of the second order, is as follows :—

I.—FOR REGULAR EPOCHS ONLY.

Ascendant in opposite sex to subject : Moon negative.

1.—As the moon is decreasing in light and above the earth, the " count " is made from the moon to the descendant, and the exact day of the epoch will be within the fourteen days *earlier* than the index date, and on the day when the moon crosses the longitude of the *descendant* of the horoscope.

2.—Calculate the time on the day of the epoch when the moon's birth longitude *sets*. This is the time of the epoch. Then calculate the longitude of the moon at this particular date and hour. This is the *descendant* of the horoscope.

3.—Calculate the time on the day of birth when this longitude *sets*. This is the correct time of birth.

II.—FOR IRREGULAR EPOCHS ONLY.

Ascendant opposite sex to subject : Moon negative.

1.—As the moon is decreasing in light and above the earth, the " count " is made from the moon to the descendant, and the exact day of the epoch will be within the fourteen days earlier than the index date, and on the day when the moon crosses the descendant of the horoscope.

2.—Calculate the time on the day of the epoch when the moon's birth longitude *rises*. This is the time of the epoch. Then calculate the longitude of the moon at this particular date and time. This is the correct descendant of the horoscope.

3.—Calculate the time on the day of birth when this longitude *sets*. This is the correct time of birth.

Second Variation.

Ascendant same sex as subject : Moon negative.

1.—As the moon is decreasing in light and above the earth, the " count " is made from the moon to the descendant and round under the earth to the ascendant, and the exact day of the epoch will fall within the twenty-eight days earlier than the index date, on the day when the moon crosses the *ascendant* of the horoscope.

2.—Calculate the time on the day of the epoch when the moon's birth longitude sets. This is the time of the epoch. Then compute the longitude of the moon at this date and time. This is the correct ascendant of the horoscope.

3.—Calculate the time on the day of birth when this longitude rises. This is the correct time of birth.

Third Variation.

Ascendant same sex as subject : Moon negative.

1.—As the moon is increasing in light and above the earth, the " count " is made from the moon to the descendant and continued round under the earth to the ascendant. The exact day of the epoch will fall within the twenty-eight days earlier than the index date, and on the day when the moon crosses the ascendant of the horoscope.

2.—Calculate the time on the day of the epoch when the moon's birth longitude *rises*. This is the time of the epoch. Then calculate the longitude of the moon at this particular date and time. This is the correct ascendant of the horoscope.

3.—Calculate the time on the day of birth when this longitude *rises*. This is the correct time of birth.

In all of the epochs derived from the four preceding processes, the moon's position *alone* determines the sex. It will always be found in an area of the same sex as the subject.

III.—FOR SEX EPOCHS ONLY.

(1) *Ascendant and Moon both in same sex as subject.*

1.—Follow the rules for an irregular epoch (1st variation). The epoch so obtained will show the moon in the opposite sex to the subject ; ascendant in same sex. Moon must, therefore, be in a quadrant of same sex as subject.

2.—Follow the rules for an irregular epoch (2nd variation). The epoch so derived will show the moon in the same sex as the subject; ascendant in opposite sex. Moon must, therefore, be in a quadrant of the same sex as subject.

3.—Follow the rules for an irregular epoch (3rd variation). The epoch so derived will give both factors in areas of the same sex as the subject.

The rules for a regular epoch cannot be employed here, as the epoch would show both factors in areas of the opposite sex.

(2) *Ascendant in same sex as subject : Moon opposite sex.*

1.—Follow the rules for a regular epoch. The epoch so obtained shows the moon in the opposite sex to the subject; ascendant in same sex. Moon must, therefore, be in a quadrant of same sex as subject.

2.—Follow the rules for an irregular epoch (2nd variation). The epoch so derived gives both factors in areas of the same sex as the subject.

3.—Follow the rules for an irregular epoch (3rd variation). The epoch so obtained shows the moon in the same sex as the subject; ascendant in opposite sex. Moon must, therefore, be in a quadrant of the same sex as subject.

The first variation of irregular epochs cannot be made use of here, as the epoch would give both factors in areas of the opposite sex to the subject.

(3) *Ascendant opposite sex to subject : Moon same sex.*

1.—Follow the rules for an ordinary regular epoch. The epoch so derived shows the moon in same sex as subject; ascendant in opposite sex. Moon must, therefore, be in a quadrant of the same sex as subject.

2.—Follow the rules for an irregular epoch (1st variation). The epoch so obtained shows both the moon and ascendant in the same sex as the subject.

3.—Follow the rules for an irregular epoch (3rd variation). The epoch so obtained shows the moon in the opposite sex to the subject; ascendant in same sex. The moon must, therefore, be in a quadrant of the same sex as subject.

The second variation of irregular epochs cannot be employed here, as it would give an epoch showing both factors in areas of the opposite sex.

(4) *Both ascendant and Moon in areas of opposite sex to subject.*

1.—Follow the rules for a regular epoch. The epoch so obtained shows both the moon and ascendant in the same sex as the subject.

2.—Follow the rules for an irregular epoch (1st variation). The epoch so obtained shows the moon in the same sex as the subject ; ascendant in opposite sex. The moon must, therefore, be in a quadrant of same sex as subject.

3.—Follow the rules for an irregular epoch (2nd variation). The epoch so derived shows the moon in the opposite sex to the subject ; ascendant in same sex. Moon must, therefore, be in a quadrant of same sex as subject.

The third variation of irregular epochs cannot be employed here, as the epoch obtained would show both factors in areas of the opposite sex.

A number of horoscopes illustrating the method of rectification when the moon is above the earth and decreasing are given in the next chapter. The rules are followed in detail, and the *modus operandi* fully explained.

CHAPTER XI.

ILLUSTRATIONS OF EPOCHS OF THE SECOND ORDER.

(1) The late Duke of Edinburgh was born August 6, 1844, at 7.50 a.m. at Windsor Castle. Lat. 51° 29′ N. Long. 0° 36′ W. This data gives the ascendant as Virgo 17° 12′, and the moon in Taurus 15° 52′, decreasing and above. The ascendant is exactly in a female degree, but as the moon is decreasing, and the moon at the epoch is found in the descending degree of the birth figure, it therefore falls in a male degree. The moon being above and decreasing, period will be more than the norm. Ten lunar revolutions measure to November 7th, 1843, and the epoch will, therefore, fall before noon of the 2nd. Moon decreasing at birth, its longitude will set at :

		H.	M.	S.
		10	21	47
Sid. time, Nov. 1st	.. ..	14	40	30
		19	41	17
Add for W. long.	.. ..		2	24
		19	43	41
Less correction	.. .. ..		3	14
		19	40	27

or. November 2nd, 7h. 40m. 27s. a.m.

The moon's longitude at this time will be 15° 48′ ✕, which is the descendant of the horoscope.

To find the birth-time proceed as follows :

		H.	M.	S.
Moon's longitude sets at	..	4	39	24
Sid. time, noon preceding birth	..	8	56	33
		19	42	51
Add for W. long.	.. ..		2	24
		19	45	15
Less acceleration	.. ..		3	14
		19	42	1

equal to August 6th, 7h. 42m. 1s. a.m., the correct moment of birth. In the epochal figure the ascendant is negative, but the moon is within two degrees of a male point, thus determining the sex to be male.

(2) The Rt. Hon. David Lloyd George was born at Manchester on January 17th, 1863, at 8.55 a.m. Lat. 53° 29′ N. Long 2° 14′ W. This data yields:

R.A.M.C.	..	..	16h. 31m. 13s.	
Ascendant	..	..	9° 30′	♒
Moon ..	..	..	24° 32′	♐

The moon is above and decreasing, and the ascendant is in a female degree. The "count" being made to the descendant brings the moon into a male degree, as required, and the period is longer than the norm.

The index date is January 18th, 1862, and the epoch falls *before* noon of January 9th.

The following calculations determine the epoch:

	H.	M.	S.
Sid. time, moon's place sets ..	21	13	31
„ „ Jan. 8th, 1862 ..	1	5	57
	20	7	34
Add for W. long.		8	56
	20	16	30
Less correction ·		3	19
	20	13	11

or, January 9th, at 8h. 13m. 11s. a.m.

The moon's longitude at that time is 10.22 ♌, which is the descendant of the horoscope:

	H.	M.	S.
This degree sets at	16	33	11
R.A.M.C. at birth	16	31	13
Difference	1	58	

showing the birth-time to be 1m. 58s. later, or 8h. 56m. 58s. a.m. of January 17th, 1863.

The epochal figure shows the moon within 2° of a male degree denoting the required sex.

(3) The late Rt. Hon. Joseph Chamberlain was born in London on July 8th, 1835, at about 2.45 in the morning. Lat. 51° 34′ N. Long. 25s. W.

R.A.M.C.	..	..	21h. 48m. 57s.
Ascendant	..	..	0° 19′ ♋
Moon ..	..	..	13° 5′ ♉

The moon is above and decreasing, and negative. The ascendant is female. The " count " being made to the descendant brings the moon at the epoch into the required sex, but the moon's place rises. The index date is October 9th, 1835, and the moon's distance from the descendant brings the day of the epoch to September 28th, afternoon.

	H.	M.	S.
Sid. time, moon rising	19	19	3
„ „ Sept. 28th, 1835 ..	12	26	10
	6	52	53
Add for W. long.			25
	6	53	18
Less correction		1	8
	6	52	10

equal to 6h. 52m. 10s. p.m. on September 28th, 1835. The moon's longitude at that time is 28° 16′ ♊, the descendant of the horoscope. This points sets with :

	H.	M.	S.
Sid. time of	21	39	58
„ „ July 7th	7	1	56
	14	38	2
Add for W. long.			25
	14	38	27
Less correction		2	24
	14	36	3

or, 2h. 36m. 3s. a.m. of July 8th.

The ascendant of the epoch being negative, the moon has sole rule over the sex. It is found close to a male degree, thus correctly determining the sex.

(4) Backhaus, the noted Russian pianist, was born at Leipzig on March 26th, 1884, at 10.30 a.m. (G.M.T. 9.30, L.M.T. 10h. 19m. 24s. a.m.). Lat. 51° 21′ N. Long. 12° 21′ E.

R.A.M.C.	..	..	22h. 36m. 32s.
Ascendant	..	..	10° 22′ ♋
Moon ..	..	..	24° 43′ ♓

The moon is decreasing and above, and just on the limits of a negative area. The ascendant is female. The " count " is made to the descendant, bringing the moon at the epoch to a male area. The index date is June 26th, and the day of epoch June 21st.

	H.	M.	S.
Sid. time, moon's place sets ..	5	30	10
„ „ June 20th	5	53	25
	23	36	45
Subtract for E. long.	0	49	24
	22	47	21
Less correction		3	44
	22	43	37

or, June 21st at 10h. 43m. 37s. a.m. The moon's longitude at this time is 8° 45′ ♑, the descendant of the horoscope. This point sets at birth with a sidereal time of :

	H.	M.	S.
	22	28	42
Sid. time, March 25th	0	13	24
	22	15	18
Subtract for E. long.		49	24
	21	25	54
Less correction		3	31
	21	22	23
Equal to March 26th, 1884 ..	9	22	23 G.M.T.
	10	22	23 Stan. T.
	10	11	47 L.M.T.

The ascendant of the epoch will be negative, and the moon in a male area, thus confirming the sex.

(5) The Czar Nicholas of Russia was born on May 18th, 1868, at noon at Petrograd. Lat. 59° 57′ N. Long. 30° 18′ E.

R.A.M.C.	..	..	3h. 45m. 27s.
Ascendant	..	..	9° 4′ ♍
Moon ..	..	..	9° 17′ ♈

The moon is above the earth and decreasing, and in a male area. The ascendant is also in a male area.

The index date is August 19th, 1867, and the day of epoch falls after noon of the 16th. The moon being in a male degree, its place rises at the epoch with a sidereal time of :

		H.	M.	S.
		18	8	35
Sid. time, August 16th ..	..	9	37	39
		8	30	56
Subtract E. long.	.. ..	2	1	12
		6	29	44
Less correction ..	.. ..		1	4
G.M.T. of epoch ..	.. ..	6	28	40

or, August 16th, 1867, at 6h. 28m. 40s. p.m., G.M.T.

The moon's longitude at this time is 8° ♓ 32′, the descendant of the horoscope. This point sets with :

			H.	M.	S.
Sid. time of	..	.. ..	3	42	0
* „ „ May 17th	..	..	3	41	51
			0	0	9
Subtract for E. long.	..	..	2	1	12
			21	58	57
Less correction ..	..	..		3	36
			21	55	21

or, May 18th, 9h. 55m. 21s. a.m., G.M.T., equal to May 18th, 11h. 56m. 33s. a.m., Petrograd local time.

The epoch shows the ascendant to be male. The moon is in a female degree, but a male quadrant, thus determining the sex as male.

---

* The Sid. time on May 18th, being 3h. 45m. 47s., greater than 3h. 42m. 0s. the Sid. time of the previous noon is taken.

(6) King Haakon of Norway was born on August 3rd, 1872, at 4 p.m., Copenhagen. Lat. 55° 40′ N. Long. 12° 35′ E.

R.A.M.C.	..	..	12h. 50m. 0s.	
Ascendant	..	..	8° 30′	♐
Moon ..	..	..	3° 3′	♌

The moon is above and decreasing, and negative. The ascendant is male. The " count " being made to the descendant brings the moon into a female area, and it must, therefore, be continued round to the ascendant. The index date is November 4th, and the day of the epoch is, October 17th, 1871, after noon.

	H.	M.	S.
The moon's place sets with sid. time	16	26	15
Sid. time, October 17th ..	13	42	11
	2	44	4
Subtract for E. long.		50	20
	1	53	44
Less correction			19
Time of epoch	1	53	25

At this time the moon's longitude is 8° 24′ ♐ , the ascendant of the horoscope. This point rises with sidereal time of 12h. 49m. 21s., or 39s. earlier than at the given time. The correct time of birth is, therefore, 3h. 59m. 21s. p.m.

The ascendant of the epoch is negative, and the moon being in a male area confirms the sex.

(7) Lord Rosebery was born in London on May 7th, 1847, at 3 a.m. Long. 38s. W.

R.A.M.C.	..	..	17h. 56m. 43s.	
Ascendant	..	..	28° 3′	♓
Moon ..	..	..	5° 14′	♒

The moon is above the earth and decreasing, and both factors are in areas of the female sex. As the interchange reverses both factors, the epoch is purely regular.

The index date is August 6th, 1846, and the moon's distance from the descendant brings the day of the epoch to July 28th before noon.

		H.	M.	S.
Sid. time, moon's place sets ..		o	48	1
„ „ July 27th		8	19	8
		16	28	53
Add for W. long.				38
		16	29	31
Less correction			2	42
		16	26	49

This is July 28th, 1846, at 4h. 26m. 49s. a.m., and the moon is then in 27° 38′ ♍, which is the descendant of the horoscope. This point sets with a sidereal time of 17h. 56m. 3s., or 40s. earlier than at the recorded time, showing the exact birth-moment to be 2h. 59m. 20s. a.m.

Both factors are then in areas of the male sex, thus proving the epoch to be correct.

(8) Princess Louise, eldest daughter of the late King Edward VII, was born in London (37s. W.) on February 29th, 1867, at 6.35 a.m.

R.A.M.C.	..	..	16h. 33m. 17s.
Ascendant	..	..	13° 37′ ♒
Moon ..	..	..	19° 42′ ♍

Both factors are in female degrees, but, as a regular epoch would reverse the sex, the " count " is made from the moon to the descendant and round under the earth to the ascendant, increasing the gestative period by 15½ days. The index date is May 22nd, 1866, and the epoch falls on May 7th just after noon.

		H.	M.	S.
Sid. time, moon's place rises ..		5	1	34
„ „ May 7th		3	0	24
		2	1	10
Add for W. long.				37
		2	1	47
Less correction				20
		2	1	27

This shows the time of epoch to be 2h. 1m. 27s. p.m. of May 7th, 1866, when the moon is in 12° 54′ ♒, the ascendant of the horoscope. This degree rises with a sidereal time of 16h. 31m. 37s., or 1m. 40s. less than at the given birth-time, thus making the correct time 6h. 33m. 20s. a.m. The epoch then shows both factors in areas of the female sex.

CHAPTER XII.

RECTIFICATION OF EPOCHS OF THE THIRD ORDER.

THE preliminary calculations having been made, according to the rules given in Chapter VII, the process of calculating the epoch and rectifying the birth-time when the epoch is of the Third Order is as follows :—

I.—FOR REGULAR EPOCHS ONLY.

Ascendant same sex as subject : Moon negative.

1.—As the moon is increasing in light, and below the earth, the " count " is made from the moon to the ascendant, and the exact day of the epoch will be within the fourteen days earlier than the index date, and on the day when the moon crosses the longitude of the ascendant of the horoscope.

2.—Calculate the time on the day of the epoch when the moon's birth longitude rises. This is the time of the epoch. At the same time, calculate the longitude of the moon at this particular day and time. This is the ascendant of the horoscope.

3.—Calculate the time on the day of birth when this longitude rises. This is the correct time of birth.

II.—FOR IRREGULAR EPOCHS ONLY.

FIRST VARIATION.

Ascendant same sex as subject : Moon negative.

1.—As the moon is increasing in light, and below the earth, the " count " is made from the moon to the ascendant, and the exact day of the epoch will be within the fourteen days preceding the index date, and on the day when the moon crosses the ascendant of the horoscope.

2.—Calculate time on the day of the epoch when the moon's birth longitude *sets*. This is the time of the epoch. Then calculate the longitude of the moon at this day and time. This is the correct ascendant of the horoscope.

3.—Calculate the time on the day of birth when this longitude rises. This is the correct time of birth.

SECOND VARIATION.

Ascendant opposite sex to subject : Moon negative.

1.—As the moon is increasing in light, and below the earth, the " count " is made from the moon to the ascendant, and round over the earth to the descendant. The exact day of the epoch will be within the twenty-eight days preceding the index date, and on the day when the moon crosses the descendant of the horoscope.

2.—Calculate the time on the day of epoch when the moon's birth longitude rises. This is the time of the epoch. Then calculate the moon's longitude at this particular date and time. This is the correct descendant of the horoscope.

3.—Calculate the time on the day of birth when this longitude sets. This is the correct time of birth.

THIRD VARIATION.

Ascendant opposite sex to subject : Moon negative.

1.—As the moon is increasing in light, and below the earth, the " count " is made from the moon to the ascendant, and round over the earth to the descendant, and the exact day of the epoch will fall within the twenty-eight days preceding the index date, and on the day when the moon crosses the descendant of the horoscope.

2.—Calculate the time on the day of the epoch when the moon's birth longitude sets. This is the time of the epoch. Then calculate the moon's longitude at this particular day and time. This is the correct descendant of the horoscope.

3.—Calculate the time on the day of birth when this longitude sets. This is the correct time of birth.

In all the epochs derived from the four preceding processes, the moon's position alone determines the sex. It will always be found in an area of the same sex as the subject.

III.—FOR SEX EPOCHS ONLY.

(1) *Ascendant and Moon both in same sex as subject.*

1.—Follow the rules for a regular epoch. The epoch so obtained shows both factors in areas of the same sex as the subject.

2.—Follow the rules for an irregular epoch (1st variation). The epoch so obtained shows the moon in the same sex as the subject ; ascendant in opposite sex. The moon must, therefore, be in a quadrant of same sex as subject.

3.—Follow the rules for an irregular epoch (2nd variation). The epoch so derived shows the moon in the opposite sex to the subject ; ascendant in same sex. Moon must, therefore, be placed in a quadrant of same sex as subject.

The rules for an irregular epoch (3rd variation) cannot here be employed, as the epoch obtained would show both factors in areas of the opposite sex to the subject.

(2) Ascendant in same sex as subject : Moon opposite sex.

1.—Follow the rules for an ordinary regular epoch. The epoch so obtained shows the moon in the same sex as the subject ; ascendant in opposite sex. Moon must, therefore, be in a quadrant of same sex as subject.

2.—Follow the rules for an irregular epoch (1st variation). The epoch now derived shows both factors in areas of the same sex as the subject.

3.—Follow the rules for an irregular epoch (3rd variation). The epoch so obtained shows the moon in the opposite sex to the subject ; ascendant in same sex. Moon must, therefore, be in a quadrant of same sex as subject.

The rules for an irregular epoch (2nd variation) cannot be employed here, as the epoch so obtained would show both factors in areas of the opposite sex to the subject.

(3) Ascendant in opposite sex to subject : Moon same sex.

1.—Follow the rules for an ordinary regular epoch. The epoch obtained will give the moon in the opposite sex to the subject ; ascendant in same sex. Moon must, therefore, hold a quadrant of same sex as subject.

2.—Follow the rules for an irregular epoch (2nd variation). The epoch so obtained shows both factors in areas of the same sex as the subject.

3.—Follow the rules for an irregular epoch (3rd variation). The epoch so obtained will show the moon in the same sex as the subject ; ascendant in opposite sex. Moon must therefore be in a quadrant of same sex as the subject.

The rules for an irregular epoch (1st variation) cannot here be employed, as the epoch so derived shows both factors in areas of the opposite sex to the subject.

(4) *Ascendant and Moon both in areas of opposite sex to subject.*

1.—Follow the rules for an irregular epoch (1st variation). The epoch so derived shows the moon in the opposite sex to the subject ; ascendant in same sex.   Moon must, therefore, be in a quadrant of same sex as subject.

2.—Follow the rules for an irregular epoch (2nd variation). The epoch so obtained shows the moon in same sex as subject ; ascendant opposite sex.   Moon must, therefore, be a quadrant of same sex as subject.

3.—Follow the rules for an irregular epoch (3rd variation). This epoch will give both factors in areas of the same sex as the subject.

The rules for a regular epoch cannot be employed here, as the epoch would give both factors in degrees of the opposite sex.

In the next chapter illustrations will be given from the horoscopes of notable people, where possible, of the different processes enumerated herein.   The horoscopes chosen have the moon below the earth and increasing, and the rules as detailed above are fully explained.

CHAPTER XIII.

ILLUSTRATIONS OF EPOCHS OF THE THIRD ORDER.

(1) The late Duke of Cambridge, born March 26th, 1819, at 2.11 a.m. at Hanover. Lat. 52° 23′ N. Long. 9° 42′ E.

This data gives the ascendant Capricorn 1° 3′, and the moon in Aries 5° 42′. The moon is below and increasing.

The ascending degree is male, being within a male area, but the moon is not within orbs of a sex degree.

The moon being below and increasing, the period is more than the norm, and the moon at the epoch must be in the ascending degree of the birth-figure to obtain the required sex.

Ten lunar revolutions backward, measure to June 25th, 1818, and the epoch will be found seven days earlier, viz., June 18th. The moon being increasing, its longitude will rise at :

	H.	M.	S.
	18	9	11
Sid. time, June 18th, 1818 ..	5	44	27
	12	24	44
Subtract for E. long.		38	48
	11	45	56
Less correction		1	56
	11	44	0

equal to June 18th, 1818, 11h. 44m. p.m.

The longitude of the moon is ♑ 1° 57′ at this time, and this is the ascendant of the epoch.

The time of birth is found as follows :

	H.	M.	S.
Sid. time when 1·57 ♑ rises ..	14	25	30
Sid. time March 25th, 1819 ..	0	8	26
	14	17	4
Less for E. long.		38	48
	13	38	16
Less correction		2	14
G.M.T.	13	36	2
Local mean time	14	14	50

or, March 26th, 2h. 14m. 50s. a.m.

The ascendant of the epoch being negative, the sex is determined by the position of the moon. This orb is found within 2° of a male point, ♑ 0°, thus showing the sex to be male.

(2) The youngest son of the King of Spain, born October 24th, 1914, at 8 a.m., at Madrid, Spain. Lat. 40° 24′ N. Long. 3° 41′ W.

Greenwich mean time is used at Madrid, hence the true local mean time of birth was 7h. 45m. 16s. a.m. This data yields :

R.A.M.C.	..	..	9h. 52m. 48s.
Ascendant	..	..	15° 57′ ♏
Moon ..	..	..	9° 57′ ♑

The moon is placed in a male area, below and increasing. The ascendant is in a female area.

The index date—the tenth revolution of the moon prior to birth—is January 24th, 1914, and the moon being below and increasing, the period of gestation is longer than the norm, making the day of epoch on January 20th, in the forenoon.

The epochal computation is as follows :

	H.	M.	S.
Sid. time, moon's place rises ..	14	8	24
„ „ January 19th, 1914 ..	19	52	8
	18	16	16
Add for W. long.		14	44
	18	31	0
Less correction		3	2
	18	27	58

or, January 20th, 6h. 27m. 58s. a.m.

The moon at this time is in ♏ 15° 32′, which is the ascendant of the horoscope.

	H.	M.	S.
R.A.M.C. when 15° 32′ ♏ rises ..	9	50	41
„ at given birth-time ..	9	52	48
Difference		2	7

The birth-time was, therefore, 7h. 57m. 53s. a.m., G.M.T., or 7h. 43m. 9s. Madrid time.

The epochal figures show a male area rising, and the moon in a female area, but the moon holding a male quadrant denotes the sex to be male.

(3) The King of Spain, born May 17th, 1886, at 0.30 p.m., Madrid. Lat. 40° 24′ N. Long. 3° 41′ W.

R.A.M.C.	.. ..	4h. 10m. 33s.
Ascendant	.. ..	8° 16′ ♍
Moon	.. ..	19° 44′ ♏

The moon is below and increasing, and in a female area. The ascendant is male. The moon at the epoch will be found in the ascendant of the horoscope, but being female its place will set. The index date is August 17th, and the exact day of the epoch after noon of the 11th August.

	H.	M.	S.
Sid. time, moon's place sets ..	20	6	10
„ „ August 11th, 1885 ..	9	20	27
	10	45	43
Add for W. long.		14	44
	11	0	27
Subtract correction		1	48
	10	58	39

or, August 11th, 1885, at 10h. 58m. 39s. p.m., G.M.T. The moon's longitude at this time is ♍ 9° 23′, which is the ascendant of the horoscope.

	H.	M.	S.
♍ 9° 23′ rises with sid. time ..	4	16	12
Sid. time, May 17th, 1886 ..	3	40	26
	0	35	46
Add for W. long.		14	44
	0	50	30
Less correction			8
	0	50	22

The correct birth-time is, therefore, 0h. 50m. 22s. p.m., G.M.T., or 0h. 35m. 38s., Madrid time.

The epoch gives a male area rising, and the moon in the same sex, thus showing the required sex.

(4) Manual Garcia, a noted Spanish toreador, was born at Seville, on January 18th, 1866, at 1.15 a.m. Lat. 37° 24′ N. Long. 5° 58′ W. G.M.T., 1.39 a.m.

R.A.M.C.	.. ..	9h. 3m. 58s.
Ascendant	.. ..	7° 12′ ♏
Moon	.. ..	12° 53′ ♒

The ascendant is in a male area. The moon is increasing and below, and female. The index date is April 19th, 1865, and the " count," being made from the moon to the ascendant, brings the day of the epoch seven days earlier, just after noon of April 12th. The moon being female, its birth place sets :

	H.	M.	S.
Sid. time moon's place sets ..	2	7	25
„ „ April 12th	1	22	48
	0	44	37
Add for W. long.		23	52
	1	8	29
Less correction			11
	1	8	18

This is 1h. 8m. 18s. p.m. G.M.T., and the moon's longitude is then 7° 33′ ♏ the ascendant of the horoscope. This point rises with a sidereal time of 9h. 4m. 43s., or 45s. later than at the given time, showing the exact moment of birth to be 1h. 15m. 45s. a.m.

The epoch shows a male area rising, and the moon also in a male area, thus confirming the sex.

(5) Princess Juliana of Holland was born on April 30th, 1909, at 6.50 a.m., Greenwich time. Lat. 52° 4′ N. Long. 4° 20′ E. The true local time of birth was 7h. 7m. 20s. a.m.

The R.A.M.C. is	..	21h. 37m. 38s.
Ascendant	..	28° 21′ ♊
Moon ..	..	11° 32′ ♍

The moon is below and increasing, and negative. The ascendant is close to a female point. The index date is July 30th, 1908, and the " count," being made from the moon to the ascendant, brings the day of epoch to July 25th before noon.

	H.	M.	S.
Sid. time, moon's place rises ..	4	14	20
„ „ July 24th, 1908 ..	8	7	13
	20	7	7
Subtract for E. long.		17	20
	19	49	47
Less correction		3	15
	19	46	32

This is equal to 7h. 46m. 32s. a.m., of July 25th, G.M.T., at which time the moon is in 29° 0′ ♊ —the ascendant of the horoscope. This point rises with a sidereal time of 20h. 40m. 23s., showing the exact time of birth to be 2m. 45s. later than recorded.

The epoch shows a negative degree rising, and the moon in a female degree, thus confirming the sex.

(6) A gentleman well known in the Astrological publishing world was born at Bath on July 13th, 1869, at 5.40 a.m. Lat. 51° 21′ N. Long. 2° 21′ W.

The R.A.M.C. is ..	0h. 55m. 10s.	
Ascendant	6° 24′	♌
Moon	10° 3′	♍

The moon is below and increasing, and negative. The ascendant is male. The index date is October 12th, 1868, and the " count," being made from the moon to the ascendant, brings the day of epoch two days earlier, viz., October 10th, after noon. The moon's birth-place sets, the epoch being irregular :

	H.	M.	S.
Sid. time, moon's place sets ..	17	25	49
„ „ October 10th, 1868 ..	13	17	28
	4	8	21
Add for W. long.		9	24
	4	17	45
Less correction			42
	4	17	3

This is 4h. 17m. 3s. p.m., of October 10th, at which time the moon is in Leo, 6° 13′—the ascendant of the horoscope. This point rises with a sidereal time of 0h. 54m. 4s., showing the birth-time to be 1m. 6s. earlier than recorded, or 5h. 38m. 54s. a.m.

The epoch shows a negative degree rising, and the moon in a male degree, thus confirming the sex.

(7) Princess Arthur of Connaught (Duchess of Fife), born May 17th, 1891, at 5 a.m., London. Long. 47s. W. This data gives :

R.A.M.C. ..	..	..		20h. 37m.	40s.
Ascendant ..	..	..		11° 51′	♊
Moon	..	..		11° 27′	♍

The moon is below and increasing, and in a negative area. The ascendant is in a female area.

The moon being below and increasing, the " count " is made from the moon to the ascendant, and the period of gestation is increased by 7 days. The index date is August 17th, 1890, and the moon crosses the ascending degree between the noons of August 9th and 10th.

In Rule 2 the variation has to be made. The moon is increasing, but its place descends at the epoch as under :

		H.	M.	S.
The moon's long. sets at	..	17	28	44
Sid. time, August 9th ..	..	9	11	43
		8	17	1
Add for W. long.				47
		8	17	48
Correction	..		1	22
		8	16	26

or, August 9th, 8h. 16m. 26s. p.m. The longitude of the moon at this time is Gemini 13° 11′, which becomes the ascendant of the rectified horoscope.

The correct time of birth is obtained in the following manner :

		H.	M.	S.
Sid. time, when Gemini 13° 11′ rises		20	41	48
Sid. time, May 16th, 1891	..	3	35	39
		17	6	9
Add for W. long.				47
		17	6	56
Less correction			2	48
		17	4	8

This is equal to May 17th, 1891, at 5h. 4m. 8s. a.m.

The epoch shows a negative degree rising with the moon in a female area, thus denoting the sex.

CHAPTER XIV.

Rectification of Epochs of the Fourth Order.

The preliminary calculations having been made, according to the rules given in Chapter VII, the process of calculating the epoch and rectifying the birth-time when the epoch is of the Fourth Order is as follows :—

FOR REGULAR EPOCHS ONLY.

Ascendant opposite sex to subject : Moon negative.

1.—As the moon is decreasing in light, and below the earth, the " count " is made from the moon to the descendant, and the exact day of the epoch will be within the fourteen days following the index date, and on the day when the moon crosses the descendant of the horoscope of birth.

2.—Calculate the time on the day of the epoch when the moon's birth longitude *sets*. This is the time of the epoch. Then calculate the longitude of the moon at this particular date and time. This is the descendant of the horoscope.

3.—Calculate the time on the day of birth when this longitude *sets*. This is the correct time of birth.

FOR IRREGULAR EPOCHS ONLY.

First Variation.

Ascendant opposite sex to subject : Moon negative.

1.—As the moon is decreasing in light and below the earth, the " count " is made from the moon to the descendant, and the exact day of the epoch will fall within the fourteen days following the index date, and on the day when the moon crosses the descendant of the horoscope.

2.—Calculate the time on the day of the epoch when the moon's birth longitude *rises*. This is the time of the epoch. Then calculate the longitude of the moon at this particular date and time. This is the correct descendant of the horoscope.

3.—Calculate the time on the day of birth when this longitude *sets*. This is the correct time of birth.

Second Variation.

Ascendant same sex as subject : Moon negative.

1.—As the moon is decreasing in light and below the earth, the "count" is made from the moon to the descendant, and round over the earth to the ascendant, and the exact day of the epoch will fall within the twenty-eight days following the index date, and on the day when the moon crosses the *ascendant* of the horoscope.

2.—Calculate the time on the day of the epoch when the moon's birth longitude *sets*. This is the time of the epoch. Then compute the longitude of the moon at this particular date and time. This is the correct ascendant of the horoscope.

3.—Calculate the time on the day of birth when this longitude *rises*. This is the correct time of birth.

Third Variation.

Ascendant same sex as subject : Moon negative.

1.—As the moon is decreasing in light, and below the earth, the "count" is made from the moon to the descendant, and round over the earth to the ascendant, and the exact day of the epoch will be within the twenty-eight days following the index date, and on the day when the moon crosses the *ascendant* of the horoscope.

2.—Calculate the time on the day of the epoch when the moon's birth longitude *rises*. This is the time of the epoch. Then calculate the longitude of the moon at this particular day and hour. This is the correct ascendant of the horoscope.

3.—Calculate the time on the day of birth when this longitude *rises*. This is the correct time of birth.

In all the epochs derived from the four preceding processes the moon's position alone determines the sex. It will always be found in an area of the same sex as the subject.

FOR SEX EPOCHS ONLY.

(1) *Ascendant and Moon both in the same sex as subject.*

1.—Follow the rules for an irregular epoch (1st variation). The epoch so obtained shows the moon in the opposite sex to the subject; ascendant in same sex. Moon must, therefore, be in a quadrant of the same sex as the subject.

2.—Follow the rules for an irregular epoch (2nd variation). The epoch so obtained shows the moon in the same sex as the subject; ascendant in opposite sex. Moon must, therefore, be in a quadrant of same sex as subject.

3.—Follow the rules for an irregular epoch (3rd variation). The epoch so obtained shows both factors in areas of the same sex as the subject.

The rules for a regular epoch cannot be here employed, as the epoch so obtained would show both factors in areas of the opposite sex to the subject.

(2) *Ascendant same sex as subject : Moon opposite sex.*

1.—Follow the rules for a regular epoch. The epoch so obtained shows the moon in the opposite sex to the subject; ascendant in same sex. Moon must, therefore, be in a quadrant of same sex as subject.

2.—Follow the rules for an irregular epoch (2nd variation). The epoch so derived shows both factors in areas of the same sex as the subject.

3.—Follow the rules for an irregular epoch (3rd variation). The epoch so obtained shows the moon in the same sex as the subject; ascendant in opposite sex. Moon must, therefore, be in a quadrant of the same sex as subject.

The first variation of irregular epochs cannot be made use of here, as the epoch would give both factors in areas of the opposite sex to the subject.

(3) *Ascendant opposite sex to subject : Moon same sex.*

1.—Follow the rules for a regular epoch. This epoch will give the moon in the same sex as subject; ascendant in opposite sex. Moon must, therefore, be in a quadrant of same sex as subject.

2.—Follow the rules for an irregular epoch (1st variation). This epoch will give both factors in areas of the same sex as subject.

3.—Follow the rules for an irregular epoch (3rd variation). The epoch so obtained will show the moon in the opposite sex to the subject; ascendant in the same sex. The moon must then be in a quadrant of the same sex as subject.

The second variation of irregular epochs cannot be employed here, as the epoch would show both factors in areas of the opposite sex to the subject.

(4) *Ascendant and Moon both in areas of the opposite sex to subject.*

1.—Follow the rules for a regular epoch. The epoch so derived gives both factors in areas of the same sex as the subject.

2.—Follow the rules for an irregular epoch (1st variation). The epoch so obtained shows the moon in the same sex as the subject ; ascendant in opposite sex. Moon must, therefore, be in a quadrant of same sex as subject.

3.—Follow the rules for an irregular epoch (2nd variation). The epoch so derived shows the moon in the opposite sex to the subject ; ascendant in same sex. Moon must, therefore, be in a quadrant of same sex as subject.

The third variation of irregular epochs cannot be employed here, as the epoch obtained would show both factors in areas of the opposite sex to the subject.

Illustrations of the Fourth Order of Epochs will be given in the next chapter.

CHAPTER XV.

ILLUSTRATIONS OF EPOCHS OF THE FOURTH ORDER.

SEVERAL horoscopes are given in this chapter, with the moon placed below the earth and decreasing, thus conforming to the Fourth Order of Epochs. The rules given in the preceding chapter are followed in detail in explaining the process of rectification.

(1) The Grand Duchess Marie of Russia, born at Petrograd, on June 26th, 1899, at noon. Lat. 59° 56′ N. Long. 30° 18′ E.

The moon in this case is decreasing and below, and the ascendant is in a male degree.

The data of birth yields the following positions for the two factors :

R.A.M.C.	.. ..	6h. 17m. 15s.
Ascendant	.. ..	2° 41′ ♎
Moon ..	.. ..	13° 48′ ♒

The moon being decreasing, the " count " is made to the descendant, and, this being a degree of the required sex, the moon will be found therein at the epoch. Ten revolutions of the moon measure to September 26th, 1898, and the actual date of the epoch is three days later.

Although the moon is decreasing at birth, its radical place will *rise* at the epoch :

		H. M. S.
Moon's place rises	.. ..	17 9 53
Sid. time, Sept. 29th, 1898	..	12 33 5
		4 36 48
Deduct for E. long.	.. ..	2 1 12
		2 35 36
Less correction ..	.. ..	25
		2 35 11

Time of epoch, September 29th, 1898, at 2h. 35m. 11s., p.m., G.M.T.

Moon's longitude and descendant of horoscope : ♈ 1° 54′.
The R.A.M.C., when this degree sets, is 6h. 12m. 14s.,
or 4m. 49s. less than at the given birth-time. The correct
time of birth will, therefore, be 11h. 55m. 1s.
The epoch shows the moon in 1° 54′ ♈ a *female* degree.

(2) The late King Carlos of Portugal, born September
28th, 1863, at 1.35 p.m., Lisbon. Lat. 38° 42′ N. Long.
9° 8′ W.

R.A.M.C.	.. ..	14h. 2m. 26s.
Ascendant	.. ..	9° 43′ ♑
Moon ..	.. ..	21° 24′ ♈

The ascendant is male ; the moon is decreasing and below,
and also male. The index date is December 29th, 1862, but,
as the descendant is female, the " count " has to be made
from the moon to that point and round over the earth to
the ascendant, curtailing the gestative period by 20½ days.
(moon from ascendant, 267° ÷ 13 = 20½ days.) The epoch
falls before noon of January 18th, 1863, and the moon's
place rises :

	H.	M.	S.
Sid. time, moon's place rising..	18	54	37
„ „ January 17th ..	19	45	39
	23	8	58
Add for W. long.		36	32
	23	45	30
Less correction		3	54
	23	41	36

equal to January 18th at 11h. 41m. 36s. a.m., G.M.T. The
moon's longitude at this time is ♑ 11° 19′—the ascendant
of the horoscope.

	H.	M.	S.
This point rises with sid. time ..	14	8	40
Sid. time, September 28th ..	12	27	4
	1	41	36
Add for W. long.		36	32
	2	18	8
Less correction			23
Time of birth G.M.T.	2	17	45

This is equal to Lisbon mean time of 1h. 41m. 13s. p.m. The epoch shows both factors in male areas giving the required sex.

(3) Mr. George R. Sims ("Dagonet" of the *Referee*) was born in London on September 2nd, 1847, at 6 p.m.

The R.A.M.C. is	..	16h. 45m. 2s.
Ascendant ..	..	18° 53′ ♒
Moon	..	20° 20′ ♊

This is a regular epoch of the Fourth Order. Both factors are female, but as the "count" is made from the moon to the descendant, and the moon's place sets, their sex positions are reversed at the epoch. The index date is December 3rd, 1846, and the moon is found in the descendant *before* noon on the 8th :

	H.	M.	S.
The moon's place sets with sid. time	13	27	43
Sid. time, December 7th ..	17	3	30
	20	24	13
Correction		3	21
	20	20	52

or, December 8th, at 8h. 20m. 52s. a.m.

The moon's longitude at this time is 18° 22′ ♌ the descendant of the horoscope. This point sets with a sidereal time of 16h. 43m. 54s., or 1m. 8s. less than at the recorded time, showing the true moment of birth to be 5h. 58m. 52s. p.m.

(4) Prince George of Wales was born on December 20th, 1902, at Sandringham, at 7.35 p.m. Lat. 52° 52′ N. Long. 0° 32′ E.

The R.A.M.C. is	..	1h. 30m. 55s.
Ascendant ..	..	13° 40′ ♌
Moon	..	15° 29′ ♍

The moon is decreasing and below, and female. The ascendant is male. The "count" has, therefore, to be made right round the map to the ascendant, decreasing the period of gestation by 25 days. The index date is March 22nd ; the epoch, therefore, falls on April 16th after noon. The moon's place, however, rises :

		H.	M.	S.
Sid. time, moon's place rises	..	4	36	9
„ „ April 16th	..	1	34	47
		3	1	22
Subtract for E. long.	..		2	8
		2	59	14
Less correction	..			29
		2	58	45

This is April 16th, 1902, at 2h. 58m. 45s. p.m., and the moon's longitude is then 13° 25′ ♌—the ascendant of the horoscope. This point rises with a sidereal time of 1h. 29m. 32s., showing the exact birth-time to be 1m. 23s. earlier than recorded, or 7h. 33m. 37s. p.m.

The epoch shows a female degree rising, with the moon in a male degree and a male quadrant, thus determining the sex to be male.

(5) Princess Mary of Wales was born in London on April 25th, 1897, at 3.30 p.m. Long. 45′ W.

The R.A.M.C. is	..	5h. 44m. 52s.
Ascendant	.. ..	27° 19′ ♍
Moon ..	.. ..	26° 22′ ♒

The moon is below and decreasing, and negative. The ascendant is male. The " count " is therefore made to the descendant, and the period of gestation is decreased by a little over two days. The index date is July 26th, 1896, and the epoch will, therefore, fall on July 29th before noon.

		H.	M.	S.
Sid. time, moon's place sets	..	2	48	15
„ „ July 28th	..	8	26	36
		18	21	39
Add for W. long.	..			45
		18	22	24
Less correction	..		3	1
		18	19	23

This is 6h. 19m. 23s. a.m. of July 29th, and the moon's longitude is then 28° 12′ ♓ the descendant of the horoscope. This point sets with a sidereal time of 5h. 50m. 0s., showing the exact birth-time to be 3h. 35m. 8s. p.m.

The epoch shows a negative degree rising, and the moon in a female degree, thus confirming the sex.

(6) The late Mr. R. Hutton, once editor of the *Spectator*, was born at Leeds on June 2nd, 1826, at 7 p.m. Lat. 53° 48′ N. Long. 1° 32′ W.

The R.A.M.C. is	..	11h.	42m.	50s.
Ascendant	..	.. 28°	35′	♏
Moon ..	..	.. 9°	24′	♉

This is a difficult case, as the ascendant is just on the border line between areas of different sexes. It is really male, but a couple of minutes earlier would make it female. However, I will treat it as an ordinary regular epoch of the fourth order. The index date is September 2nd, 1825, and the epoch should fall about noon of the 4th, probably just before. The moon is female.

	H.	M.	S.
Sid. time, moon's place sets ..	9	45	45
„ „ September 3rd ..	10	49	19
	22	56	26
Add for W. long.		6	8
	23	2	34
Less correction		3	47
	22	58	47

As the sidereal time when the moon's place sets was less than that of September 4th, it shows the epoch did take place before noon of that date, hence I take the S.T. of the previous day. The correction shows the time of the epoch to be 10h. 58m. 47s. a.m., of September 4th, when the moon was in 27° 50′ ♉ the descendant of the horoscope. This point sets with a sidereal time of 11h. 39m. 19s., or 3m. 31s. less than at the recorded time, showing the exact birth-time to be 6h. 36m. 29s. p.m.

The epoch shows the ascendant to be male, and brings the moon just within an area of the male sex, it being 6° 24′ from the exact point. It thus determines the sex.

(7) Mr. Edward Francis Fay, journalist, better known as "The Bounder," was born on April 6th, 1853, at 4.30 a.m., London.

R.A.M.C.	..	..	17h. 27m. 30s.
Ascendant	..	..	10° 53′ ♓
Moon ..	..	..	20° 5′ ♓

The moon is below and decreasing, and male. The ascendant is just on the border-line of areas of the opposite sex. It is in reality male, but a couple of minutes would bring it into a female area. The "count" has to be made to the descendant, so that it is complicated.

The index date is July 7th, 1852, and the epoch will probably fall just before noon of the 20th July.

		H.	M.	S.
Sid. time, moon's place sets	..	5	3	41
„ „ July 19th	.. ..	7	49	43
		21	13	58
Less correction	.. .. ..		3	29
		21	10	29

This gives 9h. 10m. 29s. a.m. of July 20th, and the moon's longitude will then be 9° 3′ ♍ the descendant of the horoscope. This point sets with a sidereal time of 17h. 24m. 16s., or 3m. 14s. less than at the recorded time, showing the birth to have taken place at 4h. 26m. 46s. a.m.

The epoch shows a female degree rising, but the moon is now in a male area, and a male quadrant, thus determining the sex.

CHAPTER XVI.

The Cause of Irregularity.

It will be observed that in the rules given for each Order of Epoch there are really only four different methods of computation—one regular and three irregular. The student at this point will doubtless ask the question: "What is the cause of this irregularity or variation?" It is a just and reasonable query, and one that demands a full and proper answer.

The causes governing irregular epochs are mainly those of sex. If the epoch is calculated in the ordinary regular manner, it either produces a birth-time which is considerably different from what is known to be the correct time, or it produces an epoch which shows the contrary sex. In the first case, although the epoch may show the proper sex, the fact that it alters the time of birth outside the limits of an ordinary error of observation, which should not in any case exceed four or five minutes, the epoch is brought into line with the birth-time by a reversal of the rising or setting of the moon, making the moon set when increasing in light, and rise when decreasing. In the case where the epoch shows the contrary sex, even though it may confirm the birth-time, it is brought into line by taking the extended "count," *i.e.* taking the moon's distance from the opposite horizon, according to the rules given in Chapter IV. This process reverses the sex, and thus shows what is required. Two illustrations of this point are appended, one of each irregularity, showing how the variation in the interchange brings things to a correct issue.

The horoscope of Princess Arthur of Connaught, given in Chapter XIII, is a good illustration of the first irregularity. The longitudes of the two factors are:—

Ascendant	..	..	11° 51′ ♊
Moon	.. ..	..	11° 27′ ♍

The moon is below and increasing, and to all appearances it is a regular epoch of the Third Order. I propose to treat it as such, and append the full calculations.

The index date is August 17th, 1890, and, the moon being distant from the ascendant 90°, equal to nearly seven days, the actual day of the epoch will fall between the noons of August 9th and 10th. The moon increasing at birth, its place will rise at the epoch, and the moon will then be in the rising sign of the horoscope.   Thus :

		H.	M.	S.
Sid. time, Moon's longitude rises		4	14	37
„ „ August 9th		9	11	43
		19	2	54
Add for W. long.				47
		19	3	41
Less correction			3	7
		19	0	34

This is equal to August 10th, at 7h. 0m. 34s. a.m., at which time the moon will be in Gemini 18° 40′—which will be the ascendant at birth.

The moon's place at the epoch being the ascendant at birth, the time when this degree rises will be the correct birth-time.

The following is, therefore, the process :

		H.	M.	S.
Sid. time, when Gemini 18°40′ rises		21	1	52
„ „ May 16th, 1891 ..		3	35	39
		17	26	13
Add for W. long.				47
		17	27	0
Less correction for 17h. 27m. ..			2	52
		17	24	8

This is equal to May 17th, 1891, at 5h. 24m. 8s. a.m.

The rectification, therefore, alters the birth-time by 24m. 8s.—an utterly impossible alteration. Reference to the epoch shows that the ascendant is in a negative area, so that the area occupied by the moon is the deciding factor. It is found in a female area, hence confirms the sex.   It is, therefore, apparent that this case is not a regular one of the Third Order.

A point of interest arises in this case, which students will do well to note. At the given time of birth, ♊ 11° 51′ rises, and the moon at noon on the day of the epoch is in ♊ 8° 59′. Assuming that the time of birth might be a few minutes earlier, to allow of the moon crossing the ascendant before noon on the day of the epoch, the following calculations will result :

		H.	M.	S.
Moon's place rises at		4	14	37
Sid. time, August 8th		9	7	47
		19	6	50
Add for W.				47
		19	7	37
Correction			3	8
		19	4	29

or, August 9th, 7h. 4m. 29s. a.m., at which time the moon will be in ♊ 6° 26′, which will be the ascendant of the birth-figure. Gemini 6° 26′ rises at 20h. 19m. 48s., making the birth-time 4h. 42m. 11s. a.m., nearly 18 minutes earlier than the recorded time. This is again a very large rectification of the birth-time, and quite against acceptance, because, as has been previously laid down, the epoch confirms the time of birth within the limits of an ordinary error of observation, and no properly noted birth-time should be rectified more than four or five minutes. If the epoch is examined, it will again be found that the sex is female, but the rectification cannot be accepted, on account of the great alteration of the birth-time. The case must, therefore, be treated as an irregular epoch (1st variation), and the moon's birth longitude made to set. In the example given in Chapter XIII it will be seen that the birth-time is then made to be 5h. 4m. 8s., and the epoch confirms the sex.

The illustration of the second variation is a very remarkable one, for while the regular epoch does not denote the sex, and the irregular confirms it, both confirm the time of birth, and the ascendants only differ by an arc of less than one-third of a degree.

The horoscope is that of Princess Louise (Princess Royal), eldest daughter of the late King Edward VII, born on February 20th, 1867, at 6.35 a.m.

The ascendant is Aquarius 11° 37′, and the moon is in Virgo 19° 42′, decreasing and above. The epoch is apparently regular of the Second Order. I propose to treat it as such.

The " count " is made from the moon to the descendant, and, the tenth revolution of the moon being on May 22nd, the day of the epoch is before noon of the 20th. The moon decreasing, its place sets with :

				H.	M.	S.
Sid. time of	..	..	..	17	42	44
„ „ May 19th	..	..	3	47	43
				13	55	1
Add for W. long.	..	..			37
				13	55	38
Correction ..	..	..	..	2	17
				13	53	21

of May 20th at 1h. 53m. 21s. a.m., when the moon is in Leo 12° 36′—which is the descendant of the horoscope.

This point sets with a sidereal time of 16h. 30m. 55s., being 2m. 22s. earlier than at the given birth-time.

The epoch, however, shows both factors in male areas, thus at once proving it to be fictitious, although confirming the birth-time. When, however, the correct rules are applied, and the " count " is taken right round to the ascendant, owing to the descendant being in an area of the wrong sex, the ascendant comes to Aquarius 12° 54′, differing only 18′ from that of the fictitious epoch, but correctly determining the sex. The time is then found to be 1m. 40s. earlier than recorded.

These two illustrations are sufficient to clearly show the cause of irregularity. In the first case the time is confirmed by varying the rising or setting of the moon, and in the second case the " count " is extended to the opposite horizon, making the day of the epoch either fourteen days earlier or later.

CHAPTER XVII.

FINAL CONSIDERATIONS.

THE full explanation of the rules governing the computation of the epoch and the subsequent rectification of the birth-time have now been given, and, in order to clear away any doubts or difficulties in the student's mind as to the proper process of rectification, I append the following additional instructions for guidance.

The preliminary steps in the calculation of all epochs are the same, and these should be carefully followed out. The first difficulty is to know which set of rules to take. In the cases of regular and irregular epochs, where the moon is always in a negative position as regards sex, the "count" should always be made to that horizon which is in the required sex. If the moon is increasing, and the ascendant is of the same sex as the subject, take the "count" to that point. If it is in the opposite sex take it to the opposite horizon—the descendant—in accordance with the rules. Up to this point the procedure is simple enough, but it becomes somewhat complicated when both the moon and ascendant hold sex positions.

When the moon is increasing, and both the ascendant and moon are in the same sex as the subject, the epoch will, in the large majority of cases, be regular. The same applies when the moon is decreasing, and both factors are in areas of the opposite sex to the subject. The two alternative processes are rarely required, and then only under exceptional conditions.

When the moon is increasing, and the ascendant is in the same sex as the subject, and the moon in the opposite sex, the "count" should be made to the ascendant, with the moon's place setting. Similarly with a decreasing moon, the ascendant in the opposite sex, and the moon in the same sex, the "count" should be made to the ascendant, with the moon's place rising at the epoch. This will serve in quite 50 per cent. of cases. The remainder will be about equally divided between the two alternative processes.

When the moon is increasing, with the ascendant in the opposite sex to the subject, and the moon in the same sex, the " count " should be made right round to the descendant and the moon's place rise at the epoch. With a decreasing moon, the ascendant in the same sex, and the moon in the opposite sex, the " count " is to be made right round to the ascendant, with the moon's place setting. This will serve in quite 50 per cent. of cases. The two alternative processes will be equally divided between the remainder.

When the moon is increasing, and both factors are in areas of the opposite sex to the subject, a regular epoch will never apply. The " count " in these cases must be made right round to the descendant with the moon's place setting. Similarly, with a decreasing moon, and both factors in the same sex as the subject, the " count " is made right round to the ascendant, with the moon's place rising. This will again serve in at least half the cases. The two alternative methods will be divided between the other half.

The best plan is to take the " count " in every instance from the moon to the horizon which is in the same sex as the subject. This gives the day of the epoch and the longitude of the moon—the latter being of first importance in the determination of the sex. In the large majority of cases this will prove correct. But it by no means follows that the " count " should not be made to an horizon of the opposite sex to the subject when the sex area occupied by the moon is the same as that of the subject. For example, in the horoscope of the youngest son of the King of Spain, given in Chapter XIII, the " count " is made from the moon to the ascendant, which is female. The position of the moon counteracts this, and, its quadrant position at the epoch being also male, gives two male influences to one female. A similar state occurs in the Queen of Spain's horoscope Although the ascendant is male, the " count " is made from the moon thereto, but the moon being female, and in a female quadrant at the epoch, the sex is also female.

Again, should the ascendant, for example, be in the required sex, and the " count " to be made thereto, it will occur in some cases that the " count " is continued round to the opposite horizon, and to the opposite sex. Such anomalies would occur where the moon at the epoch held the proper sex area, and also a quadrant of the same sex as the subject.   Instances such as these are very rare, and are the exceptions which prove the rule.

Suffice to say, the ascendant or descendant at birth which becomes the moon at the epoch holds the chief prerogative of sex.   The lunar position at birth has the next power, while the quadrant is only brought into use when one factor is in an area of a different sex to the other.

It must, of course, be clearly understood that these hints, as well as all the previous rules, relate exclusively to full nine months births, *i.e.* all those where the index date is at the tenth revolution of the moon, or the 273rd day previous to birth.   The application of the rules to longer and shorter period births will be given later.

The final point in the calculation of the epoch and the rectification of the birth-time is what is known as the " adjustment of the epoch."   It will have been observed, from the several illustrations given, that the time of the epoch is deduced from the rising or setting of the longitude of the moon at the given time of birth, and that when the rectification has been performed the longitude of the moon will have altered some few minutes.   Thus, in the horoscope of the late Duke of Edinburgh the longitude of the moon at the given time of birth was Taurus 15° 52′, but the rectified time is 8m. earlier, showing the moon to be then in Taurus 15° 48′.   The epoch is computed for the former position, and is found to be November 2nd, 1843, at 7h. 40m. 27s.   The adjustment is now to be made by computing the epoch with Taurus, 15° 48′, setting.   The sidereal time for this is 10h. 21m. 11s., which makes the epoch 36s. earlier.   The moon's longitude at that time is not altered, so that it does not affect the time of birth.

This process of adjustment should always be carried out when the birth-time is altered more than a couple of minutes.

SECTION III.

Some Astro-Physiological Problems.

CHAPTER XVIII.

THE PERIOD OF GESTATION.

The student will have observed that the question of the exact period of gestation is an important factor in the computation of the correct epoch, and that the general laws of the epoch allow for the normal period to be increased or decreased by either one to fourteen days, or one to twenty-eight days, according as to whether the " count " is taken from the required horizon or to that horizon and round to the opposite. According to Scotch law and the French code, a period of 301 days is to be allowed, and the extended " count," 28 days over 273 days, equals this period.

It will naturally be assumed that when the moon at birth is increasing and below the earth, or decreasing and above, the period of gestation will always be more than the norm, and less than the norm when the moon is placed in the opposite two positions. This assumption, however, is not always correct. The whole question turns on the exact gestative period of the particular subject. A child may be born at the eighth month of pregnancy. The birth-figure shows the moon increasing and below, and, therefore, one would look for an epoch in excess of the normal time. Such cases do occur, but they are of a very minute percentage, and, although an exception to the general law of the epoch, are still covered by that law.

The general law of the epoch allows for births taking place so many days earlier or later than the tenth revolution of the moon, the 273rd day before birth. At the same time, a child may be born with the moon in the required position to give an excess period, and yet the birth may occur in the eighth month. The solution to this anomaly is that the excess period shown by the moon's position at birth is taken from the previous revolution of the moon, *i.e.* the *ninth* return of the moon to its radical place.

This particular point is better explained by the examination of horoscopes in which it occurs, and the following authentic cases are given in illustration thereof.

The first case I propose to deal with is that of " Lilian," a grandchild of the Astrologer, Raphael, given by him in the *Astrologer's Magazine* for May, 1895. In his remarks on this horoscope, Raphael made the following very pointed observation : " Our friend, Sepharial, may be interested to know that, stretching the period of gestation to the utmost limit, it could not have exceeded 36 weeks and 4 days." It is naturally to be inferred from this that the *last* day of the *last* menstrual period previous to conception was at this particular period before birth.   Now, 36 weeks and 4 days equal 256 days, and this, subtracted from August 21st, 1894, the date of birth, measures to December 8th, 1893, so that the epoch should not fall before that date.   I will, therefore, apply the rules and see how far they agree with this date, and whether the time and sex are confirmed.   The data is as follows : Female, August 21st, 1894, 3.55 p.m.   Lat. 52° 48′ N.   Long. 1° 25′ E.

				H.	M.	S.
Sid. time, August 21st	..	..	..	9	59	10
Time of birth	..	..	..	3	55	0
Correction ..	..	..	..			39
Add for E. long.	..	..	..		5	40
				14	0	29

Ascendant	25°	46′	Sagittarius.
Moon	26°	51′	Aries.

The moon is below and decreasing, hence the period is less than the norm.

Assuming this to be an ordinary regular epoch of the Fourth Order, the moon at the epoch would be found in the descendant, and the day of the epoch would be November 25th, 1893, but calculation shows that by taking such date the time of birth would be thrown several minutes out—a fact which could not be accepted, seeing that the birth-time was carefully taken—and also does not determine either the sex or the period of gestation.   The moon's distance is, therefore, taken from the ascendant in the numerical order of the houses, and it crosses this particular longitude between the noons of December 8th and 9th, as follows :

	H.	M.	S.
Moon's place sets	8	35	22
Sid. time, December 8th ..	17	9	52
	15	25	30
E. long.		5	40
	15	19	50
Correction		2	31
	15	17	19

or, December 9th, 3h. 17m. 19s. a.m. The moon's longitude at this time is 26° 12′ Sagittarius, which is the correct ascendant of the horoscope. The time is 1m. 58s. later than the observed birth moment. This rectification confirms the birth-time, shows the sex, and agrees approximately with the period of gestation.

Now, in this particular case we have no departure from the second variation of irregular epochs. The index date is November 21st, 1893, and the distance of the moon from the ascendant, taken in the order of the houses, is 239 degrees, equal to 18 days. This, added to November 21st, yields December 9th as the day of the epoch, and calculation confirms this fact. This is a normal nine months birth, the "count" being taken from the tenth revolution of the moon.

The second case illustrates the reverse of this. It is of a male child born on June 4th, 1886, at 11 p.m. We are informed that the coitus took place on September 24th, 1885. This child is a son of Raphael. Here we have a period of 253 days from coitus to birth. I give the calculations in full. Lat. of birthplace, 51° 18′ N. Long. 2° 27′ W.

	H.	M.	S.
Sid. time, June 4th, 1886 ..	4	51	24
Birth-time	11	0	0
Correction		1	48
	15	53	12
Subtract for W. long.		9	48
	15	43	24
Ascendant	25° 3″ ♑		
Moon	16° 0′ ♋		

The ascendant is in a female area ; the moon is also in a female area, increasing and below ; the child is a short period, as clearly shown from the gestative period. The moon, although increasing and below, will set at the epoch, but the epochal moon must be in Cancer to get the required sex.

How is this process to be arrived at ? The index date falls on September 4th, 1885 ; the moon is distant 13 days from the ascendant, and the epoch would, in the ordinary course, fall on August 22nd.

The fact is that, in this case, the "count" is made from the moon round to the ascendant, and then over the horizon to the descendant, making a period of 27 days in excess of the *eighth* revolution of the moon, which took place on October 29th, the epoch falling on October 2nd, which is 27 days earlier, as shown in the following calculations :—

		H.	M.	S.
Moon's place sets	.. ..	15	13	58
Sid. time, October 2nd	..	12	45	28
		2	28	30
W. long.	..		9	48
		2	38	18
Correction	..			26
G.M.T.	..	2	37	52

The moon's longitude at this time is ♋ 24.32—a male degree, giving the required sex. The ascendant will, therefore, be ♑ 24.32.

		H.	M.	S.
This degree rises at	.. ..	15	41	50
Sid. time observed at birth	..	15	43	24

The birth-time is, therefore, 1m. 34s. earlier than the observed time.

Making the necessary adjustments, very small in this case, we have the following comparison of birth and epoch :

BIRTH.		EPOCH.
June 4th, 1886.		October 2nd, 1885.
10h. 58m. 26s. p.m.	G.M.T.	2h. 37m. 49s. p.m.
10h. 48m. 38s. p.m.	L.M.T.	2h. 28m. 1s. p.m.
24° 32′ ♑ Ascd.		Moon 24°32′ ♋
15° 59′ ♋ Moon		Ascd. 15°59′ ♑

From a comparison of these two cases it will be seen that in the first the normal period of gestation is diminished by the moon's distance from the eastern horizon, measured in the numerical order of the houses, and the number of days agreeing with that distance is taken from the tenth revolution of the moon, the 273rd day before birth. In the second case, although the moon is increasing and below, and in an ordinary case would come under the formula 10L *plus* x —10L meaning ten lunar months, and x the number of days in excess of the norm—the case actually has its genesis from the *eighth* lunar revolution, and comes under the formula 8L *plus* x, *plus* 14—meaning that the index date is the eighth return of the moon to its radical place, and the increment x is the distance of the moon from the eastern horizon, *plus* 14 days more, the distance from the ascendant to the descendant.

The first case is a purely normal one of nine months, with a variation in the interchange of the factors due to the sex of the degrees involved. The moon is in a male degree, decreasing in light, and, as the subject is of the female sex, the degree held by the moon must rise at the epoch. The second case is an abnormal one—short period—of eight months' gestation, and the variation in the interchange is due to both factors being in degrees of sex contrary to that of the subject.

In the first case the rectification could have been performed accurately without knowing the period of gestation beforehand. In the second case it would have been necessary to know this period, otherwise an ordinary normal epoch confirming the birth-time and denoting the sex could not have been obtained.

These illustrations are sufficient to show that the period of gestation is one of the basic factors in the computation of the epoch, and a direct contradiction of the illogical objection that " it is absolutely impossible for the epoch to determine the period of gestation." Certainly, the second case is abnormal, and could not occur more than once in 120 births. It is a pointed illustration, and confirmation of the obstetric statement made in Chapter II : "But great variations occasionally are found, first on the side of pregnancies which may be of shorter duration, and still more on the side of those which extend beyond the period just named." Once again, obstetric science and the epoch are found to agree.

There is another point in connection with the gestative period which should be considered, and here again another authentic horoscope will serve as an illustration.

In Chapter II, the following extract from "The Modern Physician" was given, viz. : "The usual way to estimate when labour will occur is that of calculating 280 days from the *first* day of the *last* menstrual period of the woman." Now menstruation lasts, as a rule, from three to seven days ; hence, from the last day to birth would be approximately 273 days. The period usually agreed upon by obstetricians is that impregnation can only follow a coitus which takes place within five days from the last day of menstruation.

The horoscope I propose to take in connection with this point is that of Raphael's youngest son, and the following information has been given in connection with it :—

" Last monthly periodic commenced on February 12th. Child born October 27th, 1891, at 0.50 p.m."

Here a period of 257 days elapses from the first day of the last menstrual period to the day of birth. The point to which I want to draw special attention is that the mere fact that the last monthly periodic commenced on February 12th is no guide as to the duration of pregnancy. Menstruation may and does occur after the woman has conceived. I know a case where it happened for three successive months after conception. It is an abnormality, undoubtedly ; but the fact that it does occur shows that the date of the last menstruation is not always a guide as to the commencement of pregnancy.

Taking this case as an illustration, the following facts are to be noted. Assuming the periodic to have lasted three days, the earliest date at which conception could occur was February 15th. If it lasted seven days, and allowing for a further five days during which impregnation was possible, we get February 24th as the latest date on which conception could occur.

Calculation shows that the prenatal epoch in this particular instance took place on February 19th, at 5.42 p.m., within the limits shown above. In this case, the last menstruation did give a definite clue as to the commencement of the gestative period, but in the case cited in the last paragraph but one the epoch took place three months before the last monthly periodic, and the latter was no guide whatever as to the commencement of the pregnancy.

I do not put these points before students for the purpose of mystifying them or upsetting the deductions they have already drawn from the previous chapters. They are points which they should know and understand ; although they are in reality abnormal occurrences, they nevertheless exist and are occasionally met with. Obstetric science allows for them, and the prenatal epoch confirms their existence.

CHAPTER XIX.

MARRIAGE AND THE EPOCH.

THERE is another point in connection with this vexed question of the commencement of the period of gestation which it is very necessary for me to deal with at this juncture. A rather serious, though illogical, argument against the validity of the epoch as calculated is that in the case of the first child the epoch may and does occasionally occur before the marriage of the parents. My own experience on this point is that the argument cannot be sustained, and is neither valid nor scientific.

It has been laid down as an authoritative ruling that we are not justified in directly associating the prenatal epoch *in point of time* (note the italics) with either coition, impregnation, or any of the preliminary stages of generation, and, with this ruling before us, the fact that the epoch of a first child may occasionally occur before the marriage of the parents is not the slightest argument against the validity of the epoch as calculated.

Even if it were a definitely accepted fact that the epoch did agree in point of time with one of the preliminary stages of generation, the occasional occurrence of an epoch of a first child falling a few days before the parents' marriage could not be taken as either a reasonable or serious objection against the correctness of the epoch. We are concerned in this work with scientific facts, not with the failings or lapses of human nature. On this point I cannot help recalling to mind a very pertinent remark made by the well-known Australian Astrologer, Zariel, in a letter published in the *Astrologer's Magazine* for June, 1894 : " The statement made by one writer that in some cases the prenatal epoch would occur before marriage cannot be easily entertained as an argument. Such things have been and will be, both in high and low life, but I fully appreciate the value of ' mum ' where there is a doubtful case."

In the case of " Lilian," given in the preceding chapter, the epoch took place on December 9th, 1893. She was a first child, and the parents were not married until December

13th, or four days after the epoch. Is this little fact to be taken as definite proof that the epoch as calculated is merely a fallacy and without a proper basis ?

My answer to this preposterous argument is this, and I put it forward as a note of intelligence for investigators and students. It has already been shown from the birth-map that the normal period of gestation is increased or decreased according to the moon's position. Is it an unreasonable hypothesis to suppose that the actual moment of the commencement of the period of gestation may vary from the epoch in a like manner, and be determinable from the epochal map ?

In this particular case of " Lilian " the ascendant of the epoch was Libra 26° 51', and the moon was in Sagittarius 26° 12'—a distance of 60 from the ascendant, equal to nearly five days. As the epoch occurred on December 9th, why should not the conception happen on the 14th, or five days later ?

In another case, particulars of which were submitted by Raphael, the epoch occurred three days before marriage. The position of the moon at the epoch in regard to the ascendant would give a difference of twelve days later as a possible date for conception.

I do not put these suggestions forward with any absolute certainty, as I have not sufficient authentic data on which to form any reliable rule. The idea is purely hypothetical, and based on the supposition already referred to, viz., that as the birth varies from the 273rd day by a certain number of days governed by the distance of the moon from the horizon in the horoscope of birth, it is also possible that the exact moment of conception may vary from the epoch by a corresponding distance of the moon from the horizon of the epochal figure.

The final word on this hypothetical point has yet to be said. I have my own particular views thereon, and am following a line of research which I am confident will lead to a further development of the epochal theory.

CHAPTER XX.

ILLUSTRATIONS OF SHORT AND LONG PERIOD BIRTHS.

IT will have been observed, in Chapter XVIII, that horoscopes are occasionally met with in which the period of gestation is either very short or else very long, and in which such period cannot be approximately determined from the relation of the moon to the sun and ascendant by the ordinary rules.

It has been shown that the number of days due to the distance of the moon from the required horizon in such cases is taken from a previous revolution of the moon, the ninth or even the eighth, and sometimes the seventh before birth in the case of short period births, and from the eleventh lunar revolution in the case of long period births. Short-period births are of more frequent occurrence than long, but neither of them happen very often.

A few illustrations of this important point are found among well-known horoscopes, and they will be of interest and instruction to students.

(1) The late Princess Alice, second daughter of the late Queen Victoria, was born in London on April 25th, 1843, at 4h. 5m. a.m.

The R.A.M.C. is 18h. 14m. 28s.

The ascendant is 8° 41′ ♈, within orbs of a female degree.

The moon is in 15° 0′ ♓, within orbs of a male degree.

The moon is above and decreasing, and to all appearances it is an epoch of the Second Order.

The index date is July 26th, 1842, and the moon's distance from the descendant would make the epoch fall on July 14th.

The moon being in a female degree, its radical place must set at the epoch, but this date does not yield an epoch which will confirm the time.

Taking the " count " right round the horoscope, from the moon to the ascendant, according to Fig. 6, Chapter IV,

making the epoch fall on July 1st, it is still impossible
to find an epoch which will confirm the birth-time.

It is, therefore, necessary to fall back to a short period
birth, taking August 22nd as the index date, and taking
the "count" as in the preceding paragraph, making 9L
plus x (= 12) *plus* 14 = 26 days, bringing the epoch 26 days
earlier—on July 28th. The moon crosses the ascendant
of the birth-figure before noon on that date.

The following is the calculation of the epoch :—

	H.	M.	S.
Sid. time, moon's radical place sets	4	34	50
Sid. time, July 27th	8	19	1
	20	15	49
Add for W. long.			39
	20	16	28
Less correction		3	19
	20	13	9

or, July 28th, 1842, at 8h. 13m. 9s. a.m.

The longitude of the moon at this time is 9° 17′ ♈—which
is the ascendant of the horoscope.

	H.	M.	S.
The sid. time when this degree rises is	18	15	33
The sid. time at the given time of birth	18	14	28
Difference	1	5	

This shows that the correct time of birth was 1m. 5s.
later than the given time, or 4h. 6m. 5s. a.m.

The epochal figure shows a female degree rising, and the
moon also in a degree of the same sex, not only confirming the time but determining the sex.

(2) The next illustration I have to deal with is the case
of the six-and-a-half months' child sent to me by Mr. E.
Kloss, of Florence, Italy. The particulars of birth are :
Male, born 0.30 a.m., May 2nd, 1897. Florence, Italy.
Lat. 43° 47′ N. Long. 44m. 56s. E.

The moon is just past the conjunction of the sun, and,
therefore, increasing in light, and below the earth, and to
all appearances it is a regular epoch of the Third Order, with
the period of gestation longer than the norm. The doctor
in attendance certified the child as only of six-and-a-half

months' pregnancy, and the calculation of the epoch will confirm this.

The face of the child was not fully developed, the nose being completely missing, and two small holes where the nostrils should have been being the only distinctive marks. The head had the appearance of a donkey's, and the child was known as the " Donkey child."

The calculation of this epoch is as follows :—

Florence, Italy, keeps standard time, which is one hour faster than Greenwich. The recorded time of birth was 0.30 a.m. of May 2nd, 1897. The Greenwich time was 11.30 p.m. of the previous day. Florence being 44m. 56s. E, the true local mean time was 0h. 14m. 56s. a.m.

This data yields :

R.A.M.C. ..	..	..	14h. 55m. 31s.
Ascendant ..	..	..	19° 26′ ♑
Moon ..	..	..	13° 3′ ♉

Six and a-half months are equal to 202 days, and contain seven revolutions of the moon and ten days over. The seventh revolution of the moon took place on October 22nd, 1896, and the moon's distance from the ascendant was 126°, or nearly ten days. This brings the exact date of the epoch to October 12th, or before noon of the 13th.

Although the moon is increasing and below, the radical place of the moon sets at the epoch, this variation being due to the fact that it is almost within orbs of a female degree :

	H.	M.	S.
Sid. time when radical place of			
moon sets	9	45	11
Sid. time, October 12th, 1896 ..	13	26	14
	20	18	57
Subtract for E. long.		44	56
	19	34	1
Less correction		3	12
	19	30	49

equal to October 13th, at 7h. 30m. 49s. a.m.

The longitude of the moon at this time is 16° 47′ ♑, within orbs of a male degree, thus indicating the proper sex.

	H.	M.	S.
Sid. time when 16° 47′ ♑ rises ..	14	45	46
„ „ May 1st, 1897 ..	2	38	42
	12	7	4
Subtract for E. long.		44	56
	11	22	8
Less correction		1	52
	11	20	16

This denotes that the Greenwich time of birth was May
1st, at 11h. 20m. 16s. p.m.   The standard time at Florence
was May 2nd, at oh. 20m. 16s. a.m., and the true local mean
time oh. 5m. 12s. a.m.

(3) The horoscope of Princess Beatrice (Princess Henry
of Battenburg) illustrates a different type of epoch.   She
was born on April 14th, 1857, at 1.45 p.m., in London
(39s. W.).

The R.A.M.C. is	3h. 15m. 3s.
Ascendant	1° 2′ ♍
Moon	21° 1′ ♐

Both factors are in male areas.   The moon is below and
decreasing, and the epoch is apparently one of the Fourth
Order.   The index date is July 15th, and the moon
crosses the descendant on the 20th, but the time of birth
is not confirmed.

Taking the previous revolution of the moon as the starting
point—11th August, 1856—the moon crosses the descendant
on the 16th, and the time of the epoch is found by making
the place of the moon rise thereat, as follows :—

	H.	M.	S.
Sid. time, moon's place rising ..	13	31	2
„ „ August 16th	9	40	15
	3	50	47
Add for W. long.			39
	3	51	26
Less correction			38
	3	50	48

equal to 3h. 50m. 48s. p.m., on August 16th, at which time
the moon is in 29° 37′ ♒—the descendant of the horoscope.

This degree sets with a sidereal time of 3h. 7m. 0s., which makes the correct birth-time as 1h. 37m. 4s. p.m. on April 14th, 1857.

The ascendant at the epoch is male, the moon is female, and in a female quadrant, hence determines the sex as female.

(4) The horoscope of Mr. A. J. Pearce, the talented editor of "Zadkiel's Almanac," is a very pretty and instructive illustration of a long period birth, with the moon decreasing and below the earth. He was born on November 10th, 1840, at 9.20 a.m., in London. Long. 31s. W. This time Mr. Pearce has rectified to 9h. 18m. 39s., by comparing past events with primary directions. How far does the epochal rectification confirm this ?

>The R.A.M.C. at 9.20 a.m. is 12h. 37m. 54s.
>Ascendant .. .. .. 10° 26′ ♐
>Moon .. .. 27° 7′ ♉

The ascendant is male and the moon negative.

The moon is decreasing and below, and the "count" made from the moon to the descendant brings a female area into play. It is, therefore, continued round to the ascendant. The moon is negative. The normal epoch would fall on February 12th, but in this case the eleventh revolution of the moon—January 14th—is taken as the genesis of the epoch, and the epoch falls on the 29th just before noon, the moon being at a distance from the ascendant equal to 15 days. The moon's place rises at the epoch, contrary to the general rule, as follows :

	H.	M.	S.
Sid. time, moon's place rising ..	19	52	57
„ „ January 28th ..	20	27	19
	23	25	38
Add for W. long.			31
	23	26	9
Less correction		3	50
	23	22	19

or, January 30th, 1840, at 11h. 22m. 19s. a.m.

The moon's longitude at this time is 10° 18′ ♐ and this point rises with a sidereal time of 12h. 36m. 56s.—58s. earlier than the recorded time, or 23s. later than the rectified time.

The ascendant of the epoch being negative, the moon's position in a male area confirms the sex.

(5) The horoscope of King George V is a unique illustration of a short period birth, but, at the same time, one which comes within a few hours of a full-time pregnancy. The King was born at Marlborough House, Long. 37s. W., on June 3rd, 1865, at 1.18 a.m.

The R.A.M.C. is	..	..	18h. 3m. 26s.
Ascendant ..	..	..	2° 4′ ♈
Moon	..	..	1° 4′ ♎

The ascendant is female ; the moon is male, increasing and below. The " count " made from the moon to the ascendant, in the ordinary way, would bring the epochal moon to a female area, so it is extended right round to the descendant, making the excess period 27 days—but not from the tenth revolution of the moon, but the following one.

The ninth lunar return to its radical place falls on September 30th, 1864, and the excess days bring the day of epoch to September 3rd before noon. The moon being male, its place at birth will rise, as follows :

	H.	M.	S.
Sid. time, moon's place rising ..	6	7	48
,, ,, September 2nd ..	10	47	33
	19	20	15
Add for W. long.			37
	19	20	52
Less correction		3	10
	19	17	42

or, September 3rd, 1864, at 7h. 17m. 42s. a.m.

The moon's longitude at this time is 3° 19′ ♎—the descendant of the horoscope. This point sets with sidereal time of 18h. 5m. 32s., or 2m. 6s. later than at the recorded time, thus showing the correct birth-time to be 1h. 20m. 6s. a.m.

The epoch shows a male area rising ; the moon in a male area, but a female quadrant. There being two male influences, the sex is, therefore, confirmed.

(6) The horoscope of the late King Edward VII is another illustration of a short period birth, though it approximates very closely to a full nine months birth. The moon is ♍ 29° 56′, above and decreasing, but the " count " is made

to the descendant and continued to the ascendant. The
distance is 274°, making 20½ days in excess of the *ninth*
lunar revolution.

He was born on November 9th, 1841, and, instead of the
epoch falling seven days over the normal period, viz.,
10L. *plus x*—making the epoch on February 2nd—it falls on
February 16th, being 20½ days in excess of the ninth lunar
revolution, which took place on March 8th.

(7) The Queen of Roumania (Princess Marie of Edinburgh),
born October 29th, 1875, at 10.30 a.m. at Eastwell Park,
Kent. Lat. 51° 12′ N. Long. 3m. 32s. E. :

R.A.M.C.	..	..	..	13h. 2m. 56s.
Ascendant ..	..	..	15° 39′ ♐
Moon	..	..	..	8° 3′ ♏

The moon is above and increasing, and both factors are
found in areas of the opposite sex to the subject. The index
date is January 29th, 1875, but, the ascendant being male,
the " count " has to be made right round to the opposite
horizon. The moon being male, its place will set at the
epoch. The day of epoch falls just after noon of February
14th. Calculation, however, does not in any way confirm
the birth-time, and the assumption is that this is a long
period birth. The eleventh lunar revolution falls on January
2nd, and the " count," taken as before, brings the day of
epoch to the 18th, just before noon. The calculation is as
follows :

		H.	M.	S.
Sid. time, moon's place sets	..	19	9	38
„ „ January 17th	..	19	46	0
		23	23	38
Subtract for E. long.	..		3	32
		23	20	6
Less correction	..	..		3	49
		23	16	17

or, January 18th at 11h. 16m. 17s. a.m. The moon's longitude at this time is ♊ 15° 13′—which is the correct descendant of the horoscope. The sidereal time when this degree
sets is 13h. 0m. 46s., or 2m. 10s. less than at the recorded
time of birth, showing the exact birth-time to be 10h. 27m.
50s. a.m. Both factors are now in degrees of the required sex.

SECTION IV.

The Prenatal Epoch and Multiple Pregnancy.

CHAPTER XXI.

FALLACIES AND FACTS IN RELATION TO TWINS.

THE subject of twins is one of the " pegs " on which opponents of Astrology seek to base their puerile objections against the science, little dreaming that it is one of the most powerful arguments in support of Astrology as a verifiable science.

The objection is put forward in these words :—" The doctrines of Astrology cannot be true, because in large cities there are births taking place at every minute, and, consequently, every day many persons must be born with exactly the same nativity, and die at the same identical time. But, in fact, no two persons have the same events happen to them exactly."

But this argument, like others of the same nature, is both illogical and fallacious, as it ignores the main point. It is not a question of two different people born on the same day and hour, but two children born at the same identical moment and of the same parents.

Let facts, however, speak for themselves. It is on record that a certain Mr. G. Hemmings was born on the same day and hour as King George III. Both were married on the same day. Both died on the same day. I have in my collection the horoscope of a gentleman who was born on the same day and hour as Lord Rosebery. Their fathers died on the same day. Both were married on the same day. On the day Lord Rosebery became Prime Minister the other was promoted in business. I have also the horoscope of a lady born on the same day and hour as Queen Mary, with this difference that the former was born at Glasgow, and the latter in London. There is a difference of some fifteen degrees in their respective ascendants.

On the other hand, it is admitted that there are numerous cases of two people born at the same time whose lives, characters, and careers have been totally different. I can cite a very pronounced case. On April 29th, 1861, two female children were born, one at 9.15 a.m., and the other at 9.30 a.m. The latter married only once, and lived a quiet life. The former married twice, and had an eventful career. Both were born under the last decan of the sign Cancer ; hence there was only a minute difference between their respective horoscopes. They were, however, children of different parents, and herein lies one of the causes.

In the case of real twins, facts must again be considered. Cases are known of real twins, whose lives have been identical from birth to death ; of cases of twin children, whose natures and disposition have been so alike, even to the very tone of their voices, that it was impossible for the nicest eye to find out any point of difference. Instance may be made of Nicholas and Andrew Tremayne, of whom it is said that they were governed by precisely the same feelings and affections. What one liked the other liked ; what one loathed the other loathed ; if one was ill, the other sickened ; and if one was in pain, the other suffered in the same part and in the same degree. In more recent times the amusing escapades of Albert Ebenezer and Ebenezer Albert may be cited. Numerous other anecdotes could be narrated to fill several pages of actual authentic cases, which utterly and flatly disprove the before-mentioned argument.

On the other hand, however, there are equally as many cases of twins whose personal appearance, lives, characters, and fate have been widely divergent, but there are astrological as well as common-sense reasons therefor.

Astrologically, the chief causes are these. In the case of twins born within a few moments of each other, their horoscopes are but little different. The same sign of the zodiac may be rising. If only ten minutes elapse between the two births there is sufficient time for a different sign to be on the ascendant at the birth of the second child. But there are frequently much longer intervals—thirty minutes, one hour, hour and a-half, and even longer, and the student of Astrology knows that with such intervals as these the horoscopes will be widely different.

But even this explanation is not all-sufficient. To Astrologers who, like myself, have delved deep in the mysteries of generation in connection with the procreation of twins, there is a more important explanation to be found. It is impossible for me to accept the simple explanation that a difference of only five minutes will so affect the second horoscope that it will alter the entire life of the second twin. The mere erection of two separate horoscopes will not by itself suffice to explain the reason and the cause why one should die and the other live. In my collection of twin births, numbering some three or four hundred, I can produce numerous cases where only five or ten minutes elapsed between the two births, yet the two horoscopes will not show the slightest alteration as regard the hyleg, and yet one will die and the other live to maturity. What is the solution of this apparent anomaly ?

The stereotyped dictum of the orthodox Astrologer is that the horoscope of birth alone shows the life and destiny of the subject. To this, I say, let him either prove his statement or pass for ever out of recognition as a progressive and truth-seeking Astrologer. I hold to the opinion, from actual investigation and research, that the answer to this apparent anomaly is found in the prenatal epoch, and in the words used in Chapter III : " It is the key to the divergence of character and fortunes in twins," and that the horoscope of birth is not the *ultima thule* of Natal Astrology.

The purport of this section of my work is to prove the contention held by me aforesaid. I shall deal with the subject in a new and original manner, basing my deductions on personal investigations, and illustrating them by cases which have come under my notice. In order to do so, I must first of all present to students some astro-physiological facts in connection with the procreation of twins.

CHAPTER XXII.

THE ASTRO-PHYSIOLOGICAL LAWS OF MULTIPLE BIRTHS.

THE examination of the laws governing twin and multiple births demands a knowledge of obstetric science and the laws of generation, and is not a subject to be dealt with only from a mathematical and purely astrological standpoint. It is absolutely necessary that the gestative period should be thoroughly examined by means of the prenatal epoch and the chart of descent before the matter can be brought to a satisfactory conclusion.

Now I am not going to weary my readers with any long dissertation on the technical facts connected with the procreation of twins, but will go straight to the point with a few simple statements and illustrations of the facts I wish to present.

It has already been pointed out that generation is effected by the contact of the male spermatoza with the female ovum. The ovum or germ from which the body of a child is formed is in reality a *cell*—that is to say, a living body composed of living material. Each ovum is surrounded by two coverings, the amnion and chorion.

Twins may be divided into two separate classes, viz. :

(1) Con-ovate, or mon-ovate ;
(2) Bi-ovate.

Con-ovate twins are those where the lives, characters, and destinies of the two children run side by side. Twins of this class are born from a double ova, and in all probability from a single act of generation. What I mean by a double ova is this : I have no doubt that all are familiar with an egg with two yolks ; a nut with two kernels. In the egg, both yolks are endowed with the power of generation. In the nut, both kernels can germinate. In the same way, the double ova contains two germs, each of which may give rise to a separate fœtus. In these cases both germs are contained within the same amniotic sac, and then they are always of the same sex.

In the case of bi-ovate twins, these are produced from separate ova, and from either one act of generation or two separate acts. In these cases there would be two distinct bags of membranes, and the placentæ would be entirely separate. It is, therefore, obvious that in such births each twin is developed from a distinct ovum, having its own chorion and amnion. The sex of the twins so born would not necessarily be the same. I am given to understand that physiologists of to-day teach that real twins are those produced from two separate and distinct ova, each of which is impregnated.

The next point for consideration is a very important one. It has been found from the examination of twin births —and medical science confirms this view—that, in the large majority, the last born is the first conceived, and the first born is often premature. The cause is apparently due to the push of the first conceived and mature fœtus effecting the apparently premature birth of the later conception, whose extrusion has to be brought about in order to make way for the mature birth.

This point, considered in the light of the family system current in the Decan, in India, is very important, as it is acknowledged in the recognition of the *last* born of twins as the elder of the two. " Not only does the second born of twins become the head of the family, but he has the custody of the joint income and estate of the whole family, and his chief control in the subsequent marriages of other members of the same *ashram* or domestic circle. To him descends the prerogative of Guru or spiritual teacher of the family, and the *mantram*, or sacred word, is breathed into his ear on the moment of his father's death. Other privileges of equal magnitude are his by right of primogeniture. In the West it is quite otherwise. He who first sees the daylight is the elder of a twin, and, in the case of an entail, succeeds to the whole of the family estate." (Sepharial, " Modern Astrology," Vol. XII, page 27.)

In the case of bi-ovate twins—those produced from separate ova from distinct acts of generation—it may always be allowed that the last born is the first conceived and the first born is premature, its extrusion being necessary in order to allow for the birth of the mature fœtus.

There is, however, a class of bi-ovate twins—those that

are produced from a single act of generation—in which the first born is the first conceived, and the last born the last conceived, conceptions having taken place within a short time of each other.

It is also well-known—to quote the learned author of the epochal theory—that in the cases of bi-ovate twins there is always one in which the epoch is out of relations with the birth. That is to say, the horoscope of birth does not portend the life experience. The birth has been forced by the more advanced development of the prior conception. The last conceived may be born, or, in other words, may be thrust into physical life at a time when the heavens are out of relation with the individual character.

This is one of the particular points of interest which I intend to demonstrate in these pages by a practical appeal to facts, and by illustrations from authentic horoscopes. I am fully aware that my views will not be accepted by those little astrological shrimps who delight to potter about in the puddles of their own shallow mentality. I, in common with the more progressive and scientific Astrologer, prefer the intellectual excitement and development which may be gained by an exhaustive and critical search for the beauties which lie hidden beneath the deeper waters of scientific enquiry.

CHAPTER XXIII.

ILLUSTRATIONS OF TWIN BIRTHS.

THE first illustration I propose to deal with is the case of the two well-known tennis players, Messrs. C. G. and E. R. Allen—who were born at Colmworth, St. Neot's, Hunts, on December 28th, 1868—the former at 9.50 p.m., and the latter at 10 p.m. Lat. 52° 13′ N. Long. 0° 24′ W.

In accordance with the statement made in the last chapter—that the second born of twins is the first conceived—it is only logical to infer that the epoch of Mr. E. R. Allen should ante-date that of his brother.   In both cases the moon is above the earth and increasing, and the gestative period will be less than the norm, but, as the ascendant is in a female area, the "count" is made right round from the moon to the descendant.

The particulars of birth are as under :

C. G. ALLEN.		E. R. ALLEN.		
4h. 18m. 57s.	R.A.M.C.	4h. 28m. 59s.		
12° 22′ ♍	Ascendant	14° 7′	♍	
28° 37′ ♊	Moon	28° 43′	♊	

The index date is March 30th, 1868, and the moon's distance from the descendant brings the exact day of the epoch to April 18th.   The moon being in a female degree its place at birth will set with :

			H.	M.	S.
Sid. time of	..	..	14	10	30
„ „ April 18th, 1868		..	1	47	31
			12	22	59
Add for W. long. 0m. 24s.		..		1	36
			12	24	35
Subtract correction	..	..		2	2
			12	22	33

This is equal to April 19th, 1868, at 0h. 22m. 33s. a.m. The moon's longitude at this time is 13° 53′ ♓, and is the descendant of the horoscope.   This degree sets with sidereal time of 4h. 27m. 38s., which will give the correct time of birth as 9h. 58m. 40s. p.m., or 1m. 20s. earlier than the given time.

In the epoch the ascendant is within two degrees of a male point, and the moon is also in a male area, thus determining the sex as male.

The epoch of the elder brother took place on May 16th, 1868, before noon. The moon's birth-place *rises* in this case, the

			H.	M.	S.
Sid. time being	..	..	21	37	53
,, ,, May 15th	..	..	3	33	58
			18	3	55
Add for W. long.	..	..		1	36
			18	5	31
Less correction	..	.,		2	58
			18	2	33

This is equal to May 16th, at 6h. 2m. 33s. a.m., when the moon's longitude will be 12° 28′ ✕—the descendant of the horoscope. This point will set with a sidereal time of 4h. 19m. 32s., giving a birth-time of 9h. 50m. 35s., or 35s. later than the recorded time. The ascendant of the epoch is female, but the moon, being in a male area and a male quadrant, thus determines the sex as male.

The above illustration is a complete confirmation of the truth of the before-mentioned statement, and the following case yields additional proof thereof.

The twins, both male, were born in East Kent. Lat. 51° 15′ N. Long. 1° 18′ E., on August 2nd, 1898, at 0.15 p.m. and 0.25 p.m., respectively. The longitudes of the two factors are as under :

FIRST CHILD.		SECOND CHILD.
9h. 4m. 38s.	R.A.M.C.	9h. 14m. 40s.
2° 31′ ♍	Ascendant	4° 17′ ♍
14° 41′ ♒	Moon	14° 47′ ♒

The moon is just past the full, therefore decreasing in light, but, as the descendant is in a female area, the "count" has to be made right round to the ascendant, bringing the period of gestation less than the norm by an additional fourteen days. The epoch of the second child, the first conceived, takes place on November 22nd, with the moon's place at birth rising :

	H. M. S.
Sid. time, moon's place rising ..	16 35 7
,, ,, November 22nd ..	16 6 56
	0 28 11
Subtract for E. long.	0 5 12
	0 22 59
Less correction	4
	0 22 55

At 0h. 22m. 55s. p.m. on November 22nd, the longitude of the moon is ♏ 3° 56', and this becomes the ascendant of the horoscope. This degree rises with a sidereal time of 9h. 12m. 43s., which gives a birth-time of 0h. 23m. 3s. p.m.—not quite 2m. earlier than the recorded time. The ascendant of the epoch is negative, and the moon is in a male area.

The epoch of the first child, the last conceived, takes place a month later—on December 19th, at 7h. 42m. 26s.—with the moon's birth-place setting.

	H. M. S.
Sid. time, moon's place setting ..	1 42 17
,, ,, December 19th ..	17 53 23
	7 48 54
Subtract for E. long.	5 12
	7 43 42
Less correction	1 16
December 22nd ,.	7 42 26 P.M.

At this time the longitude of the moon is ♏ 2° 15'—the correct ascendant of the horoscope. This point rises with a sidereal time of 9h. 3m. 7s., which gives a birth-time of 0h. 13m. 29s. p.m. The same sex conditions prevail at the epoch as in the case of the first child.

Here again is shown the truth of the observation previously made. This case, like the first, is one of bi-ovate twins, born from separate acts of generation.

The next case illustrates a different type of double epoch. It is that of twin girls, born on October 23rd, 1875, at 4 p.m. and 9.30 p.m., local time, respectively. Both of these were premature births—seven months only—and both died immediately after birth, the former living 20 minutes, and the latter only 10 minutes.

The necessary particulars of birth are as under :

GIRL, 4 p.m.		GIRL, 9.30 p.m.		
18h. 6m. 39s.	R.A.M.C.	23h. 37m. 33s.		
♈ 3° 56′	Ascendant	♋ 22° 12′		
♌ 25° 42′	Moon	♌ 28° 42′		

In both cases the moon is below the earth and decreasing, and the period will, therefore, be less than seven months by the number of days equal to the moon's distance from the descendant divided by 13. The epochs in both cases are regular of the Fourth Order.

The epoch of the elder twin falls on March 22nd, 1875, at 4h. 56m. 8s. a.m., with the moon's place at birth setting, and the moon in ♎ 3° 32′—the descendant of the horoscope. The ascendant of the epoch is in a female area, and the moon in a male area, but being in a female quadrant determines the correct sex. The correct time of birth is found to be 41s. earlier than that recorded. The epoch of the second child falls on March 31st, 1875, at 4h. 26m. 38s. a.m., with the moon's birth-place again setting, and the moon in the descending sign. This time gives ♑ 21° 37′ as the descendant of the horoscope, and makes the time of birth 9h. 26m. 57s. p.m., or 3m. 3s. earlier than the recorded time. The ascendant of the epoch is negative, and the moon is in a female area, thus denoting the sex to be female.

In this case, the elder child was the first conceived, contrary to the two previous cases, and the assumption is that these children were con-ovate twins, produced from two separate acts of generation. My reason for this latter view is that the interval between the two epochs, viz., 9 days, is too long for the twins to be produced from one act of generation, as five days is the limit allowed by obstetricians during which, from a single act of generation, conception may follow. The spermatoza loses its vivifying power after this period.

The following case also illustrates another type of double epoch. There is an interval of seven hours between the two births, but both children lived to maturity. The data of birth are as follows :

<table>
<tr><td>FEMALE.</td><td></td><td>MALE.</td></tr>
</table>

FEMALE.		MALE.
July 13th, 1866, 10.30 p.m.		July 14th, 1866, 5.30 a.m.
17h. 56m. 16s.	R.A.M.C.	0h. 57m. 25s.
27° 47′ ✕	Ascendant	6° 44′ ♌
13° 39′ ♌	Moon	17° 41′ ♌

Both of these are full-time births, the moon being below
the earth, and increasing in light. The epoch of the girl
took place on October 4th, 1865, at 0h. 40m. 20s. a.m., the
moon then being in ✕ 27° 54′, making the time of birth 18s.
later than given. The epoch of the boy fell on October
13th, at 0h. 27m. 40s. a.m., the moon being then in ♌ 6° 3′,
making the birth-time 5h. 26m. 8s. a.m.—not quite 4m.
earlier than given. The elder twin is again the first conceived, hence it is evidently a case of bi-ovate twins
produced from a single act of generation. Although the
interval between the epochs is considerable, I do not regard
it as precluding the probability of a single coitus.

The last illustration given is that of twins born with an
interval of four hours between the two births. The first—
a girl—was born on October 7th, 1860, at 4 a.m., and the
second—a boy—on the same date at 8 a.m.

GIRL.		BOY.
5h. 4m. 4s.	R.A.M.C.	9h. 4m. 44s.
20° 7′ ♍	Ascendant	2° 32′ ♏
4° 25′ ♋	Moon	6° 35′ ♋

In both cases the moon is above the earth and decreasing,
and in negative areas. The ascendant in each case is of
the required sex, so that the count has to be made from the
moon round by the seventh house to the ascending degree.
The epoch of the girl—the first conceived—falls on December
16th, 1859, at 4h. 25m. 3s. p.m., with the moon's place
setting, giving an ascendant of ♍ 21° 37′, and a birth-time of
4h. 3m. 14s. a.m. The epoch of the boy falls three days
later, on December 19th, at 4h. 21m. 47s. p.m., the moon
being then in ♏ 2° 47′—the ascendant of the horoscope—
making the birth-time 8h. 1m. 26s. a.m.

In this case the epochs fall so closely together that one
is tempted to regard them as con-ovate, but the fact that
the children were of different sex is against this. I am,
therefore, disposed to regard them as bi-ovate twins, produced from a single act of generation, there being only three
days between each epoch.

CHAPTER XXIV.

An Illustration of a Multiple Birth.

THE question of computing the epochs and rectifying the birth-times of triplets and quadruplets is a very complicated matter, and, in view of the fact that they occur only about once in 10,000 births, the student need not concern himself much about them. The following illustration is given for the purpose of making the work complete, and for showing how the epoch falls into line with all the facts connected with multiple births.

The illustration is that of triplets, born in East Kent, on July 19th, 1873. All three children were boys, and their births took place at 0.30 p.m., 0.50 p.m., and 1.30 p.m., respectively, the longitudes of the two factors in each case being as under :

	0.30 p.m.	0.50 p.m.	1.30 p.m.
R.A.M.C.	8h. 19m. 28s.	8h. 39m. 31s.	9h. 19m. 38s.
Ascendant	23° 52′ ♎	28° 7′ ♎	5° 8′ ♏
Moon ..	29° 43′ ♉	29° 54′ ♉	0° 16′ ♊

All three children died—the first two on July 21st, only living two days—while the third only lived five minutes. This point should be particularly noted. The two first lived two days and died within 1h. 20m. of each other ; the third only survived for five minutes. Why did the little lives of the first two run parallel, while the third one appears to show a divergence from the others ? I will show the reason later.

Examination of these horoscopes elicits the following facts. The moon is above and decreasing in all three cases, but the births are premature, so that the epoch will be found earlier than 10 L *plus x.* The ascendants in the first two cases are in female areas, and in a male area in the third. The moon in the first two cases is negative, and in a female area in the third. Here is the first indication that the third birth is distinct from the other two. I am, therefore, of opinion that the two first births are con-ovate twins, and the third is an entirely separate birth. One would judge from this that the third child was the first conceived, and that the other two are later conceptions, and in order of their respective births.

I will take the third case first. The moon being decreasing and the ascendant male, the " count " is made from the moon to the descendant and round under the earth to the ascendant, and, as the moon is female, its place will set at the epoch. These conditions are satisfied by an epoch which occurs on November 28th, 1872, at 7h. 6m. 29s. a.m.—fifteen days in excess of the eighth lunar revolution. The moon's longitude at this time is 4° 44′ ♏, giving a birth-time of 1h. 27m. 38s., local time, or 1h. 22m. 26s., G.M.T.—2m. 22s. earlier than recorded.

In the first and second cases, as the ascendant is female

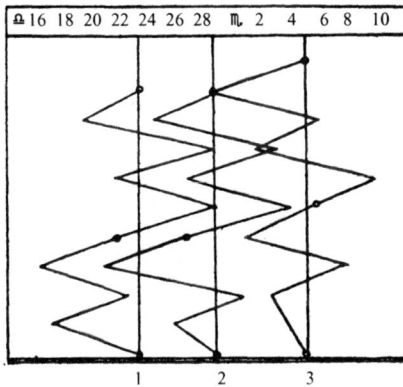

FIG. 11.

and the moon negative, the " count " must be made to the descendant, and epochs complying with these conditions are found on December 10th, 1872. In the first birth, the moon's radical place sets, giving a time of 6h. 16m. 18s. a.m., with the moon in 23° 42′ ♎, and a birth-time of 0h. 29m. 6s. p.m., local time—54s. earlier than the given time. In the second case, the epoch falls at 2h. 38m. 29s. p.m. of the same date, with the moon in 28° 21′ ♎, which gives a birth-time of 0h. 51m. 18s. p.m., local time—a little more than 1m. later than that recorded.

Fig. 11 is the Chart of Descent of these three cases.

This chart, on inspection, gives a real clue to the query propounded. The first two children died within 1h. 20m.

of one another ; the third barely survived its birth. The
epochs of the first two fall within a few hours of each other ;
the third is a separate epoch, twelve days earlier, and,
therefore, born under quite distinct influences from the
other two, whose epochs are very similar.

In the case of the third it is observed that eight days
before birth Mars crosses the ascendant of the horoscope,
but what are more important are the transits of Mars over the
line of impulse and the moon's librations during the gestative
period. On March 17th, the moon was in 9° 52′, and
Mars in 15° 12′ of Scorpio. On April 13th the moon was in
5° 28′, and Mars in 11° 57′ of Scorpio. On May 10th the
moon was in 0° 50′ and Mars in 2° 38′ of the same sign. On
July 4th the moon was in Scorpio 2° 27′ and Mars in 2° 31′
of the same sign. So that the evil planet, Mars, was
afflicting the moon during the greater part of the gestative
period.

In the face of all this violent affliction, it is only logical
to infer that what little vitality the child had could not
sustain life, and it died immediately after birth.

In the other two cases the line of central impulse is not
so heavily afflicted. Mars is in opposition to the moon at
the first libration of both on January 6th, and also at the
libration of June 19th. The chief affliction in these two
cases is from Neptune, whose longitude covers from Aries
23° 41′ on December 10th to 28° 33′ on July 19th—the
actual limits of the two descendants. The vitality of these
two children was not so affected, and consequently they
survived the third child by two days.

The argument may be put forward that all three horoscopes
show the sun to be hyleg, and in opposition and parallel
with Saturn, and the moon also in parallel with Saturn, and
that the indications of early death were clearly shown. I
do not deny it, but, on the other hand, I can produce horoscopes with far heavier affliction where the subjects have
lived to an advanced age. If the horoscope is the sole
factor in determining such matters, how can such contra-
dictions be explained ? My answer is : By reference to
the epoch and the chart of descent.

There is another remarkable point in connection with
this case of triplets. The position of the moon at the epoch
of the second child is coincident with its position at the

first libration of the third child.   It starts, as it were, from
the longitude of the moon at the first libration in the
third child's chart.   In other words, the line of impulse of
the second commences exactly at the point of the first
libration of the moon in the third.   This is no chance
occurrence, and, from investigation, I believe it to have a
scientific basis.   It has already been noted in connection
with the subject in current astrological magazines.

CHAPTER XXV.

DIVERGENCE OF CHARACTER AND FORTUNE IN TWINS.

I HAVE now come to a matter of prime importance in relation to twin births, and one which has been the cause of some considerable discussion and difference of opinion among astrologers, viz., the divergence of character and

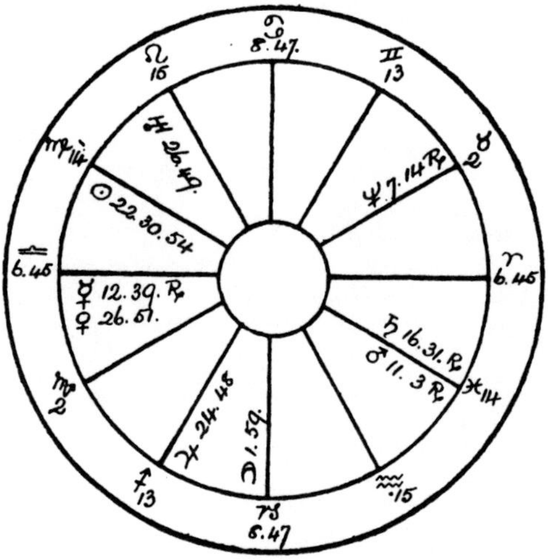

FIG. 12.

fortune. Twins are born within a few minutes of one another ; one child dies, and the other lives to maturity ; one has an eventful life, and the other the reverse ; one is quick and forward mentally and physically, the other dull and weakly. The horoscopes of birth are inadequate to show these divergencies, being in most cases almost identical. The prenatal epoch is the sole and only factor by which such divergencies can be accounted for.

The first case I have to present in illustration of this important point is that of twins—girl and boy—the former born on September 15th, 1877, at 7 a.m., and the latter at 11.30 a.m. of the same day. The particulars were given to me by a lady correspondent some years ago, and the following interesting and remarkable comments were also appended :—"The girl was very puny and backward in all ways ; never gave any signs of intelligence until three months after birth, and has always developed slowly, both physically and intellectually. The boy was full-grown, strong and healthy, developed quickly, and when older was always thought to be at least a year older than the girl. There were two separate after-births, and it appears to be most probable that the girl was a seven months child and

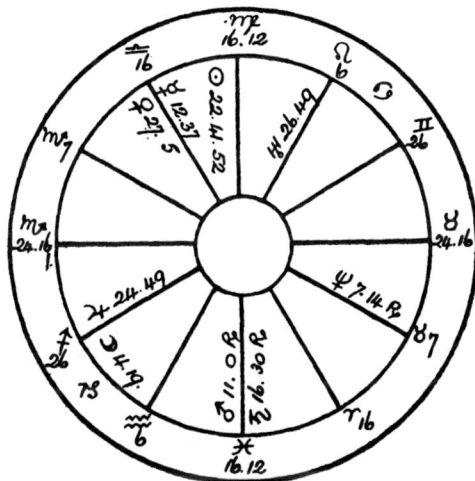

FIG. 13.

was born simply because the boy's time had come and could not be delayed."

The particulars of birth are as follow :

GIRL (Fig. 12).		BOY (Fig. 13).
6h. 37m. 24s.	R.A.M.C.	11h. 8m. 8s.
6° 36′ ♎	Ascendant	24° 4′ ♏
1° 59′ ♑	Moon	4° 19′ ♑

The moon in both cases is below the earth and increasing in light, and in the second case the epoch occurs on November 30th, 1876, the moon being then in the descending degree of the horoscope, and the moon's birth-place rising. The "count" is made from the moon to the ascendant, but, in consequence of that degree being in a female area, it is continued round to the descendant, making the excess period sixteen days. The time of the epoch is 9h. 52m. 27s. a.m., with the moon in 24° 16' ♉. This point sets on the day of birth at 11h. 31m. 5s. a.m., or 1m. 5s. later than the recorded time.

The epoch of the girl is, as surmised, a short period one, falling on February 2nd, 1877, seven days in excess of the eighth return of the moon to its radical place, at 5h. 30m.

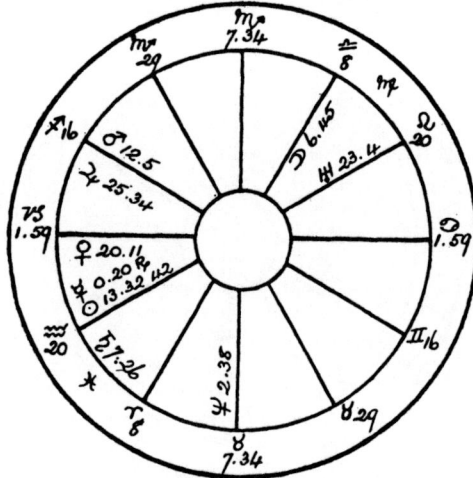

FIG. 14.

45s. a.m., at which time the moon is in 6° 45' ♎—the correct ascendant of the horoscope. This point rises on the day of birth at 7h. 0m. 50s. a.m., or 50s. later than the given time. Figs. 12 and 13 show the two horoscopes.

The horoscope of the girl shows Mercury rising in Libra, retrograde, but unafflicted save for a semisquare of Uranus. Here there is nothing to account for the backwardness intellectually. The ascendant is hyleg, separating from the square of the moon, but Venus—ruler of the ascendant—is rising, well aspected by Jupiter and Uranus. Certainly Mars and Saturn are in the sixth house, the latter only a few degrees separated from the opposition of the sun, but that luminary is not hyleg. The position of the two malefics would make the child backward physically, and delicate, but scores of horoscopes have the same position, and nothing untoward has occurred. The fact is that the horoscope does not show the defects above stated.

The boy's horoscope shows Scorpio rising, but Mars—ruler—is weak, while the sun here is hyleg, and afflicted by the opposition of Saturn, and sesquiquadrate of Neptune. Mercury is no better placed than in his sister's horoscope, and is nearer the square of the moon, yet he was intellectually

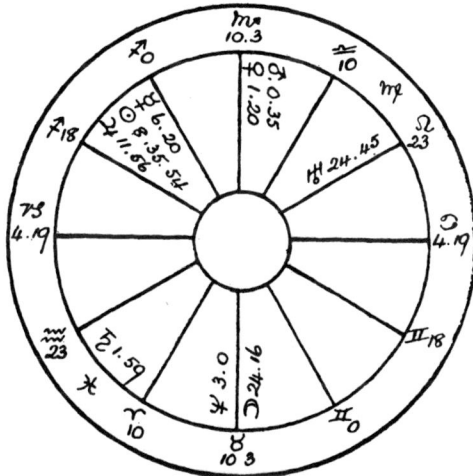

FIG. 15.

her superior, and physically stronger and better developed. There is nothing whatever in the horoscope to account for this, so where is the solution?

The maps of the prenatal epochs of each child are given in Figs. 14 and 15.

In the epoch of the girl, Mercury is again found in the ascendant, but in square to Neptune and semi-square to Mars. It is true that it is near a trine of the moon, but Mercury is retrograde, and the aspect is separating. Moreover, during the prenatal period, Neptune was in square to Mercury, and at nearly every libration of the moon Mercury was heavily afflicted. The ruler of the ascendant Saturn was afflicted by a square of Mars and a semi-square of Venus, and this was sufficient to make the child weakly and backward.

What does the epoch of the boy show ?   Saturn ruler of the ascendant, trine Mars, trine Venus, and the moon apply-ing to its trine as well—all indications of physical strength and well-developed body.   Mentally, Mercury is found in the eleventh house, in conjunction and parallel with both the sun and Jupiter—indications of a splendid mind, quick intellect, and unusual cleverness.   The ascendant has also

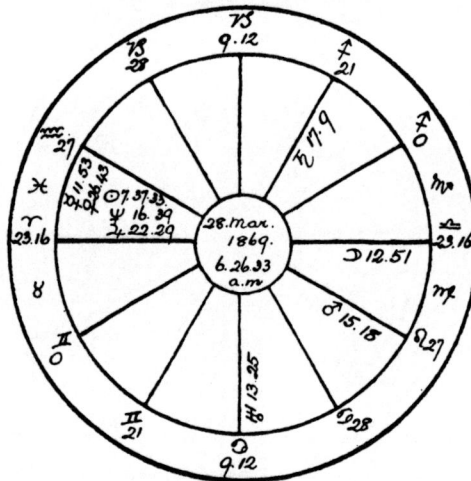

FIG. 16.

the sextile of Mars and Venus, and the trine of Neptune, and the sun is conjoined with Jupiter.

The comparison of the two epochal maps shows the divergence in a remarkable manner ; the horoscopes do not show it at all

My second illustration is a well-known one, having been commented on in astrological magazines some years since. It is a very remarkable one, and gives further proof of the validity of the epoch as calculated, and of its paramount importance in prefiguring the destiny and the directions for events in life.   It is the case of twin ladies who were born near Bath on March 28th, 1869—one at 6.25 a.m., and the other at 8 a.m. On May 1st, 1889, they were out driving, when the second lady alighted to adjust the bit which the servant had allowed to slip between the horse's teeth ; she removed the head-piece, and the horse bolted. The elder remained in the trap, and was uninjured. The younger lady was killed instantly.

The rectified times are respectively 6h. 26m. 33s. a.m., and 7h. 54m. 47s., as will be seen from the maps of the horoscopes (Figs. 16 and 17).

The horoscope of the elder lady shows Aries rising. She

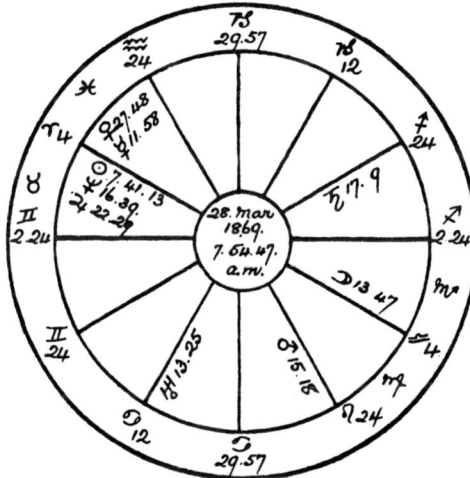

FIG. 17.

was tall and dark. Mars, her ruler, was in Leo, giving height, and Jupiter, rising in Aries, darkened the hair. There is little in the horoscope to indicate danger while travelling—the only position being that of Mercury, ruler of the third, in square to Saturn. At the time of the accident (planets' places April 17th, 8.38 a.m.), the moon was in the third house near a semi-square of ♂ R. The sun was conjoined with Jupiter P. The progressed ascendant is Taurus 29° 8', just past the semi-square of Uranus, whose progressed position is on the cusp of the third house, showing the slight danger to herself.

The horoscope of the younger lady does not show the

danger any more pointedly, while there is nothing to indicate the danger of a violent death. Uranus, on the cusp of the third, afflicts both the luminaries, but neither of these are hyleg, hence do not indicate the danger. The same directions are in force as in her sister's case, though the moon is a little closer to the semi-square of Mars. The ascendant, which is hyleg, certainly has the parallel of Saturn, but it is also in sextile with both Venus and the sun. The ascendant, by direction, was near the parallel of Uranus, and the Sun in parallel to Neptune conversely.

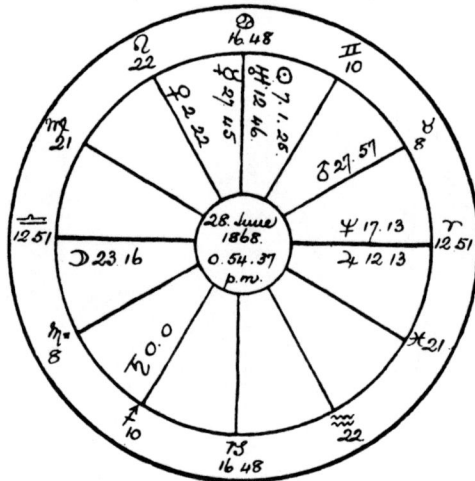

FIG. 18.

Both ladies had the sun in square to Saturn by converse motion, but why should it kill in one case and not in the other?

A very contradictory point occurs in this case. In the elder lady's horoscope the moon is hyleg, as, owing to it having over 4° N. Lat., it is only just over two degrees below the west horizon. It is afflicted by a square of Uranus and the opposition of the sun; hence, greater violence is shown in her case than in her sister's. In the younger lady's horoscope neither luminary is hyleg, and the ascendant is not sufficiently afflicted to indicate a violent death.

How is the question to be decided? The maps of the

prenatal epochs (Figs. 18 and 19) will show the cause, and give directions to account for the sad event.

Reference to the epoch of the elder lady, which took place on June 28th, 1868, at oh. 54m. 37s. p.m., shows no serious danger of accident. At the time of the event the sun was conjoined with Mercury and sextile to Mars, and the moon conjoined with Mercury P. By converse direction the sun was in parallel with Venus P. The moon, however, was in parallel with Mars, and close to the square of Neptune and opposition of Uranus. The progressed ascendant was in

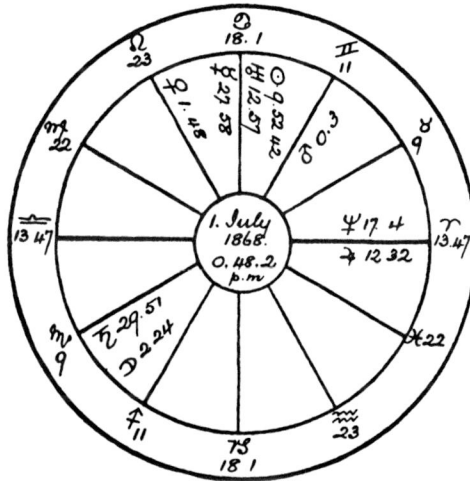

FIG. 19.

square to Mercury, accounting for the death of the sister.

The epoch of the younger sister, (July 1st, 1868, oh. 48m. 2s. p.m.) however, shows different influences, and these very serious ones. The moon is conjoined with Saturn, and in opposition to Mars, the two latter being in close opposition, and the entire influence falling across the horizon of the horoscope of birth. By direction, the sun is in parallel with Mars R., and the moon has just separated from square Mars, square Saturn, square moon, all acting on the epochal indications of danger. By converse direction, the sun is in parallel with Uranus, and Mars has progressed to the parallel of the radical moon. The ascendant of the converse lunar equivalent has the exact parallel with the progressed Mars and the radical moon.

Here again the prenatal epoch has been proved to be paramount in determining the divergence of fortune in twins. In the horoscopes dealt with, nothing is clearly shown that the younger lady would die a violent death ; nor are there directions to account for the event. Reference to the epoch shows the cause and nature of the whole occurrence, and produces directions to account therefor.

SECTION V.

The Epoch in Relation to Prenatal Affections.

CHAPTER XXVI.

THE CHART OF DESCENT.

PROBABLY the most important of the many practical values of the epoch in connection with the scientific exposition of Natal Astrology is that one connected with the cause and nature of all prenatal affections, accidents *in utero*, physical and mental abnormalities and defects, malformations and the like. A child is born minus a hand or a foot, blind or imbecile, possessing peculiar marks or blemishes on some part of the body, or endowed with some remarkable mental gifts or physical abnormalities.

The horoscope of birth which relates to the physical birth, and from then onwards, is totally inadequate to determine the cause or the nature of defects which arise previous to the hour of birth, and it is to the prenatal epoch, and what is known as the chart of descent, that reference must be made for the unravelling of the cause, nature, and time of formation of all antenatal affections and abnormalities.

It had been put forward by opponents of the epoch, as an objection against its verity, that epochs could be found every month—both before and after birth—and that in every month from epoch to birth there was a certain day and time when the interchange of the two factors at birth and epoch was possible, and that the longitude of the moon at such day and time varied only slightly from the actual longitude of the moon at the epoch.

Such, indeed, was an actual fact, and was not denied, but, instead of being in any way a logical or scientific objection against the validity of the epoch, it turned out to be a *thesis* of remarkable beauty and scientific interest, an important adjunct to the epochal theory, and one which yielded the most far-reaching results in the determination of many points connected with the inter-uterine life of the subject. In my own opinion, it was one of the most marvellous discoveries of modern astrological science.

It is, therefore, an important point to be remembered that each rising or setting of the birth moon—according as to which is required—on the date in each month from epoch to birth, when the moon is nearest to the ascending or descending degree at birth, should be noted, and a diagram made showing the moon's actual positions at such time, as shown in the figure appended. This diagram represents what is known as the "Descent of the Monad." Sepharial, in introducing this *thesis* twelve years ago, referred to it in these terms :—" In order to further illustrate the remarkable agreement of the epoch with the moment of birth, we may trace the genesis of the monad from the epoch to the moment of birth, a *thesis* of singular beauty and charm, the parallel of which will be found in Professor Crookes' ' Genesis of the Atom,' read before the Society of Engineers at Birmingham. In that address he shows how the atom is differentiated from the protyle, takes up a definite rate and mode of motion in a mean free path of vibration, and finally becomes established as a permanent chemical body with specific properties and characteristics."

The calculation of the chart of descent is somewhat complicated, and requires some little skill in order to determine the proper longitude of the moon on the several days required. The student should obtain some cross-ruled paper, as shown in the diagram in the next chapter, rule the same in the manner indicated, and head the vertical lines for about six or eight degrees on each side of the moon's longitude at the epoch.

As an illustration of computing the chart of descent, I give the necessary calculations, showing how the moon's longitude is arrived at. The first date represents the epoch, taking place on February 20th, 18h. 35m. (6h. 35m. a.m. of the 21st) when the moon is in Aries $1° 46'$—the descendant of the horoscope. The first position of the moon in the month following should always be to the left of the line of impulse, denoted by the thick line drawn from the top to the bottom of the diagram, just to the left of the line headed " 2." This is the line of impulse from the moon at the epoch to the descendant at birth, this being a decreasing moon. With an increasing moon, the line would be from the moon to the ascendant at birth.

The first return of the moon to its epochal place takes place on March 20th, and when the moon's place at birth sets (March 19th, 16h. 45m.) the moon will be in Pisces $24° 11'$, which should be marked with a dot on the second line. The second return is on April 17th, with the moon's place setting—(the exact time April 16th, 14h. 49m.), and the moon at that time is in Aries 1° 0′. The third return is on May 14th, and the moon will be in Pisces 24° 10′, at the time of the setting of the moon's birth longitude, 1h. 9m. a.m. In the same manner, the fourth return takes place on June 10th, at 11h. 23m. p.m., when the moon is in Aries 3° 11′.

The fifth return, which is the half-way period, takes place on July 7th, and the moon will be nearest its epochal position at 9.37 p.m., and in Pisces 28° 52′. This point should be marked with a small circle, because here, as in all *regular* epochs, the libration of the moon from left to right continues in the same line, and does not go back as at the other dates.

The remaining returns of the moon to its epochal position, and the nearest longitude of the moon thereto, at the moment of the setting of the birth moon are as follows :

Aug.	3rd : 7h. 51m. p.m.	..	24° 27′ ♓
„	31st : 6h. 1m. p.m.	..	3° 12′ ♈
Sept.	27th : 4h. 14m. p.m.	..	26° 12′ ♓
Oct.	25th : 2h. 44m. p.m.	..	3° 16′ ♈
Nov.	21st : 0h. 38m. p.m.	..	25° 38′ ♓

The last line in the chart represents the birth hour, and the descendant of the horoscope is marked on the line of impulse.

Each of these points are now to be connected by lines as shown in the diagram, taking care to continue the line from the fourth return to the sixth, instead of reversing it at the fifth. These charts of descent vary in a very remarkable degree, some being extremely lopsided, *i.e.* the librations of the moon extending several degrees on one side of the line of central impulse, and only just crossing it on the other side —sometimes not even crossing it, as shown at the second return in this illustration. In normal cases the libration is fairly regular, but in all abnormal births the librations are invariably very irregular and lopsided. So far as experience goes, in all regular epochs the continuation of the moon's libration from the fourth to the sixth return is uniformly maintained, but in irregular epochs, as shown in the third diagram in the next chapter, this may occur twice, and it is a peculiarity which is uniformly observed in such epochs.

The subject of the chart of descent is receiving some considerable attention and investigation at the present time, and further developments will undoubtedly be arrived at.

CHAPTER XXVII.

Illustrations of Prenatal Abnormalities.

In this chapter I give full details of four very interesting and instructive cases of prenatal abnormalities, in order to definitely prove that what is claimed for the epoch is no plausible delusion or fancy, but can be substantiated by a direct appeal to authentic facts, and confirmed by observation.

The claim I put forward is one which was the cause of some criticism a few years ago, opponents of the epoch representing that the horoscope of birth was the be-all and end-all of human destiny, in opposition to the fact that authentic cases had been produced where the epoch was the paramount factor. I am of opinion, founded on observation and investigation, that the horoscope of the prenatal epoch is the final and conclusive factor in all matters affecting the life, character, physical and mental characteristics and destiny of the subject, and, in support of my contention, I am producing facts and statements from authentic births. It will be well, therefore, for all opponents of the theory to reconsider their positions in the face of what is known to be the truth.

I. Abdominal Nœvus.

The first case is particularly interesting from the fact that the horoscope of birth shows nothing whatever of the peculiarity, the zodiacal sign governing the part of the body affected not being occupied by any of the planets. It is the horoscope of my eldest daughter, who was born on December 1st, 1901, at 1h. 32m. 23s. a.m. The doctor in attendance reported the time of birth as 1.40 a.m. I personally recorded the first cry at 1.32 a.m., and the epoch confirmed this time within 23s. The ascendant is Libra 1° 46′, and the moon in Leo 15° 56′, above and decreasing. The diagram given on page 153 is based on the setting of the moon's place at birth on each succeeding month from the epoch to birth when the moon is nearest in longitude to the descending degree of the birth figure.   The variations of the moon on each side of the " direct line of impulse " from epoch to birth are particularly lopsided, showing some abnormality.   It is to be noted that on April 16th the moon does not cross the central line, and it is interesting to know that a few hours before the time given the mother experienced a violent flooding, and it was thought that a miscarriage had taken place.   The child was born with a *nævus* to the left of the umbilicus, and, owing to its position, could not be removed by the surgeon's knife, and had to be burned away gradually by the application of caustic. The horoscope gives no planets in the sign Virgo, the sign

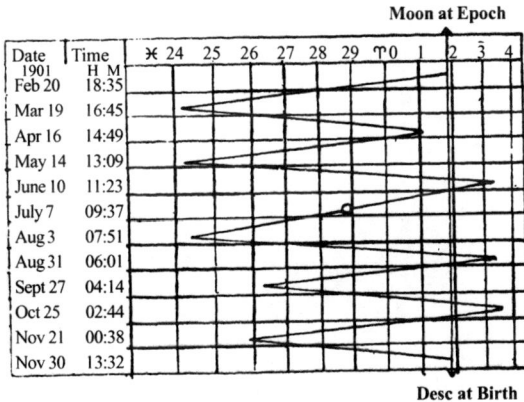

Fig. 20.

ruling the abdominal region, but the prenatal epoch shows Mars in Virgo in opposition to the sun.   Now I would like to ask those self-satisfied astrologers who disbelieve in the prenatal epoch how they could have judged from the horoscope this peculiarity, and whether they could give any idea when it was caused.

Reference to the chart of descent shows that the moon moves backward and forward until July 7th, when, instead of reversing, as it did at all the other times, it continues straight on.   The July 7th was the half-way period—that of quickening.   The moon was then in Pisces 28° 52′, and Mars on that day was in Virgo 27°, in opposition to the moon, and in the sign ruling the part of the body afflicted.

The horoscope shows nothing of this affliction, but the epoch does, and the chart of descent points to the time when the *nævus* was first formed. As the cause of this affliction was antenatal, it was not to be seen in the horoscope, and, therefore, the epoch and the chart of descent had to be examined to trace its formation.

The following is the map of the prenatal epoch of the above case :

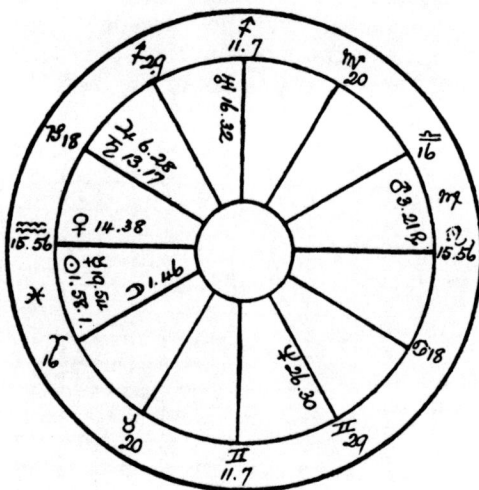

FIG. 21.

II. DONKEY-FACED CHILD.

The second case is that of the " Donkey-faced child," the rectfication of whose horoscope was given in Chapter XX. The following is the comparison of the birth and epoch :

BIRTH.		EPOCH.
1st May, 1897.		12th October, 1896.
12h. 5m. 12s.	L.M.T.	20h. 15m. 19s.
11h. 20m. 16s.	G.M.T.	19h. 30m. 23s.
Ascdt. 16° 47′ ♑		Moon 16° 47′ ♑
Moon 12° 58′ ♉		Ascdt. 12° 58′ ♏

The case is not of very great importance, as it is an ordinary one of premature birth, the child having been *in utero* only six and a-half months, but it will be interesting to examine the chart of descent and the epochal figure in order to determine the cause of the premature birth and the nasal disfigurement.

The following is the diagram of the chart of descent:

Moon at Epoch

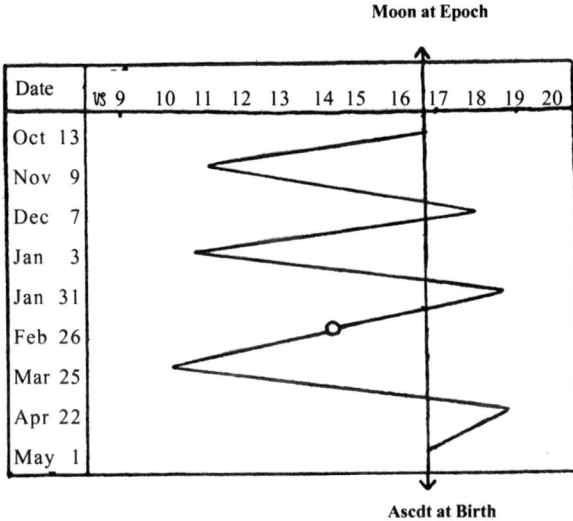

FIG. 22.

It will be observed that the librations of the moon are extremely lopsided, indicating some abnormality, but it will be also noticed that these librations are very regular, and, up the seventh return, go from left to right in a perfect pendulum swing. The child had quickened on February 26th, and up to that period there was nothing to indicate any disaster. On the various dates up to and including March 25th, there were no evil transits to the extremities of the lunar elongations, but on April 22nd we find the following :

Moon's libration	..	..	18° 55′	♑
Mars	..	..	..	..	15° 55′	♋
Central line	..	..	..	16° 47′	♑

Now, at the epoch, we find the ascendant in 12° 58′ ♏, ♄ in 18° 7′ ♏, and Venus 15° 57′ ♏, and on April 22nd we find Venus in ♉ 13°—the opposition of the epochal ascendant.

It is evident, therefore, that on this date something must have occurred to have disturbed the equilibrium and brought about the expulsion of the *fœtus* before its proper time. Personally, I should judge the cause to have been an over-indulgence in pleasure (Venus in Taurus) and intoxicants (Mars in Cancer, crossing the extremity of the Moon's libration on April 22nd). A possible alternative is that it was due to shock caused by fire (Mars opposition ascendant at birth).

Turning to the epochal figure, which is appended, for the cause of the disfigurement or non-development of the nasal organs, Scorpio 12° 58′ is rising, with Venus, Saturn, and Uranus conjoined just below the ascendant.

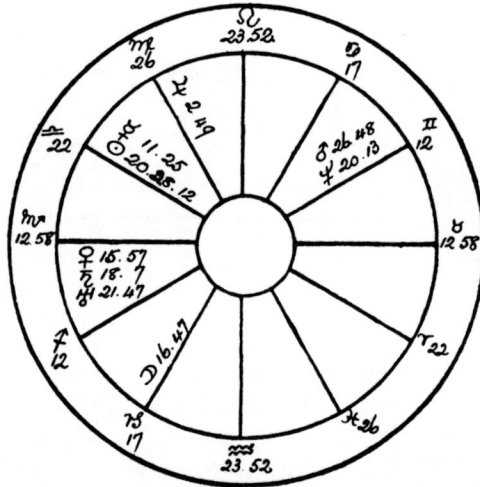

FIG. 23.

The rising sign governs the head, and the sign Scorpio has a special government over the nose. Venus is conjoined with the two malefics, Saturn and Uranus—a very rare configuration—hence the nasal deformity is clearly indicated in the epochal figure.

The horoscope of birth does not show any such deformity, for, although Saturn and Uranus are conjoined at the end of the sign Scorpio, they are close to a trine of Mars, and are not placed in the ascendant, nor do they throw any evil aspects to that point.

Here again is another indication of the superiority of the epochal figure over the horoscope, and the value of the chart of descent in determining the cause and nature of any antenatal deformity.

III. L'Enfant Grenouille (The Frog Child).

This case is one of the most remarkable I have ever met with, and will be of more than ordinary interest to students as I am able not only to give the details of a most peculiar deformity of the hands and feet but to reproduce the photograph of the child in question.

The child, which was of the male sex, was born at Holvenen, Antwerp, Lat. 51° 12′ N., Long. 4° 24′ E., on July 25th, 1909, at 4 a.m. (local mean time, 4h. 17m. 36s. a.m.).

At the recorded time of birth, Leo 0° 34′ was rising, and the moon was placed in Libra 28° 0′, increasing and below, and in a female degree.   The period of gestation was longer than the norm by seven days, the moon being at this distance from the ascendant.   The moon at the epoch is found in the ascending degree of the horoscope, but the radical place of the moon descends at the epoch in order to obtain the required sex.

The following is the comparison of the birth and epoch :

	BIRTH.		EPOCH.
	25th July, 1909.		17th October, 1908.
3h. 53m. 29s. a.m.	G.M.T.	4h. 48m. 28s. p.m.
4h. 11m. 5s. a.m.	L.M.T.	5h. 6m. 4s. p.m.
29° 59′ ♋	Ascdt.	26° 57′ ♈
26° 57′ ♎	Moon	29° 59′ ♋

The child was known by the nickname of " L'Enfant Grenouille," or " The Frog Child," owing to its peculiar appearance, as will be seen from the photograph, Fig. 24.

" It was born with the *right* arm only from the elbow to the shoulder, the right forearm and hand being missing.   Both legs are present from the groin to the knee, and that part from the knee to the ankle is missing.   The feet and toes are stuck to, or rather start from, the knee."

Why was this child born like this ?   An examination of the chart of descent and the epochal figure should determine the cause of the deformity, and whether it is indicated in the latter. Fig. 25 is the chart of descent, and a more abnormal one, I think, it will be hard to find.

Now, it will be observed that in this chart the librations of the moon are abnormally lopsided, on only three occasions out of ten crossing the line of central impulse, and on one occasion not crossing at all. Also, it will be observed that

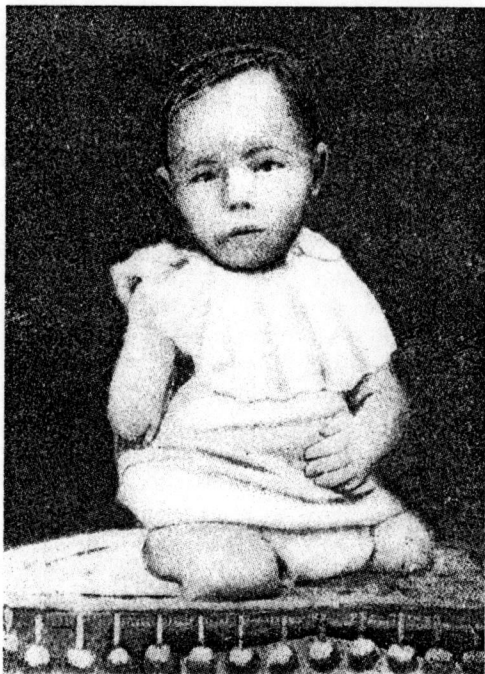

FIG. 24.

instead of the libration continuing at the fifth month, as in the first chart given in this chapter, this peculiarity occurs at two distinct times—the *third* and *sixth* months. This is a distinct irregularity, and, from investigation, I believe that it is always noticeable in irregular epochs. In a regular epoch this continuation would only occur at the fifth month.

In regard to the peculiar deformities or malformations in

the limbs of the child, what disturbing influences are to be found along the path of the moon from epoch to birth ? There are several very important ones.

At the first return of the moon (November 13th) to ♋ 24° 53′ Mars is found in ♎ 22° 13′ in square thereto.

At the third return (January 7th) to ♋ 26° 28′, Mercury is in ♑ 25° 13′ in opposition.

At the fourth return (February 3rd) to ♋ 22° 17′, Uranus is in Capricorn 18° 43′, and Venus in 23° 0′ of the same sign, both in opposition to the epochal moon.

Moon at Epoch

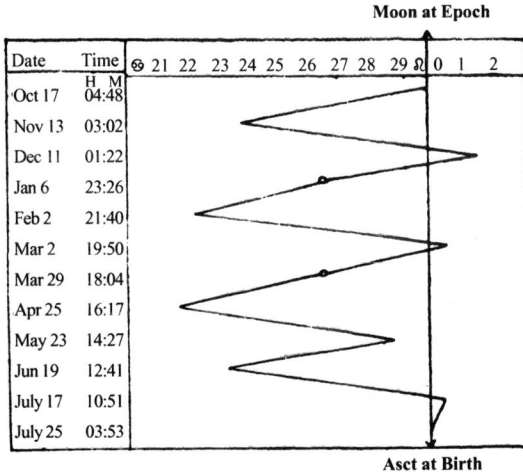

Date	Time
	H M
Oct 17	04:48
Nov 13	03:02
Dec 11	01:22
Jan 6	23:26
Feb 2	21:40
Mar 2	19:50
Mar 29	18:04
Apr 25	16:17
May 23	14:27
Jun 19	12:41
July 17	10:51
July 25	03:53

♋ 21 22 23 24 25 26 27 28 29 ♌ 0 1 2

Asct at Birth

FIG. 25.

The sixth return (March 30th) is the most remarkable. Here the moon is in Cancer 26° 37′. Mars is in Capricorn 21° 55′ and Uranus in 20° 47′ of the same sign. These two planets are conjoined in opposition to the moon.

The seventh return (April 26th) brings the moon to Cancer 21° 50′, and Uranus *stationary* in Capricorn 21° 5′.

At the ninth return (June 20th) the moon is in Cancer 23° 18′ and Uranus in 19° 59′ of the opposite sign.

It will, therefore, be seen that at six of the ten lunar returns, either Mars, Mercury, or Uranus, notably the latter, are afflicting the moon—a more than remarkable coincidence. I will now examine the figure for the prenatal epoch

(Fig. 26) in order to determine whether this peculiar deformity is shown therein.

This figure shows Saturn in Aries 5° 26′ in the twelfth
house, ruling the feet—showing a deformity in those organs—
in opposition to Mars in Libra 4° 48′, in the sixth house, ruling
the hands—denoting a deformity in those organs. The
opposition of Uranus and Neptune from Capricorn and
Cancer—the former ruling the knee and the latter the elbow—
accounts for the absence of the calves and the feet stuck on
at the knees, also the loss of the forearm. The sun is placed

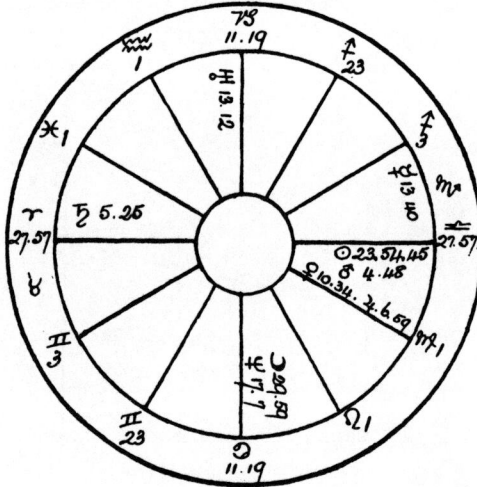

FIG. 26.

at the epoch on the radical place of the moon, and the
opposition of the moon and Saturn at birth falls right
across the horizon of the epochal figure. The opposition
of Mars and Saturn at the epoch falls exactly across the
meridian of the horoscope.

But to return to the horoscope of birth. Is this malformation shown therein? Truly, Mercury and Neptune
are conjoined in the twelfth house, ruling the feet, in
opposition to Uranus and square to Saturn, but how many
other children were born on or about this time with the same
configuration? Jupiter, in the third house, ruling the
arms, is not seriously afflicted, while it is well aspected by

three planets. The malefics are elevated, it is true, but one is in trine with the sun, and neither are in a sign ruling the hands or feet. Moreover—and this is the point which I wish to bring strongly forward—the child was born in the condition described, and, therefore, the *cause* was antecedent to the birth, and such cause cannot be found in the horoscope.

IV.—IMPERFECT SEX.

The next case is one of a sex deformity, and the particulars were forwarded to me by a gentleman from Hull. The child was born on July 9th, 1913, at 6.15 a.m., at Hull, and the following are the particulars given by my correspondent : " A sexless child, medically described as an imperfect boy. It had been fairly healthy, although not very strong, and was making good progress when its death occurred on December 11th. It was found dead, and apparently died of convulsions. The infant was born with an imperfect or dwarfed male organ, by which water was passed, but there were no testicles. The period was believed to be a short one, and the mother attributed malformation to a shock."

The following are the particulars and comparison of the birth and epoch :

	BIRTH.		EPOCH.	
July 9th, 1913.			Nov. 29th, 1912.	
6h. 10m. 52s.		L.M.T.	1h. 19m. 55s.	
6h. 12m. 12s.		G.M.T.	1h. 21m. 15s.	
11° 52′ ♌		Ascdt.	24° 47′ ♓	
24° 47′ ♍		Moon	11° 52′ ♌	

The period, as stated, is a short one, being only 8 L + *x*, that is, exceeding eight lunar months by the moon's distance from the ascendant divided by 13, and, in order to obtain the required sex, the moon's place at birth sets at the epoch, and the moon thereat is found in the degree rising at birth, according to rule.

Examination of the chart of descent (Fig. 27) will at once disclose a remarkable abnormality, the librations of the moon being particularly lopsided, only just crossing the line of central impulse to the right, but extending on the left from six to ten degrees.

Now, taking each return of the epochal moon to its own place, it will be found that on the third return—February 19th, 7h. 59m. a.m.—the moon is in ♌ 5° 9′, Mars in ♒ 0° 0′, and Uranus in ♒ 5° 0′, the two latter being conjoined and opposed to the moon. It would be interesting to note whether the fright, to which the mother attributes the cause of the deformity, occurred on February 25th or 26th, the two planets Mars and Uranus being in conjunction in ♒ 6, the moon at the time being in the sign Scorpio, ruling the afflicted parts.

Again, at the return on April 14th, the moon was in Leo 6° 59′ and Uranus 7° 13′. This being the central

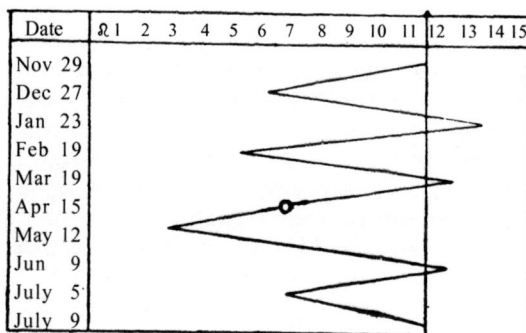

FIG. 27.

point where the moon continues her librations instead of returning—the point of sex formation—the conjunction of Uranus with the moon within only 14′ is particularly worthy of note. At the return previous to birth, the moon was in 6° 54′, Leo and Uranus in Aquarius 6° 29′.

The ascendant of the epoch was Pisces 24° 47′, the Scorpio decanate of the sign, and Mars was in the last degree of Scorpio in the eighth house, in opposition to Saturn—the same malefic influence as in the case of the " Frog child."

Examining the horoscope of this child, there are no indications of the deformity. The sign Scorpio is not occupied by any of the planets. Here again is shown the superiority of the epochal figure demonstrated in the determining of the indications of antenatal deformities.

CHAPTER XXVIII.

THE DATE OF QUICKENING.

A FURTHER important point in connection with the chart of descent is the determination of the date of quickening.

According to medical authorities, quickening is often called that of " feeling life," or " stirrage," and it is due to the movement of the fœtus in the womb. Importance is attached to the period at which quickening occurs. This period may be set down, as a rule, as occurring at the end of the fourth month of pregnancy, approximately at the half-way point between conception and birth. Very frequently, the first movement of quickening causes a sensation of faintness or sickness in the woman. Many nurses calculate the date when the confinement will take place from the occurrence of the quickening.

With these notes in view, it will be interesting to see how far the epoch can be brought into play in determining the date of the quickening, and whether the date of the fifth libration of the moon shown in the chart of descent will coincide with such date.

The following facts came under my personal observation in the year 1903, but it was not until eleven years afterwards that I was able to bring to light a very important discovery in connection with the chart of descent and the librations of the moon over the line of lunar impulse. I give the full details, so that students shall have the opportunity of examining the whole matter.

" A lady relative, who was known to be *enceinte*, related to my wife that about one o'clock in the middle of the day on August 11th, 1903, she experienced a turning movement *in utero*, came over very faint, and was very sick."

The lady gave birth to a boy on December 26th, 1903, at 3.47 a.m., rectified time. The ascendant was Scorpio 12° 17′, and the moon was in Pisces 22° 49′, increasing and below.

On August 11th, at 1.15 p.m., the moon was in Pisces 22° 49′, exactly the same as at birth, and the ascendant was in the middle of Scorpio, close to the birth ascendant.

At the epoch on March 16th, 1903, the ascendant was

22° 49′ Pisces—the place of the moon at birth—and the moon
was in Scorpio 12° 17′—the ascendant of the horoscope.

Such a series of coincidences—if one may properly call
them such—are not by any means fortuitous. They cannot
have happened by chance, or be merely a play on the moon's
motion. There must have been some reason for the exact
coinciding of the moon's place and ascendant at three
distinct and separate dates, some natural law in operation
regulating such coincidence.

Reference, however, to the chart of descent of this
particular case gives no clue as to the quickening taking

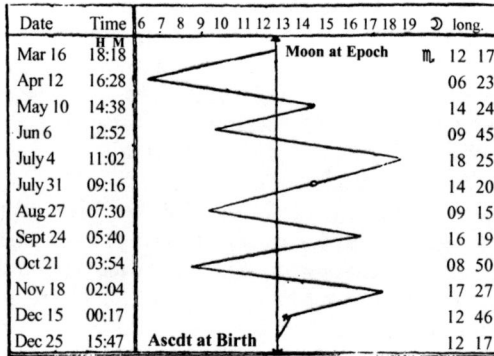

Date	Time	6 7 8 9 10 11 12 13 14 15 16 17 18 19 ☽ long.
Mar 16	18:18	Moon at Epoch ♏ 12 17
Apr 12	16:28	06 23
May 10	14:38	14 24
Jun 6	12:52	09 45
July 4	11:02	18 25
July 31	09:16	14 20
Aug 27	07:30	09 15
Sept 24	05:40	16 19
Oct 21	03:54	08 50
Nov 18	02:04	17 27
Dec 15	00:17	12 46
Dec 25	15:47	Ascdt at Birth 12 17

FIG. 28.

place on this date. The dates of the moon's librations on
either side of the line of central impulse nearest to this date
are July 31st and August 27th, as shown above.

But a point now arises which opens up another phase
in this *thesis* of the chart of descent, and one which has an
important bearing on the subject of the date of quickening.
It should be pointed out that the several dates given in the
chart of descent are the days when the moon is nearest to
the radical ascendant, at the time of the rising or setting,
as the case may be, of the radical moon. In other words,
the ascendant at such dates is the ascendant at the epoch,
and the moon is nearest to its epochal position, the line
of central impulse being from the epochal moon to the
ascendant of the horoscope.

On this particular date, however, we find the positions reversed. The moon is close to its *birth* longitude at the rising of the *birth* ascendant, and this, therefore, gives rise to an entirely new chart of descent, based upon the radical position of the two factors instead of the epochal, giving a line of central impulse from the epochal ascendant to the radical moon, instead of from the epochal moon to the radical ascendant, as shown in the following diagram.

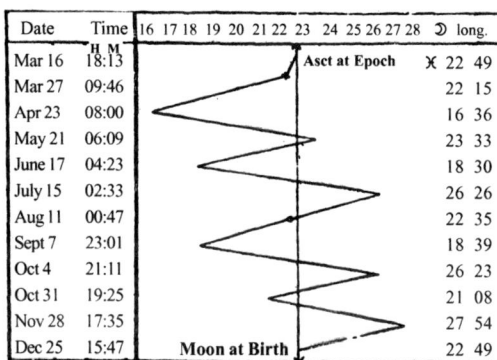

Date	Time	16 17 18 19 20 21 22 23 24 25 26 27 28 ☽ long.
	H. M.	
Mar 16	18:13	Asct at Epoch ♓ 22 49
Mar 27	09:46	22 15
Apr 23	08:00	16 36
May 21	06:09	23 33
June 17	04:23	18 30
July 15	02:33	26 26
Aug 11	00:47	22 35
Sept 7	23:01	18 39
Oct 4	21:11	26 23
Oct 31	19:25	21 08
Nov 28	17:35	27 54
Dec 25	15:47	Moon at Birth 22 49

FIG. 29.

As previously stated, the occurrence took place about 1 p.m. on August 11th, 1893, and, on referring to the chart, it will be seen that on that date, at 0h. 47m. 4s. p.m. the birth ascendant was rising, and the moon was in Pisces 22° 35'—distant only 14' from its radical place. It will also be noted that this is the fifth return of the moon to its radical place—the half-way point, where the moon's libration continues in the same direction instead of being reversed as at other dates. We have here the centre point agreeing exactly with the date and time of quickening, as given above—another emphatic proof of the validity of the epoch as calculated.

There is a marked peculiarity in this case which should be observed independently of its connection with the date of quickening. In the original chart of descent at date December 15th, it will be seen that the moon does not cross the central line of impulse, but stops short approximately half a degree therefrom. In the new chart the same peculiarity is to be noticed, but this time it is on March 27th— the first libration—and here again it stops short half a degree from the line of central impulse. The latter chart appears to be the complement of the former.

This is another point in connection with the epoch on which the last word has yet to be written—that there is a law, at present only in part known, which governs the question of the date of quickening. That the facts stated in this chapter must be relegated to the realms of coincidence is a suggestion which no earnest seeker after the truth will admit. Moreover, there are no such things as coincidences where natural laws are concerned. The fact has been shown that the date and time of quickening happened at the exact moment when the birth ascendant was rising, and at the fifth return of the moon to its radical place. It was no " fake," no chance occurrence ; it was in conformity with a well-defined law, which is capable of further demonstration.

SECTION VI.

The Prenatal Epoch as a Factor in Directing.

CHAPTER XXIX.

DIRECTING FROM THE PRENATAL EPOCH.

IT is one of the four fundamental conditions of the epochal theory that every correctly calculated epoch should be capable of producing directions to account for all the events of life, in exactly the same manner as the horoscope of birth. I use the term "correctly calculated epoch" because this question of directing therefrom is one of the four proofs that the epoch has been correctly calculated.

As more than once stated in these pages, it is only too easy to find a fictitious epoch which agrees with the birth-time merely as a time measure—that is to say, it shows that the time of birth has been correctly noted. Such fictitious epoch may even correctly denote the sex of the subject; but unless it yields directions to account for the various events of life, even though it should agree in the other two particulars, it may be safely assumed that it is not correct.

Directions may be taken from the epochal figure in exactly the same way as from a horoscope, either by the progressive method—both direct and converse, or, more correctly speaking, post-epochal and pre-epochal—or by the primary method. The age of the subject, however, must be reckoned from the date of the epoch.

Directions from the prenatal epoch, although measuring to, and agreeing with, the nature of the events in life, should always be co-ordinated with those from the horoscope—post-epochal with the postnatal, and pre-epochal with the prenatal. It is not possible, in the scope of this work, to give the full detailed rules for the calculation and judgment of directions from the epoch, and the student must, therefore, be referred to the several Astrological works dealing with the subject. In the *British Journal of Astrology*, I gave a series of lessons on the progressive system of directing, with a number of illustrations from both horoscopes and epochs, and the student would be well-advised to purchase these volumes and make himself fully conversant with the rules for calculation and judgment. The principal rules for the calculation of the progressed epoch—both direct and converse—are given in the next chapter.

The lunar equivalent and diurnal horoscope—two theories of remarkable utility in directing—can be applied to the prenatal epoch in exactly the same way as the horoscope. Illustrations of these will also be given.

The value of directions computed from the epoch cannot be too highly estimated. They fill in many of the gaps found in directions from the horoscope, and supply the solution to the many anomalies which are found in judging the effects of directions. They show why directions from the horoscope are held over, or accentuated, and why some do not appear to act at all. In the horoscopes of infants and those who die young they solve completely the time of death, and are also the positive solution to the whole vexed and anomalous question of infant mortality. Experience gained from an investigation of some dozens of infant horoscopes has enabled me to make the following authoritative statement : " Children are born at favourable moments with little affliction shown in their horoscopes, yet their lives are short—perhaps only a few months, a few weeks, or even a few days. Events occur for which there are no corresponding directions in the horoscope. Where lies the solution to this apparent anomaly ? Turn to the epoch, and there will be found the master key." It has also been found that events occur in life, and no directions in accord with the nature of the event can be traced from the horoscope. The epoch supplies this deficiency.

From the metaphysical aspect of the science, the question of directions from the epoch is one capable of the highest development. It solves the eternal question—" WHY ? " It shows why certain directions act more powerfully than others, and why events occur in the life for which no adequate cause is to be found in the horoscope. A full discussion on the metaphysical aspect of the epoch is outside the limits of this present work. I am, herein, only concerned with the practical and scientific side of the theory, and its application to the horoscope of birth.

CHAPTER XXX.

How to Calculate Directions from the Epoch.

In order to assist the student to thoroughly understand the importance of directions from the prenatal epoch, I now give the principal rules for the calculation of the progressed epoch and of the directions therefrom.

The progressed epoch is a map or figure of the heavens erected on each succeeding and preceding day from the epoch date, and at certain times to be afterwards explained. It contains the planetary longitudes at these times, and shows the progress of the planets through the zodiac and the epoch, as well as the motion of the epoch itself.

I. How to Calculate the Progressed Epoch.

There are three methods of calculating the progressed epoch, viz. :

- (1) For the epochal anniversary.
- (2) For the January 1st in any year.
- (3) For the date in each year which measures to the exact noon on the succeeding and preceding days to the epoch.

The first two methods are not to be recommended for general practice, on account of the numerous calculations involved, and especially so when the directions are required to be taken out for a period of twelve months at a time, and I shall, therefore, not give the rules.

The second method is, however, of great utility when working out the directions for any particular date or event in the past, and it will be illustrated in the examples given in Chapter XXXII.

The third method is the one recommended for general adoption, and the complete rules will be given. It is by far the easiest and most accurate one, and enables the aspects, and especially the lunar parallels, to be more correctly computed. It does away with all the calculations of the planets' places, and renders the entire process one of simplicity. The key to this method is what is termed the "index date," because all the calculations—both of the progressed epoch and directions—hinge on this particular date.

1. *To calculate the direct or post-epochal directions.*

Rule 1. (*a*) When the time of epoch is before noon, add to the time of epoch so many hours and minutes as will bring the time to noon, and turn this odd period into months and days at the rate of two hours for a month and four minutes for a day, and add it to the date of epoch. The date found is that for which the progressed epoch should be erected.

(*b*) When the time of epoch is after noon, turn the time of epoch after noon into months and days at the rate of two hours for a month and four minutes for a day and subtract it from the date of epoch ; this will be the date for which the progressed epoch should be erected.

Rule 2. Find the age of the native in days, hours and minutes on the date found, and add the progress for such age to the R.A.M.C. at the epoch; this will give the R.A.M.C. of the progressed epoch.

Rule 3. Add the age thus found to the day and hour of epoch, deducting the number of days in the epoch month if required, and this will give the date for which the planets' places should be calculated.

Note.—The date found by Rule 3 will always be an *exact* noon.

In the illustration of the epoch of the late Princess Alice, the time is before noon. The amount required to be added to the epoch time is 3h. 47m.—equal to 1 month 27 days—and this is to be added to the date of epoch, bringing the index date to September 25th.

On September 25th, 1878, the age of the native from the epoch, was 36 years 1 month 27 days—equal to 36d. 3h. 47m.—and the progress for this period taken from the table on page 174, 2h. 22m. 34s., added to the R.A.M.C. of the epoch, gives 6h. 57m. 30s. This is the R.A.M.C. of the progressed epoch for September 25th, 1878.

By Rule 3, the age of the native on the index date, as found in the last paragraph, 36d. 3h. 47m., added to the date and time of the epoch, gives September 2nd, 1842, at noon, exactly, and the planets' places have merely to be taken from the ephemeris, and inserted in the figure. There need be no fear of a mistake here, as the time obtained from this rule is always an exact noon.

2. *To calculate the converse or pre-epochal directions.*

Rule 1. (a) When the time of epoch is before noon, add to the time of epoch so many hours and minutes as will bring the time to noon, and turn this odd period into months and days at the rate of two hours for a month and four minutes for a day, and subtract it from the date of epoch. The date found is that for which the progressed epoch should be erected.

(b) When the time of epoch is after noon, turn the time of epoch after noon into months and days at the rate of two hours for a month and four minutes for a day, and add it to the date of epoch; this will be the date for which the progressed epoch should be erected.

Rule 2. Find the age of the native in days, hours and minutes on the date found and subtract the progress for such age from the R.A.M.C. at the epoch; this will give the R.A.M.C. of the progressed epoch.

Rule 3. Subtract the age thus found from the day and hour of epoch, adding the number of days in the previous month if required, and this will give the date for which the planets' places should be calculated.

Note.—The date found by Rule 3 will always be an *exact* noon.

By Rule 1, the amount required to be added to the epoch time is 3h. 47m.—equal to 1 month 27 days—and, as this is to be subtracted from the date of the epoch, the index date will become June 1st.

On this date in 1878, the age of the native from the epoch was 35 years 10 months 3 days—equal to 35d. 20h. 13m. The progress for this, taken from the table, is 2h. 21m. 18s., and, subtracted from the epochal meridian, gives 2h. 13m. 38s. as the R.A.M.C. of the converse progressed epoch for June 1st, 1878.

The age of the native on June 1st, subtracted from the date of the epoch, yields June 22nd at noon. Thus :

		D.	H.	M
Date and time of Epoch ..	July	27	20	13
Add days in June		30	0	0
		57	20	13
Subtract age .. ,. ..		35	20	13
Date for which planets' places are taken	June	22	0	0

Here again there need be no fear of a mistake, as the date found will always be an *exact* noon.

I now give the table for calculating the progressed epoch, to which reference has been made in the examples.

TABLE FOR CALCULATING THE PROGRESSED EPOCH.

Days.	Progress.	Days.	Progress.	Days.	Progress.	Hours.	Progress.
	H. M. S.		H. M. S.		H. M. S.		M. S.
1	3 57	35	2 17 59	69	4 32 2	12	1 58
2	7 53	36	2 21 56	70	4 35 59	13	2 8
3	11 50	37	2 25 52	71	4 39 55	14	2 18
4	15 46	38	2 29 49	72	4 43 52	15	2 28
5	19 43	39	2 33 46	73	4 47 48	16	2 38
6	23 39	40	2 37 42	74	4 51 45	17	2 48
7	27 36	41	2 41 39	75	4 55 42	18	2 57
8	31 32	42	2 45 35	76	4 59 38	19	3 7
9	35 29	43	2 49 32	77	5 3 35	20	3 17
10	39 26	44	2 53 28	78	5 7 31	21	3 27
11	43 22	45	2 57 25	79	5 11 28	22	3 37
12	47 19	46	3 1 21	80	5 15 24	23	3 47
13	51 15	47	3 5 18	81	5 19 21	24	3 57
14	55 12	48	3 9 15	82	5 23 17		
15	59 8	49	3 13 11	83	5 27 14		
16	1 3 5	50	3 17 8	84	5 31 11	Min.	Progress.
17	1 7 1	51	3 21 4				S.
18	1 10 58	52	3 25 1			4	1
19	1 14 54	53	3 28 57			8	1
20	1 18 51	54	3 32 54	Hours.	Progress.	12	2
21	1 22 47	55	3 36 50		M. S.	16	3
22	1 26 44	56	3 40 47	1	10	20	3
23	1 30 41	57	3 44 44	2	20	24	4
24	1 34 37	58	3 48 40	3	30	28	5
25	1 38 34	59	3 52 37	4	39	32	5
26	1 42 30	60	3 56 33	5	49	36	6
27	1 46 27	61	4 0 30	6	59	40	7
28	1 50 23	62	4 4 26	7	1 9	44	7
29	1 54 20	63	4 8 23	8	1 19	48	8
30	1 58 17	64	4 12 19	9	1 29	52	9
31	2 2 13	65	4 16 16	10	1 39	56	9
32	2 6 10	66	4 20 13	11	1 48	60	10
33	2 10 6	67	4 24 9				
34	2 14 3	68	4 28 6				

II. How to Calculate Directions from the Prenatal Epoch.

The mathematical principles of directing from the epoch are very simple, and require only a knowledge of elementary Astrology, the erection of horoscopes, calculation of planetary positions and declinations, with simple addition, subtraction, and rule of three.

Just as in the progressive system of directing, the meridian, ascendant, sun, moon and planets, by their diurnal progression, form aspects to the places they held at the epoch, and also to one another as they move along in the zodiac. The aspects are termed directions, and are measured by accounting each twenty-four hours before and after the hour of epoch as equal to one year of life.

Directions are formed in two distinct ways :—

1. By the approach of one body to the conjunction or aspect of the radical place of another.

   (a) The meridian and ascendant, by their progression, will form aspects to the radical places of the sun, moon, and planets.

   (b) The sun, by its motion through the zodiac, will form aspects to the radical meridian and ascendant, to its own radical place, and to the radical places of the moon and planets.

   (c) The moon, by similar motion, will form aspects to the radical meridian, ascendant, and sun, to its own radical place, and to the radical places of the planets.

   (d) The planets, by their motion through the zodiac, will form aspects to the radical meridian, ascendant, sun, and moon, and to their own radical places.

2. By the combined approach of two bodies to the conjunction and aspects of each other.

   (a) The progressed meridian and ascendant will form aspects to the progressed positions of the sun and planets only.

   (b) The sun, by its progressive motion, will form aspects to the progressed places of the planets only.

   (c) The moon, in progression, will form aspects to the progressed meridian, ascendant, sun, and planets.

   (d) The planets, by their progressive motion, will form aspects among themselves.

There are three classes of progressive directions, viz. :

PRIMARY, PLANETARY, AND SECONDARY.

The following table will show the formation and division of the various directions :

PRIMARY DIRECTIONS.

The M.C. progressed to	⟨ ☉ ☽ and planets radical. ⟨ ☉ and planets progressed.
The Asc. progressed to	⟨ ☉ ☽ and planets radical. ⟨ ☉ and planets progressed.
The ☉ progressed to	⎧ M.C., Asc., ☉ ☽ and planets ⎨ radical ⎩ Planets progressed *only*.
The M.C., Asc., ☉ and ☽ Radical to the	⎰ Planets progressed.

PLANETARY DIRECTIONS.

The seven planets progressed to	⎰ Their own radical places. ⎱ Their progressed places.

SECONDARY DIRECTIONS.

The moon progressed to	⎧ The M.C., Asc., ☉, ☽ and ⎨ planets radical. ⎪ The M.C., Asc., ☉ and ⎩ planets progressed.

Having erected the progressed epoch for the index date in the year required (in the example given it will be the 25th September, 1861 ; *see* map on page 179), insert the planet's places therein for the progressed date, which will be August 16th, 1842 at noon, and also note their declinations and the declinations of the progressed meridian and ascendant.

Then note whether the sun makes any aspects to the radical M.C., ascendant, moon, or the planets' places, and note them down. Similarly with the M.C. and ascendant ; and also note whether the planets make any aspects to the radical sun, moon, M.C., and ascendant. See also whether any parallels of declination are formed in the same manner.

Then note whether the planets make any aspects to their own radical places, or form any parallel of declination.

Then note whether the sun, M.C., or ascendant form any aspects with the progressed places of the planets, and note these down.

Next note whether the planets are forming any mutual aspects on the progressed date.

The lunar directions are computed as follows : Note the moon's position on the progressed date and on the day after, and subtract the two. This gives the moon's motion's for the year. Divide this by 12, and this will give the monthly increment. Add this successively to the moon's position on the progressed date, and this will give its progressed position for each month of the year, on the same date as the index date. Proceed exactly the same way with the moon's declination.

Then note in what month the moon makes aspects with the radical M.C., ascendant, sun, moon, and planets, and note them down opposite the month. Similarly place opposite the month the aspects formed by the moon to the progressed M.C., ascendant, sun, and planets.

The converse directions are taken in exactly the same way, but care must be taken to note that the M.C., ascendant, sun, moon, and planets are moving backwards in the zodiac (unless any planet is retrograde), and also, in computing the lunar directions, the moon's position on the progressed date is subtracted from its position on the day *previous*, and the monthly amount is successively subtracted from the longitude on the progressed date.

This process completed, the whole of the directions operating during a single year are then tabulated. It is not possible in the scope of this work to give the rules for judging directions, and I must, therefore, refer students to my work on " Predictive Astrology," to be published later.

CHAPTER XXXI.

Epochal Directions Illustrated.

As an illustration of the method of computing directions from the prenatal epoch, as outlined in the previous chapter, I will take the epoch of the late Princess Alice, which took place on July 28th, 1842, at 8h. 13m. 15s. a.m., and compute the directions operating for the year in which her father died.

The following is the map of the epoch :

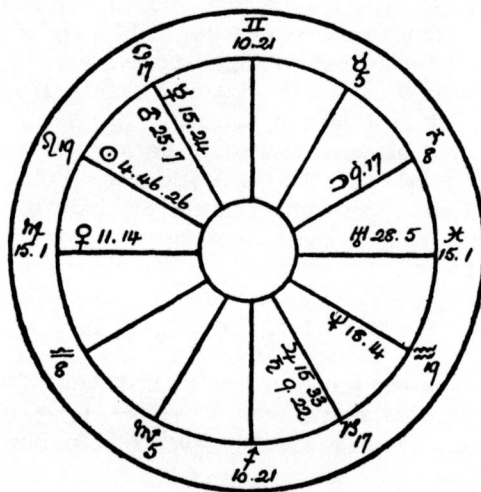

Fig. 30.

☉ 19° 5′ N.	♀ 8° 30′ N.	♄ 22° 38′ S.
☽ 8° 26′ N.	♂ 22° 7′ N.	♅ 1° 29′ S.
☿ 20° 24′ N.	♃ 22° 51′ S.	♆ 15° 36′ S.

The index date, as previously shown, is September 25th, and the progressed date for that day in 1861 is August 16th, 1842, at noon, and the planets' places are taken for that

day. The age of the Princess on September 25th, 1861, was
19 years 1 month 27 days—equal to 19d. 3h. 47m.—and the
progress for this time, taken from the table, is 1h. 15m. 32s.
This added to the R.A.M.C. at the epoch gives 5h. 50m.
28s., and the progressed epoch is erected with this R.A.M.C.

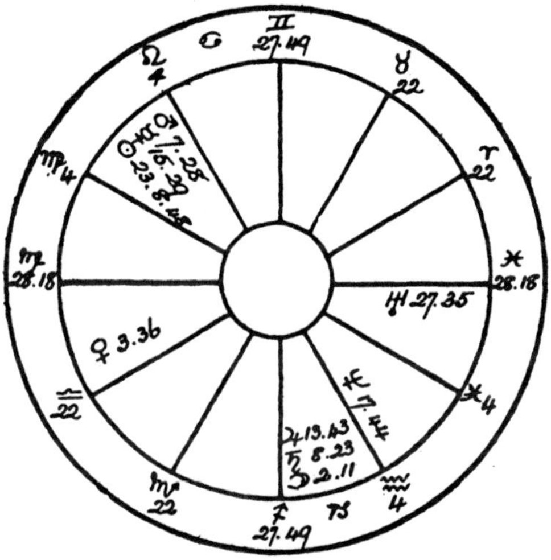

FIG. 31.

☉ 13° 49′ N.	♀ 1° 11′ S.	♄ 22° 44′ S.
☽ 25° 5′ S.	♂ 19° 29′ N.	♅ 1° 41′ S.
☿ 17° 41′ N.	♃ 23° 5′ S.	♆ 15° 45′ S.

Reference to the map will show that the meridian has
reached the square of Uranus, both R. and P., and that
the progressed ascendant is forming the opposition of the
same planet. These are typical directions for the death of
a parent. The sun is also in exact sesquiquadrate with
Saturn P.

The longitude of the moon on August 16th is 2° 11′ ♑,
and on the following day 14° 29′ ♑, showing an increment of
12° 18′—which is a little more than 1° 1′ per month. This
monthly increment is added to the longitude on August 16th,
as in the following table. The declinations are not given,
as they are very high, and no parallels are formed during the
period in question.

It will now be seen that in October the moon is in semi-square with Neptune, so this direction is noted down opposite the month. In November, the moon is in square with Venus P. ; in March, it is conjoined with Saturn P., and in sesquiquadrate with the Sun P ; in April, it is conjoined with the radical Saturn and in square to its own radical place. All these directions are noted down opposite the months in which they are formed. It is of interest to note that Venus is applying to the square of Saturn P., and that the moon is passing from the square of the former to the conjunction of the latter, being about midway between the two aspects in the month of December, when the father died.

The following is the table referred to above :

1861.	Sept. 25th	♑ 2° 11′		
,,	Oct.	3° 13′	☽ ∠ ♆ R.	
,,	Nov.	4° 15′	☽ □ ♀ R.	
,,	Dec.	5° 17′		
1862.	Jan.	6° 19′		
,,	Feb.	7° 21′		
,,	March	8° 23′	☽ ♂ ♄ P.	⚏ ☉ P.
,,	April	9° 24′	☽ ♂ ♄ R.	□ ☽ R.
,,	May	10° 25′		
,,	June	11° 26′		
,,	July	12° 27′		
,,	Aug.	13° 28′		
,,	Sept.	14° 29′		

The prenatal or converse directions are computed in exactly the same manner, care being taken to note that the planetary longitudes are decreasing (unless retrograde), and in computing the lunar directions the moon's position on the progressed date must be subtracted from that on the *previous* day. I append an illustration of converse directions, taking the same event as before.

The index date for converse directions is June 1st, and the age on that date in 1861 is 18 years 10 months 3 days—equal to 18d. 20h. 13m. The progress for this period is 1h. 14m. 17s., and this is to be subtracted from the R.A.M.C. of the epoch, making 3h. 20m. 39s., and a figure erected with this R.A.M.C. The progressed date, found by subtracting the age from the date and time of the epoch, is July 9th at noon.

Reference to this map will show the sun between the opposition of Jupiter R. and P. This planet is ruler of the fourth house, indicating the parents. It is also in parallel with Saturn R. and P. Venus P., ruler of the progressed tenth, is in exact opposition to Neptune.

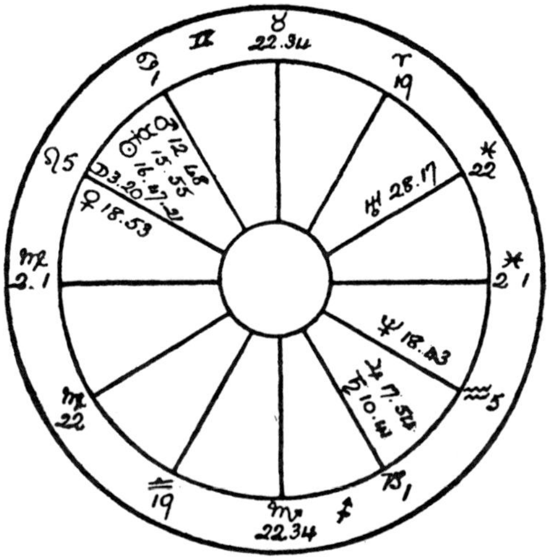

FIG. 32.

☉ 22° 24′ N.	♀ 16° 47′ N.	♄ 22° 31′ S.
☽ 18° 18′ N.	♂ 23° 44′ N.	♅ 1° 23′ S.
☿ 17° 45′ N.	♃ 22° 31′ S.	♇ 15° 28′ S.

The moon is in 3° 20′ ♌ on July 9th, and on the previous day—the directions being backward from the epoch—in 18° 40′ ♋, showing a difference of 14° 40′—equal to just over 1° 13′ per month. This amount is to be subtracted from the longitude on July 9th, as shown on page 182.

In October, the moon will be found in trine with Uranus, both R. and P., and in December—the month of the event—it will pass the exact conjunction of the radical Mars.

The moon's declination is given in the table below for each month, it being calculated in exactly the same manner as the longitude, the difference between its declination on July 9th and the previous day being divided by 12, the amount added successively to the declination on July 9th.

Three parallels are formed, as shown below :

1861.	June 1st.	3° 20′ ♌	18° 18′ N.	
,,	July	2° 6′	18° 41′	
,,	Aug.	0° 52′	19° 3′	
,,	Sept.	29° 38′ ♋	19° 25′	
,,	Oct.	28° 24′	19° 47′	☽ △ ♅ R. and P.
,,	Nov.	27° 11′	20° 8′	
,,	Dec.	25° 58′	21° 28′	☽ ☌ ♂ R.
1862.	Jan.	24° 45′	21° 48′	
,,	Feb.	23° 32′	21° 8′	
,,	March	22° 19′	21° 27′	
,,	April	21° 6′	21° 45′	
,,	May	19° 53′	22° 3′	☽ ∥ ♂ R.
,,	June	18° 40′	22° 21′	☽ ∥ ♃ P.
				☽ ∥ ♄ P.

In the next chapter, further illustrations are given from the epochs of notable people, and conclusive evidence is produced of the validity not only of the epoch as calculated but also of the scientific accuracy of epochal directions.

CHAPTER XXXII.

ILLUSTRATIONS OF EPOCHAL DIRECTIONS.

Now that the general rules for the calculation of directions have been given, the student will doubtless like to test the principles involved by computing directions for past events from various epochs. This is an excellent practice, and one to be strongly recommended, and I, therefore, append a few additional rules for this purpose.

1. Find the age of the subject on the date of any particular event, and turn it into time by allowing one day for each year, two hours for each month, and four minutes for each day.

2. Add this time to the date and time of the epoch, and this will give the date and time for which the progressed positions of the planets are required. Subtract the time if the converse or pre-epochal directions are required.

3. Take out from the table on page 174 the progress for the time found by Rule 1, and add it to the R.A.M.C. of the epoch, and erect a figure with the R.A.M.C. so found. Subtract the progress if the converse directions are required, and erect the progressed epoch with the R.A.M.C. so obtained.

4. Insert the planets' places for the date and time found by Rule 2, in the progressed map, and compute the directions as already shown. The moon's longitude being given for the date of the event, it is not necessary to make a monthly table.

Continuing with the example in the last chapter, I will give the directions for marriage and death.

The marriage took place on July 1st, 1862. Age of subject, 19 years 11 months 3 days—equal to 19d. 22h. 12m.

POST-EPOCHAL				PRE-EPOCHAL.			
	D.	H.	M.		D.	H.	M.
July	27	20	13	Date of epoch July	27	20	13
	19	22	12	+ Age at event —	19	22	12
August	16	18	25	Progressed date	7	22	1
	H.	M.	S.		H.	M.	S.
	4	34	56	R.A.M.C. epoch	4	34	56
	1	18	33	+ Progress for age —	1	18	33
	5	53	29	Progressed R.A.M.C.	3	16	23

At this time Venus has progressed to ♎ 4° 29′ in sextile to the radical sun, an influence conducive to marriage. The moon has progressed to ♑ 11° 37′ △ ♀ R., and close to the ☌ and ∥ of ♃ P., this planet being ruler of the seventh house—that of marriage.

The pre-epochal directions are ☉ P. parallel ♃ P., moon P. ∥ ☉ P., ∥ ♃ P., the lunar secondaries agreeing with the solar primary.

Following the same process for the native's death, the post-epochal directions measure to September 2nd, 1842, 5.17 p.m., and the meridian is 6h. 58m. 22s., ascendant 10° 17′ ♎.

This gives the directions ascendant □ ♄ R., ascendant 8 ☽ R., the moon being in the eighth house at the epoch. The sun is nearly ∠ ♂ R., lord of the eighth, and the moon is in parallel with Mars P. and Neptune P. The sun is also just past the parallel of the moon R.

The converse or pre-epochal directions are remarkable. The progressed date is June 21st, 1842, 11.9 p.m. The sun is in ♋ 0° 4′ 15″, ♂ in ♋ 1° 9′, and Uranus in ♓ 28° 14′. The sun is, therefore, between ☌ ♂ P. and □ ♅ P., leaving the former and applying to the latter.

Two points of interest may be noted from this epoch. The progressed date for marriage was August 17th, 6.25 a.m. A figure erected for this time—the lunar equivalent—gives ♍ 10, ascending ☌ ♀ R. at the time of the epoch.

A similar figure erected for the father's death, which was August 16th, 5.17 p.m., gives ♏ 16 on the M.C. and ♑ 10 ascending. The ascendant of this figure is ☌ ♄ R., and Mars on the date of the father's death was transitting the meridian—♏ 16.

The next illustration of epochal directions is taken from the prenatal epoch of the late King Edward VII. (Fig. 33).

Death of Father, December 14th, 1861. Age from epoch, 20 years 9 months 29 days. Progressed date, March 8th, 4h. 10m. p.m. Progressed M.C., ♋ 18° 5′. Progressed ascendant, ♎ 13° 49′. The following directions will be found operating at this time, viz., ☉ P. ☌ ♅ R., ☉ P. ∥ ♅ R., ☉ P. □ ♃ R. The moon is in exact parallel with the sun and Uranus, acting on the solar directions to that planet, and is also in □ ♄ P. The progressed M.C. is in parallel ♄, and the progressed ascendant is leaving 8 ♀ R. and ∥ ♅ R.

Marriage.—March 10th, 1863. Age from epoch, equal to 22d. 1h. 32m. Progressed date, March 9th, 9.46 p.m. The progressive ascendant, ♎ 14° 40', is in ‖ ♀ R., in the seventh house. The progressed M.C. is in exact ‖ ♃ R., ruler of the seventh. The moon has progressed to ♎ 19° 10', exactly ♂ ♀ in the horoscope. By converse direction, the moon is conjoined with the sun in the fifth house, and Venus is conjoined with Uranus.

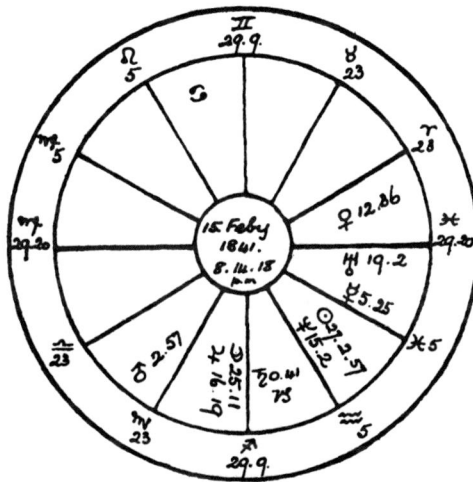

FIG. 33.

DECLINATIONS.

☉ 12° 51' S.	♀ 5° 44' N.	♄ 22° 25' S.
☽ 27° 36' S.	♂ 10° 18' S.	♅ 5° 1' S.
☿ 10° 49' S.	♃ 22° 5' S.	♇ 16° 28' S.

Illness : Typhoid Fever.—November, 1871. Age from epoch, 30 years 9 months. Progressed date, March 18th, 2.14 p.m. The sun is midway between □ ☽ R., and ☍ ascendant R., ♂ ♄ R. The moon is in exact □ ♂ P. The progressed ascendant is ∠ ♂ P.

Attempted Assassination.—April 4th, 1900. Age, 59 years 2 months 19 days. Progressed date, 16th April, 1.30 a.m. The sun is then between the parallels of the radical and progressed Mars. Mercury is nearly in opposition to the ascendant.

By converse direction, Venus is in exact square with Mars R., while the mid-heaven is in exact ☌ ♂ R., and □ ♀ P.

Death of Queen Victoria and Accession to Throne.—January 22nd, 1901. Age from epoch, 59 years 11 months 7 days. The directions operating were :

	Mother's Death.	*Accession.*
Post-epochal.	☉ P. ☍ ♂ P.	☉ R. △ ♂ P.,
		M.C.R. △ ♂ P.
	☉ P. ∥ ♂ R.	☽ P. ✶ ☉ P.
	Asc. R. ☍ ☿ P.	☽ ☌ ☉ R.
	M.C. prog. ☍ ☉ R.	☽ △ ♂ P.
Pre-epochal.	☉ P. ☌ ☽ R.	
	☉ P. ☌ ♄ P.	

In May, 1901, at the time of the *Shamrock* accident, the moon was in Pisces, a watery sign, in parallel to Mars P., and also in square to Venus P. in Gemini.

The operation for appendicitis on June 24th, 1902, at age from epoch of 61 years 4 months 9 days. The sun was in exact of ☍ ♂ P., and the ascendant close to ∥ ♅ P. and the moon separating from ∥ ♅ P. Conversely the ascendant was in ∥ ♅ R.

The lamented death of our subject took place on May 6th, 1910, at age from epoch of 69 years 2 months 21 days. The progressive date is April 26th, 1841, 1.38 a.m. The sun is just past ☍ ♂ R. and ∠ ♅ R. The moon is ☍ ♄ P. The M.C. is in □ ☿ R. and the ascendant is □ ♅ P.

The converse directions measure to December 8th, 1840, at 2.50 p.m. The sun is then in exact □ ♅ P. and close to ∥ ♄ R.

The epoch of the late Duke of Edinburgh occurred at 7.40 a.m. on November 2nd, 1843, as shown in Fig. 34.

There are several events in the life of the Duke which will repay investigation. He had an attack of fever in February, 1863. The progressed sun, moon, and ascendant were con-

joined at this time, and the moon was in parallel with Mars
R.   Mars from the epoch, was exactly square to the moon
at birth, and by transit was in Taurus ☌ ☽ R. □ ♂ P.
from the horoscope.

His father, the Prince Consort, died on December 14th,
1861.   The sun, by converse motion, was □ ♄. Mars, by
direct motion, was in ♒ 13°, exactly opposition to the sun in
the horoscope.   Mars by transit was on the ascendant of
the epoch.   The meridian of the lunar equivalent was ♋

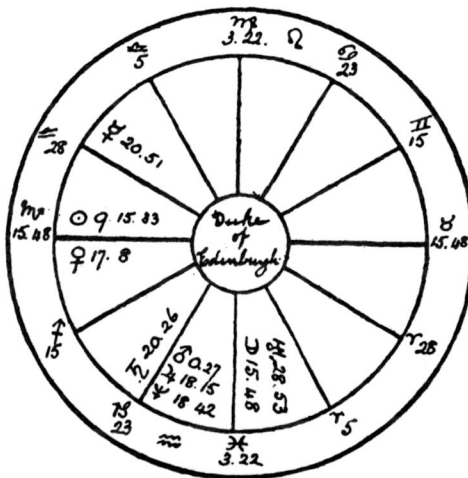

FIG. 34.

5°, ☌ ☽ P.   The moon, by converse motion, was in ♋ 5°,
parallel ♂ R., parallel ♄ R.

On March 12th, 1868, an attempt was made to assassinate
the Duke while travelling in Australia.   By converse motion
the sun was in square to Mars, and the moon opposition
Mercury, square Saturn.   The M.C. was opposition ♅ R.,
and M.C. □ ☉ R. converse, while the ascendant was only
just past the square of ♂ R. by converse motion.

The Duke was married on January 23rd, 1874, his age
from the epoch being 30 years 2 months 21 days.   The
directions are so remarkable as to merit being given in full,
and I may say that I hardly remember such a remarkable

confirmation of the truth of the epoch, and of converse
directions, than the following :

			D	H	M
Epoch, November	..	..	I	19	40
Add October	..	..	31	0	0
			32	19	40
Deduct age	..	..	30	5	24
October	..	..	..	2	14	16

Progressed ☉ 9° 12′ Libra.
       „   ♀ 9° 20′ Libra.
       „   ☽ 9° 5′ Aquarius.

Here are ☉ P. conjunction Venus, moon trine sun,
trine Venus, Venus ruler of the seventh.   Ascendant of lunar
equivalent, Taurus 16°, the seventh house of the epoch.

Ascendant of diurnal horoscope 25° Capricorn, on
January 23rd, 1874, Mercury and Venus were conjoined
in Capricorn 25°, the exact ascendant of this figure.

Where are the critics of the epoch now ?   Where are
those learned gentlemen who call converse directions
unscientific and opposed to Astrological reason ?   After this
I feel a little pity for those who reject things before they
examine them.

On June 21st, 1882, the Duke was nearly drowned in
Corrie Bay.   The sun was then in opposition and parallel
to Uranus, and parallel the radical moon, by converse
motion acting on the radical parallel of the moon and
Uranus in watery signs.   The ascendant was also in square
to Saturn.   The ascendant of the diurnal horoscope was
Virgo 15°, and on the day of the accident Uranus was
transmitting this degree, which is also the opposition of the
radical moon.

The death of the Duke took place on July 30th, 1900,
at age from the epoch of 56 years 8 months 28 days.
The following converse directions were then in force :—

☉ P. ∥ ☿ R. (☿ being □ ♄ acts as a malefic).
☉ P. 8 ☽ R.   ☉ R. ∠ ♂ P.
☽ P. ☌ ♅ R.   □ ♀ R.

The ascendant by direct motion was □ ♅ R.

The ascendant of the converse lunar equivalent was
♐ 13°, □ ☉ P. □ ☽ R., acting on the second of the solar

directions. Saturn, on the day of death, was crossing the
progressed ascendant.

The next illustration is that of the prenatal epoch of
the Right Hon. J. Chamberlain, which took place on
September 28th, 1835, at 6.52 p.m., as shown in Fig. 35.

It will be worth while to look at this figure, which is
particularly remarkable. Venus, ruler of the map, is
conjoined with the sun and in trine to Neptune The
triple conjunction of Mars, Saturn, and Mercury—a most
uncommon configuration—is trine with Uranus. The moon

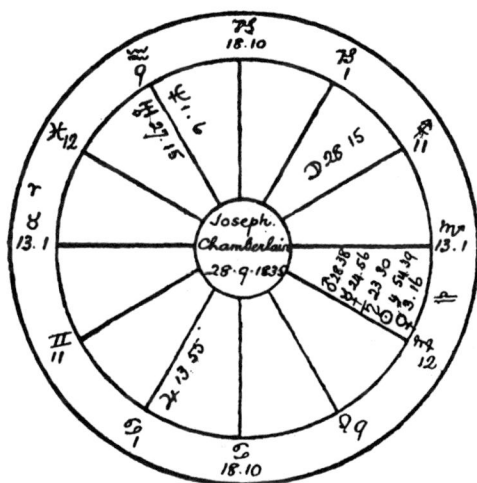

FIG. 35.

is in close sextile with Mercury, Mars, Saturn, and Uranus.
Seven planets occupy airy signs, while six are placed in
cardinal signs.

The map is particularly significant of the man and his
rise in life to an exalted position. The moon on the cusp
of the ninth, so splendidly aspected, shows his ability and
success in foreign and colonial affairs, and, as will be
remembered, he held the position of Colonial Secretary with
exceptional distinction.

The conjunction of Mars, ruler of the seventh, with
Mercury and Saturn, is strong evidence of the intense

hatred of his political opponents, and of the enmity to which he was subject. The position of Uranus in the eleventh is another important influence in the map.

Our illustrious subject entered Parliament in 1876, under the directions of sun parallel Uranus—a typical direction for such an event—and ascendant trine Saturn.

At the time of the Home Rule split, and the formation of the Liberal Unionist Party, the sun was in square to Uranus, and Mars in sextile to the sun. It is interesting to note that the directions from the horoscope at this time were sun opposition Uranus, sextile Mars. Note the peculiar correspondence. Surely not another coincidence ! By converse direction, the ascendant was conjunction Neptune, and the meridian sextile Neptune and Venus.

He became a Cabinet Minister and Colonial Secretary in 1895, under the direction of sun sextile Venus, parallel Mercury. At the time of the Boer War the ascendant was conversely in opposition to Jupiter, and the sun in semi-square to Saturn and Mercury.

His long illness during the first decade of this century was caused by the slowly forming direction of sun conjunction progressed Mars, and by the converse squares of the sun to Mercury, Saturn, and Mars.

The death of the right hon. gentleman occurred on July 2nd, 1914, at age from epoch of 78 yrs. 9m. 4d. The progressed date is December 16th, 1835, at 1.8 p.m. The sun was then in ☌ ♂ P., and the ascendant ♉ ♅ R. The moon, by direction, was in ♏ 7°—the exact degree held by the moon at the time of death. The ascendant of the lunar equivalent was ♉ ♂ R.

The converse directions measure to July 12th, 1835, at 0.36 a.m. The sun is in □ ♄ P., and the ascendant ☌ ☽ R. The meridian of the lunar equivalent was ♐ 28° ☌ ☽ R.

A study of the prenatal epoch of Queen Victoria of Spain is one of more than ordinary interest to students of epochal directions in view of the dastardly attempt at assassination on her wedding day. It is for the purpose of showing from the epoch how both these events are signified by the directions in operation at the time that the map has been chosen. The data of the birth and epoch, with the calculations, are given in full on pages 59 and 60.

Fig. 36 is the map of the prenatal epoch.

The two chief events are dealt with as follows :

Father's death, January 20th, 1896.—The following directions measure to this event :

M.C. ∠ ☉ R.
Asc. P. ☌ ♂ P.
Asc. P. ⎐ ♄ R.

The meridian of the lunar equivalent is ♐ 16°. Neptune is in transit in the opposite degree.

By converse direction we find the moon in square to Venus R. and Mars P., and the sun in semi-square to the

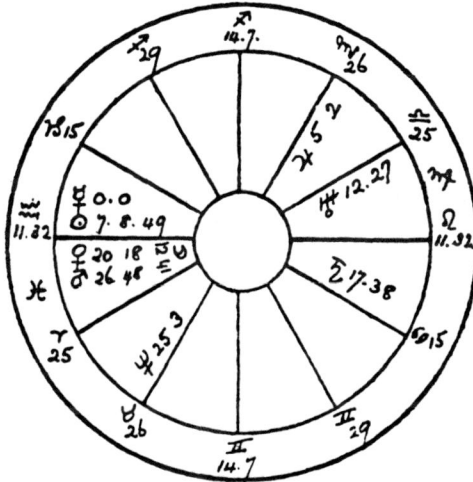

FIG. 36.

radical moon. It is interesting to note that the primary direction of ☉ ☌ ♂ z. d. 8° 59′ is due at the time of the father's death. The arc required is exactly the same as the direction.

Marriage and attempted assassination, May 31st, 1906.— The directions operating at this time show the two events in a very remarkable manner.

By direct motion we have as follows :

For marriage—

♀ P. ☌ ☽ R.   ♀ P. par. ☽ R.
Asc. P. ✶ ☉ R. ruler of seventh.
☽ P. par. ♀ R.

For attempted assassination—

⊙ P. ☌ ♂ R.   ☽ ⊔ ☿ P.
♂ P. ☌ ☽ R.
⊙ P. □ ♇ R.

The ascendant of the lunar equivalent is ♌ 25°, opposition ♂ R., acting on the direction of sun conjunction Mars.
By converse direction we have :

For marriage—

⊙ P. par. ♀ P.   ☽ △ ♀ R.
Asc. P. ✳ ☽ R.

For attempted assassination—

♂ P. ☌ Asc. R.   ☽ P. par ♂ P.
M.C. ☍ ♇ R.
M.C. □ ♂ R.

The predominance of the planet Mars at this time may be noted, but it must be pointed out that neither this planet nor Neptune afflict either the sun, moon, or ascendant at birth ; therefore, their power for evil by direction is greatly minimised.

CHAPTER XXXIII.

Primary Directions and the Epoch.

THE argument was put forward some years ago, in a private communication to me from a certain experienced Astrologer and supporter of the primary system of directing, that, after a horoscope had been rectified by the epoch, the primary directions from such rectified figure did not measure to known events in life. Since then I have heard the same argument propounded, but my experience, based on the examination of various rectified horoscopes, is quite to the contrary ; in fact, I have proved that the primary directions from horoscopes rectified by the epoch tally more closely with recorded events than those from horoscopes rectified by primary directions themselves. Of course, if the argument is put forward that every primary direction must measure exactly to the event, then I leave the matter alone, as I am quite unable to accept such a dictum. I propose to prove this point by an appeal to a horoscope, and give the calculations in full in order that students may be able to verify the proof.

The following particulars were supplied me by a client, in order to arrive at the correct time of his birth.

Male, born at Nottingham, November 21st, 1876, between 2.30 and 7 a.m. Mother died May 17th, 1902 ; married June 11th, 1903.

During the hours mentioned, the signs Libra and Scorpio were rising, and as the gentleman's handwriting forcibly suggested the latter sign, I erected a figure with the beginning of that sign rising, and found that it gave an epoch which yielded progressive directions for the two events, and the usual calculations fixed the ascendant as 8° 28′ of the sign, giving a birth-time of 5h. 45m. 16s. a.m. Fig. 37 shows the figure.

R.A.M.C. of the horoscope, 145° 53′
R.A. of Moon, with 3° 50′ S. Lat., 300° 14′.
R.A. of Venus, with 1° 58′ N. Lat., 199° 26′, M.D. 53° 33′,
    S.A. 81° 52′.

Up to this time I had made no calculations from the horoscope itself, and, in order to test the accuracy of the figure, I computed the speculum of the moon and Venus as given above, and worked out a few primary directions operating at the time of the two events.

The death of the mother took place on May 17th, 1902, in the 26th year of life, the exact arc required being 25° 29'.

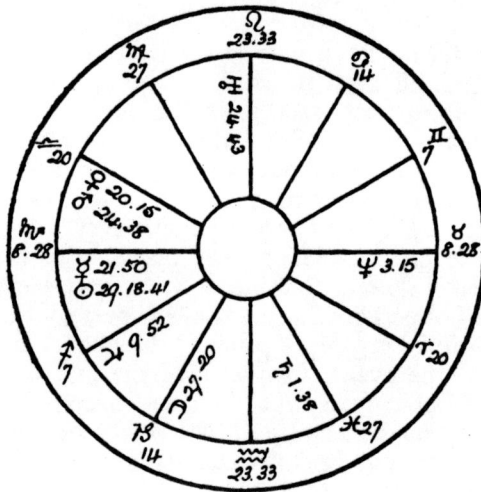

FIG. 37.

The direction of the meridian to the opposition of the moon, mundo. con., measured to 25° 39'.

R.A. of the 8 of the Moon	120° 14'
R.A. of the M.C.	145° 53'
Difference	25° 39'

The date of the marriage was June 11th, 1903, requiring an arc of 26° 33'.

The following directions measure thereto:

M.C. sextile Venus, m.d.	26° 16'
Ascendant conjunction Venus, z. con.	26° 33'

The calculations of the first direction are:

Meridian distance of Venus	53° 33'
One third of semi-arc of Venus	27° 17'
Difference	26° 16'

The second direction is found by adding the ascensional difference of Libra 20° 15'—the place of Venus—to its R.A., and subtracting the result from the oblique ascension of the ascendant. Thus :

R.A. of longitude of Venus	198° 41'
Ascension difference	10° 37'
	209° 18'
Oblique ascension of ascendant	235° 53'
Difference	26° 35'

This direction measures exactly to the time of the event.

The fallacy of this argument is again shown by computing primary directions from the epoch itself. Taking the epoch of the Queen of Spain, given on page 191, it was pointed out that the primary direction of sun conjunction Mars, zodiac direction, measured 8° 59' in arc. The death of the father took place on January 20th, 1896, just one week less than nine years after the epoch—equal to an arc of 8° 59'—exactly the same as the direction. Many further illustrations could be given, but the above must suffice.

SECTION VII.

The Prenatal Epoch and Infant Mortality.

CHAPTER XXXIV.

INFANT MORTALITY.

THE value of the prenatal epoch in the judgment of infant horoscopes and the determination of the question of vitality and life cannot be over-estimated by the astrological student. In Chapter III, in dealing with the practical uses of the epoch, I stated as follows :

" In the question of infant mortality, the prenatal epoch has a most important and far-reaching influence. Children are born at apparently favourable moments, with little or no affliction to the hyleg, yet their lives are short, perhaps only a few weeks or a few months, or even only two or three days. The horoscope of birth is utterly inadequate to explain these apparent anomalies. Turn to the epoch, and there will be found the master key. The death in infancy is due to the affliction of the moon at the epoch . . . ."

This is a question to which I have given very considerable thought and investigation ; in fact, it was the very matter which led to my study of the epoch in 1898. The results of my study are outlined in the paragraph quoted above, and from the decision arrived at therein I am not disposed to withdraw. I could fill many pages with illustrations of infant horoscopes, wherein there is absolutely nothing to indicate the early demise of the child, nor yet directions to account for the death at the particular time.

The power of the epoch in determining this question is unchallenged. In dealing with the question of twins in the *British Journal of Astrology*, I gave an illustration of a case wherein one child lived to maturity, and the other died a minute after birth from asphyxiation. It was shown in the epoch that at the time of birth of the second child the moon was directed to the exact opposition of the sun, and was forming the square of Saturn, the major luminary at the same time being in square to Saturn also, and these directions fell in fixed signs, indicative of the nature of the death.

This is only one case ; others equally convincing to the mind of the progressive astrologer can be produced. In the next chapter I am illustrating this point from the horoscopes

of infants who have lived only a short while. In none of
these do the horoscopes afford any real evidence of early
death, or give directions to measure to the date of death,
but the whole matter is solved, absolutely and entirely, by
the epoch.

Of course, I am fully aware that numerous horoscopes do
show most emphatically that the children will not live,
but even these, in the majority of cases, do not give directions
to account for death, or even show the actual cause.   Even
in those cases where death in infancy is clearly denoted,
the epoch is the final arbiter.   An illustration of one of such
cases will be given in the next chapter.

As a note of instruction to all students of Astrology : Never
judge the probabilities of life in an infant horoscope from
the horoscope alone.   Take the epoch in conjunction with
it.   Many children are born who live for a short while, merely
on a precarious vitality stored up within their little frames
during the gestative period. Their epochs are out of
harmony with the horoscope ; the in-coming ego cannot
function through the environmental conditions set up in
the horoscope ; the result is that death supervenes—the
child wastes away physically.   All these points are fully
explained by a study of the epoch in conjunction with the
horoscope.

CHAPTER XXXV.

ILLUSTRATIONS OF INFANT HOROSCOPES.

THE first case I present for examination is that of a male child born in East Kent, Lat. 51° 13′ N., Long. 1° 24′ E., on January 27th, 1848, at rectified time of 5h. 0m. 19s. a.m. The following is the horoscope :

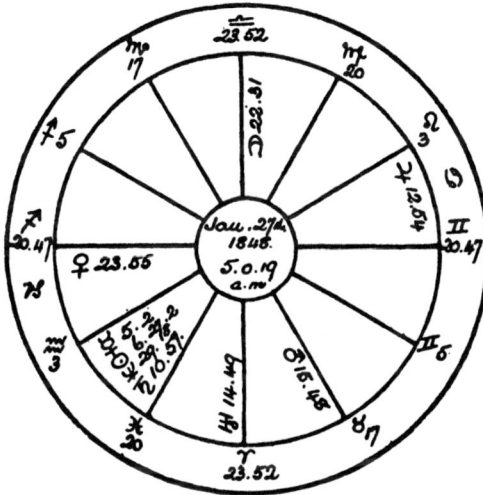

FIG. 38.

What astrologer would predict the death of this child before it was twelve months old ? The sign Sagittarius rises with Venus ascending in sextile to the moon—the hyleg. Jupiter, ruler of the ascending sign, is dignified, in trine Saturn and sextile Mars. The moon is barely within orbs of the sesquiquadrate of Saturn, and the sun is more than half a degree from the parallel of Mars. Suffice to say, there is nothing whatever in the map to show early death. I have seen scores of horoscopes of people who have lived to maturity with ten times the affliction that this map possesses, and yet this poor little chap did not live a year. He died on December 5th, 1848.

What does the epoch say ?   Aries rises, with Uranus on the ascendant in square to Venus in the fourth.   The moon, which is the birth ascendant, is heavily afflicted by a square of Mars, and is applying to the opposition of Jupiter.   Mars —ruler of the ascendant—is conjoined with Saturn, square moon and Jupiter.   The sun—ruler of the sixth—is in square to Saturn.   The   child   died   from   atrophy—a   wasting

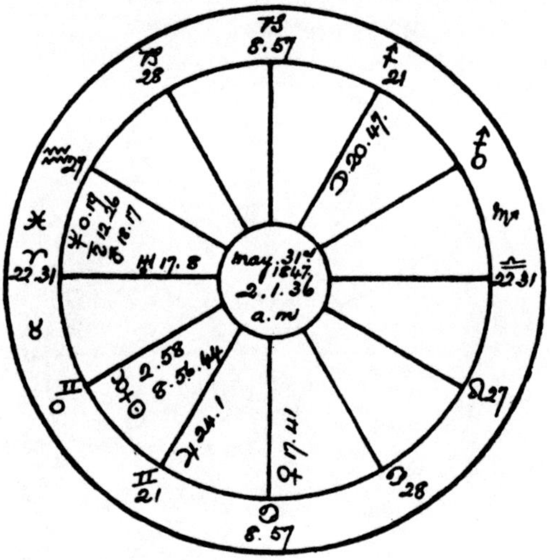

FIG. 39.

disease. All the affliction occurred from common signs, there being no less than seven planets in those signs. At the time of death the moon was conversely directed to the opposition of Mercury and square of Neptune.

Here is a case in which the child was born with a favour-able horoscope, but the fact remained that it was weakly and delicate—due to prenatal conditions—and it could not properly function in its horoscope.

II. The second case is quite different, for here the horo-scope clearly shows that the child will die, but it does not give any directions that measure to the time of death.

It is an accepted rule that "if the rays of two malefics be bad to the sun and moon, the child will die." The sun is in an angle, afflicted by Mars in the eighth house, this planet being also ruler of the ascending sign, and the moon is afflicted by a square of Uranus. Nothing can be clearer, or more precisely shown.

Fig. 40 shows the horoscope.

Let the epoch, however, be examined as well. Venus rises in Capricorn, in trine with the moon and sextile to

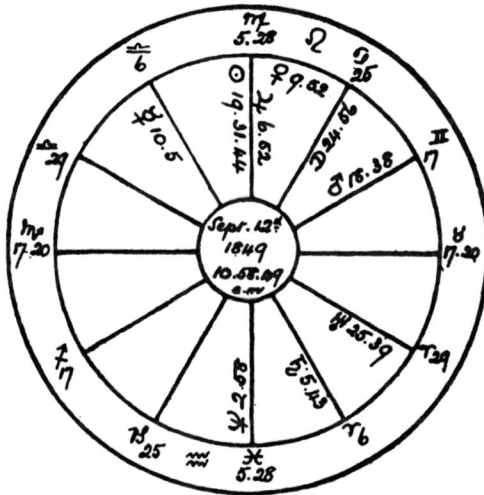

Fig. 40.

Saturn, the two latter being also in sextile. The sun, however, has the square of Saturn, and is in opposition to the place of Mars at birth. The rulers of the first and eighth in the horoscope are conjoined at the epoch.

Fig. 41 shows that the evil indications at birth were transferred from the epoch, and that, although the child possessed a fair amount of vitality, it was born into a bad environment and could not exist.

The epoch shows a very interesting feature. The child died on December 12th, 1849—one year and four days after the epoch, measuring to December 9th, 1848, at

10.44 a.m.   A figure erected for this time shows the following :

M.C.	..	..	..	2° 46′ ♐
Moon	..	..	..	2° 42′ ♊
Mars	..	..	..	0° 30′ ♐
Mercury	..	..	..	1° 19′ ♐

The moon is exactly on the cusp of the fourth house—in opposition to Mars and Mercury.

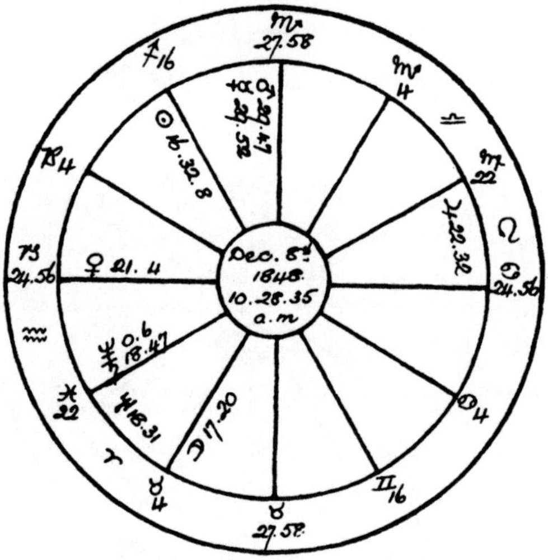

Fig. 41.

The particulars of birth and epoch are :

Birth.—September 12th, 1849, 10h. 58m. 49s. a.m.
Lat. 51° 15′ N.   Long. 5m. E.
Epoch.—December 8th, 1848, 10h. 28m. 35s. a.m.

III. The third case is more interesting, but it still shows the weakness of the horoscope in determining the time of death. It is that of a child born on June 12th, 1847, at 2h. 59m. 48s. a.m., rectified time (birth recorded as 3 a.m.), and who died on July 13th of the same year from the effects of an overdose of opium administered unintentionally by the mother. The horoscope is shown in Fig. 42.

The sun and moon are angular, and both heavily afflicted
—the former by Mars, and the latter by Saturn.   Here are
clear indications of death, and not by ordinary causes.
Mercury, the disposer of the luminaries, is afflicted by Mars,
and Jupiter, although conjoined with the sun, is also
afflicted by Mars ; hence, it was powerless to save life.   The
nature of the death is also clearly shown in the horoscope,
Pisces being a sign notoriously connected with poisons and
drugging.

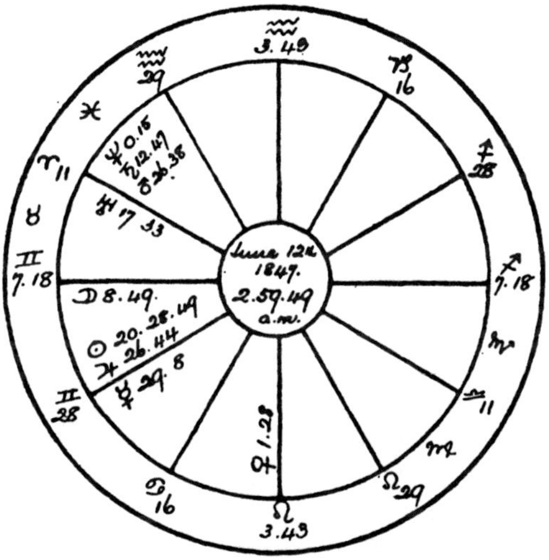

FIG. 42.

The horoscope shows nothing to account for the death
at the time stated, but the epoch is remarkably clear as to
this, as is shown in Fig. 43.

Here is found the sun conjoined with Mars in the sign
Virgo, ruling the bowels—a particularly weak organ for the
administering of such a drug as opium.   Mars is ruler of the
fourth house, and so represents the mother of the child.
Jupiter here is close to the moon, but is again heavily
afflicted by Mars as in the horoscope, and, therefore, particularly weak.

In the matter of the directions to account for the event,
it will be found that the child was ten months and two days
old from the epoch, and this gives September 12th, at 9.10

a.m., at which time the moon was exactly in square with
the sun and Mars. Measured conversely, the time is 4.54
p.m., of September 10th, when the moon is in square to
Saturn, Venus, and Neptune. At this time the moon's
radical place is exactly on the cusp of the fourth house.

These three cases are sufficient to prove the practical
value of the epoch in matters to do with infant mortality.
Numerous cases could be given, enough to fill dozens of
pages, but these three were particularly chosen to illustrate

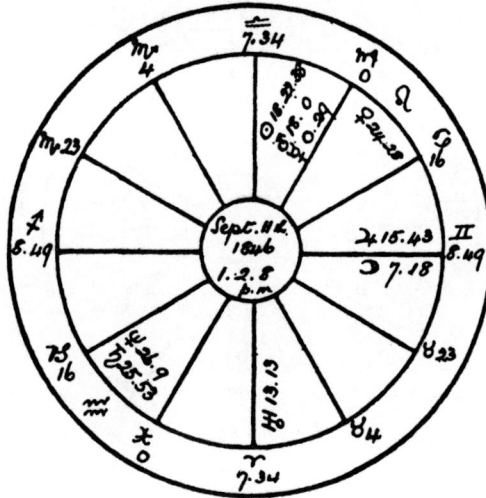

FIG. 43.

the paramount importance of the epoch, both as regards
the cause and time of death, and to demonstrate, as in the
first case, that the horoscope is not the be-all and end-all
of human destiny.

CHAPTER XXXVI.

The Procreation of Children.

King Solomon, the wisest man who ever lived, wrote: "To everything there is a season, and a time to every purpose under the heavens; a time to be born and a time to die; a time to plant and a time to pluck up that which is planted. . . . ." William Shakespeare, the greatest of all great poets, wrote: "There is a tide in the affairs of men which taken at the flood leads on to fortune."

But what has this to do with the prenatal epoch? More, perhaps, than many of us dream.

Solomon said, "There is a time to be born; there is a time to sow." The farmer sows his wheat at a propitious time, and reaps a bountiful harvest. The cottage gardener or allotment holder sows his beans and peas under favourable planetary influences, and obtains an abundant yield. The investor buys securities or shares at a favourable time, and later on sells out at a large profit. But do we ever hear of the sowing of the seed which in after days will develop into a human form and be the home or dwelling-place of a Divine Spirit—the soul—at a time when the influences are favourable for such an act?

The gardener prepares his ground, selects the best and strongest seeds, and the young plant thrives, grows strong, and yields an abundant harvest. Does man prepare his own seed, or select the best and purest of virgin soil, and thus obtain a strong child, physically, mentally, and morally as near perfection as possible—the *beau ideal* of a veritable superman? Is it not more often the case that the seed is tainted by habits of bad living, physical imperfections, hereditary diseases, and the soil unprepared, equally tainted, and similarly imperfect and diseased?

And yet, what is the difference in the sowing of the seed of the plant and that of the human form divine? In the sowing of the plant seed there is the union between the seed and the soil. Then follows the germinative period—the darkness beneath the ground—and then the thrusting

207

forth of the young shoot to face the winds and storms, and the danger of destruction from being trodden under-foot.

In the human life we have the same parallel. The sowing of the male spermatoza to meet the ovum of the female is the same as the union of the plant seed and the soil. Then follows the gestative period—the darkness of the womb—followed by the thrusting forth of the living child to face the dangers and trials of earthly life.

The question which I am now propounding is this : If the farmer, by astrological rules, can select a favourable time for the sowing of the plant seed, after having properly prepared his soil, why should not humanity select similar propitious times for the procreation of children, thereby ensuring a sound progeny, physically, mentally, and morally superior, capable of uplifting and benefiting the world ?

I am putting forward no fanciful theory or plausible delusion. I am making no suggestion which cannot be put into a practical and concrete form. Moreover, I am bringing forward no new theory, or invention of my own. It is part and parcel of the laws of Astrology. If, by Astrology, man is advised to avail himself of certain planetary positions for particular purposes, is it logical to suppose that the question of procreation is not one of these particular purposes ? A man makes an " election " for commencing a business, for taking a journey, or making a change. Why should he not do so for reproducing his kind ? In the Hindu writings we are given the facts that a man should avail himself of particular planetary positions if he desires an excellent issue. Parasara, who was a great Astronomer and Astro-loger, finding that such an hour for *Nisheka* (conception) had approached, joined a boatman's daughter in an island on the Jumna, and the issue was the great Vedavyasa. A Brahmin astrologer, under similar circumstances, joined a potter's daughter, and the issue was the great Salivahana.

In modern days several attempts have been made to improve the race by preventing the marriage of the unfit, and in the science of eugenics much has been done in this respect, but, without the science of Astrology to aid us, all these attempts will be futile and to no purpose.

From my investigations along a certain line in connection with the prenatal epoch, I believe that the solution lies in

the inter-relationship of the ascendant at the act of generation (coitus) with the moon at birth, these having also the
usual inter-relationship with the moon and ascendant at
the epoch, and the ascendant and moon at birth.

The following remarkable case is put forward in support
of my views, it being the first known case of its kind, and
the one which led me into a definite line of research.

In November, 1905, a gentleman resident at Sittingbourne,
Kent, acquainted me with the fact that he was about to
become a father, and that he had computed the birth of
the child, which would be of the male sex, to take place on
December 23rd, 1905, at 3.35 p.m.

The date and time of the coitus in this case had been noted
as occurring at 11 p.m., on March 26th, 1905, and from
this the epoch had been computed as taking place on the
following day at 7.34 a.m. No reason was assigned for this
particular computation, and I was left to ascertain the
modus operandi myself.

Now, I propose to make a detailed examination of this
particular case with a view of explaining and illustrating
the relationship of these three times and the connecting link
with each other.

The three times are as follows :

> Coitus : March 26th, 1905. 11 p.m.
> Epoch : March 27th, 1905. 7.34 a.m.
> Birth : Dec. 23rd, 1905. 3.35 p.m.

The particular and most astonishing point in connection
with this case is that the father of the child correctly computed the time of its birth some weeks before it happened,
and with no other factor to work from than the date and
time of the coitus. If there were any mathematical basis
for this procedure in one case, there should be no difficulty
in arriving at the *modus operandi* in other cases.

Examination of this particular case yields the following
points :

At the coitus—March 25th, 11 p.m.—the R. A.M.C. was
11h. 17m. 47s. ; ascendant, Scorpio 26° ; moon in Sagittarius, 24° 3′.

At the time of the epoch it is noted that the degree rising
at the coitus is now exactly setting, 26° 39′ ♉ being on the
ascendant ; the moon had progressed to ♐ 28° 50′—an

increment of 4° 47'. At the time of birth the positions are reversed, the ascendant being 28° 50' ♊, and the moon 26° 39' ♏.

The point to be noted is that the ascendant at the coitus was the moon's place at birth. The period of sex formation —the fifth return of the epochal moon to its radical place,

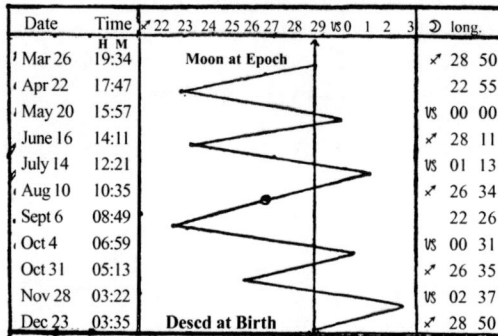

Date	Time	♐ 22 23 24 25 26 27 28 29 ♑ 0 1 2 3	☽ long.
	H M		
Mar 26	19:34	Moon at Epoch	♐ 28 50
Apr 22	17:47		22 55
May 20	15:57		♑ 00 00
June 16	14:11		♐ 28 11
July 14	12:21		♑ 01 13
Aug 10	10:35		♐ 26 34
Sept 6	08:49		22 26
Oct 4	06:59		♑ 00 31
Oct 31	05:13		♐ 26 35
Nov 28	03:22		♑ 02 37
Dec 23	03:35	Descd at Birth	♐ 28 50

FIG. 44.

shown on the chart of descent by the circle, on August 10th, at 10h. 34m. 57s. p.m.—shows 26° 39' ♉ again ascending with the moon in 26° 31' ♐.

The distance of the moon at this time from the line of central impulse is 2° 19'—approximately half the distance moved by the moon between the coitus and the epoch.

Examining the position of the moon and ascendant at the four periods, the following is obtained :

Coitus	..	26° 39' ♏.	Ascendant.
Epoch	..	26° 39' ♉.	,,
5th Return		26° 39' ♉.	,,
Birth	..	26° 39' ♏.	Moon.

Thus, at all the four points there is found the same identical longitude of either Scorpio or Taurus, the opposite sign. The transposition is due to the moon at birth being decreasing. With an increasing moon, all four would be in the same sign. A connecting factor is thus shown to exist, the ascendant or its opposite at the first three stages becoming the moon's longitude at the fourth stage—that of birth.

CONCLUSION.

My task for the present is now completed. There are several other matters intimately associated with the prenatal epoch which might have been included in this work, and others which at the present moment are awaiting further investigation and development, all of which, in due course, will be published for the benefit of astrological students.

As a fitting conclusion to my labours, I will briefly run over the principal features of the theory which I have explained and illustrated in these pages. I have a great dislike in going over old ground, but, in view of the many weeds of prejudice and ignorance which ill-informed and misguided critics continue to sow in my field of scientific facts, I feel it is necessary to plough over the ground once more. I would, therefore, ask my readers to carefully distinguish between the facts and the weeds, so that they may be able to gather the real fruit from the information which I have planted before them.

First of all, it was clearly proved that the objections made by certain Astrologers were both shallow and devoid of reason, arising entirely from a complete ignorance of the principles of the theory, and a lack of systematic and unbiassed study.

The astro-physiological basis of the epoch was then fully dealt with, and extracts from modern medical works were given in order to show that the laws of the epoch were in accord with obstetric science and statistics. The practical values of the epoch in relation to the horoscope were then explained, and it was clearly shown that the figure for the epoch was equally as important as the horoscope, and, in many respects, the latter was valueless in determining a number of important details affecting the life and destiny.

The laws of the epoch were then fully explained, showing how the period of gestation varied according to the distance of the moon from the horizon, and the method of taking the " count " from the moon to the required horizon was shown by means of diagrams. The paramount law of sex then received attention, and it was there shown that the entire interchange of the two factors at birth and epoch was regulated by the sex of the area in which they were placed.

The entire question of rectification was then dealt with, illustrated by the horoscopes of well-known people, and the whole process placed on a simple foundation. The cause of irregularity was explained, and it was clearly demonstrated that, while the prime law of the epoch remained unchanged, the irregularity was merely a variation in the interchange of the factors, due to the sex of the areas in which the moon and ascendant were placed.

The validity of the epoch was further demonstrated from the horoscopes of twins, and illustrations were given of the divergence of character and fortune in children born within a short while of each other. Illustrations of prenatal affections and abnormalities were then given, showing the utmost importance of the epoch in dealing with matters which had their genesis during the gestative period, and showing the subordinate position of the horoscope in such cases.

The question of directions from the epoch received a lengthy explanation, and it was clearly proved that the events in life could be computed from the epochal figure with equal facility as from the horoscope, in many cases showing the time and nature of the event far more distinctly than did the horoscope.

Finally, the vexed question of infant mortality was discussed, and here again the paramount importance of the epoch was demonstrated beyond the shadow of a doubt.

There now remain a few points for consideration. First of all it must be remembered that the entire calculation of the epoch depends upon the gestative period. The normal period is 273 days, equal to 10 lunar months, and that it varies on either side of this period to the extent of from one to fourteen days or from one to twenty-eight days, according as to whether the " count " is taken from the moon to the horizon, or extended round to the other horizon. It has been proved from obstetric statistics that 85 per cent. of cases comply with this requirement, and that the other 15 per cent. are either long or short period births, and derive their genesis from the seventh, eighth, or eleventh lunar return, as explained in Chapter XX.

The next point for consideration is an equally important one, and students should be very particular to realise it, as it will save much disappointment in their studies. It by no means follows that because an ordinary regular epoch confirms the time of birth, or properly determines the sex, it is the correct epoch. The fact that, within the limits of the gestative period, there can be found certain times when the interchange of the two factors becomes possible has given rise to the most illogical contention that it is possible to find several epochs for the same birth. This contention, however, is a direct violation of the principles of the epochal theory, which lays down as an emphatic law that every epoch must conform to four primary conditions, viz. :

(1) It must confirm the time of birth within the limits of an ordinary error of observation.

(2) It must approximately determine the exact period of gestation of the particular case.

(3) It must determine the sex of the subject.

(4) It must produce directions agreeing with the main events of life.

As the learned author of the epochal theory has more than once said, and I can personally testify to the absolute truth of his assertion : " It is only too easy to find a fictitious epoch which agrees with the birth merely as a time measure."

It has been demonstrated from authentic cases that the four stages—coitus, epoch, quickening, and birth—are related to each other by a definite factor or line, which is termed the line of lunar impulse, and that it is possible to determine the birth of the child from the act of generation.

This is a question which is at present receiving further investigation, and, from certain facts which have come to my knowledge, I believe I am on the verge of an important discovery. The drawback to any great progress is the want of precise information and accurate data.

The calculation of the exact time of birth from past events only is another subject which is receiving additional investigation. I have on many occasions succeeded in demonstrating the possibility of this procedure, and a complete set of rules is in course of preparation.

The metaphysical basis of the epoch is another most important subject, but, as this volume was intended to be an exposition of the mathematical and astrological basis of the epoch, and its paramount importance from a purely scientific point of view, it was decided to omit any discussion on that side of the question.

Finally, let me point out that every statement put forward by me in these pages has been substantiated by facts and illustrations. I have put forward nothing that I cannot prove, nor propounded any theory that I have not facts behind me to illustrate. This my critics have never done. They have continually made statements, persistently contradicted facts, but when challenged to prove their assertions have been silent.

In conclusion, let me add that sufficient has been written to prove to the student and investigator that the theory is not to be relegated to the realms of " delusions " or " fancies "; in fact, that it is no longer a theory, but an actual, verifiable truth, and one of the most important foundations of the whole Astrological fabric.

I do not intend to delude anyone by asking them to " take my word for it." The entire rules and principles of the theory have been put forward in a simple and logical manner with the necessary examples, and anyone who will take the trouble to test the entire subject *on the lines laid down*, must, I think, arrive at the same conclusion as myself.

Of course, if there are still some who will persist in mistaking " potatoes for principles," and who refuse, out of mere caprice and personal feeling, to accept truth in one of its many phases, the loss to them in this age of mental progress will be more than they can properly afford. I have but stated the plain and unvarnished facts anent this remarkable theory : I have but given the results of many years of constant investigation and research, and I am content to leave it at this. I should, however, be lacking in gratitude if I did not express my deep appreciation of the assistance and collaboration of my friend and colleague, Sepharial, and for the many suggestions I have received from him. As stated in the Introduction, I claim no originality in regard to the Epochal theory. I have but elaborated its principles, and developed its many practical uses. The results of my labours I leave to the chastening hand of time.

SECTION VIII.

Appendix.

APPENDIX.

SOME ASTRO-MATHEMATICAL RULES.

IN the rules given in the chapters on Rectification (Section II) there are certain statements which require careful explanation. In Rule 2 the following statement appears, viz., "calculate the time on the day of the epoch when the moon's birth longitude rises" and "sets." In Rule 4 are the words, "calculate the time on the day of birth when this longitude rises (sets)."

The student will naturally enquire as to the method of computing these particular times, and in order, therefore, to facilitate the proper computation of the times of the epoch and of the correct birth moment, I have thought fit to devote a chapter giving a number of rules and examples of the calculations involved.

It is necessary to say that it is most important that this part of the epochal theory should be thoroughly understood, for unless the details of calculation are properly performed serious errors will creep in, and render the whole proceeding futile and useless.

The ordinary rule for finding the time at which any particular degree rises or sets is to turn to the table of houses for the required latitude, and subtract the sidereal time at noon on the day of birth or epoch from the sidereal time at which the required degree rises or sets. For example, in the latitude of London, ♐ 11° 41' rises with the sidereal time of 12h. 44m. 8s. On August 1st, 1915, the sidereal time at noon is 8h. 36m. 3s. The calculation is, therefore, as follows :

	H.	M.	S.
Sid. time when ♐ 11° 41' rises	12	44	8
„ at noon, August 1st, 1915	8	36	3
	4	8	5
Less correction			40
Time on August 1st, 1915, when ♐ 11° 41' rises	4	7	25

In the same way, the ordinary rule for finding when a
particular degree sets is to calculate the sidereal time when
the opposite degree rises, and proceed as above. Thus, if it
were required to find when ♐ 11° 50′ sets, look in the
table of houses for the sidereal time when ♊ 11° 50′, the
opposite point, rises, and subtract the sidereal time at noon
on the particular day therefrom.

But a second factor has to be taken into account when
dealing with these epochal problems, and it is very essential
that this second factor should be carefully noted, otherwise
it may frequently throw the day of epoch as much as twenty-
four hours out.

In order to illustrate this point, it is assumed that the
ascendant at birth is Virgo 18°, and the moon is in Sagittarius
11° 41′, increasing and below, and that the day of the epoch,
as found by Rule 2, is November 3rd, 1915. Reference to
the Ephemeris will show that the moon's longitude at noon
on November 3rd is Virgo 18° 53′, and, therefore, the moon
will cross the ascendant of the birth figure *previous* to that
noon.   In such cases, subtract the sidereal time at the noon
previous to the day of epoch from the sidereal time at which
the degree rises.

In this particular example the calculation will be as
follows :

		H.	M.	S.
Sid. time when ♐ 11° 41′ rises		12	44	8
Add 24 hours because the sid. time at noon on November 2nd is greater	.. .. ..	24	0	0
		36	44	8
Sid. time Nov. 2nd, 1915	..	14	42	43
		22	1	25
Less correction	.. .. ..		3	36
		21	57	49

This gives November 2nd, 21h. 57m. 49s., which is equal
to November 3rd, 9h. 57m. 49s. a.m.

To put it briefly, students should take care to observe whether the moon crosses the longitude of the ascendant *before* noon or *after* noon on the day of the epoch. In the latter case, proceed as shown in the first example given in this chapter, taking the sidereal time at noon on the actual day of the epoch. In the former case it is safer and more uniform to subtract the sidereal time at the noon *previous* to the day of epoch, as shown in the second example given.

It is, however, necessary to point out that the two examples given only apply to places on the same meridian as that of Greenwich, and students must understand that, as all time in Great Britain is invariably given in terms of Greenwich, a further correction is necessary when the place of birth is not on the same meridian as Greenwich.

The rule is as follows :—

(*a*) Subtract the sidereal time at noon on the day required from the sidereal time when the degree given rises or sets, taken from the table of houses for the proper latitude.

(*b*) If the place of birth is *west* of Greenwich, add to the result the difference in longitude turned into time, and subtract the correction for the result. The answer is the Greenwich time for the moment of the degree rising or setting.

(*c*) If the place of birth is *east* of Greenwich, subtract the difference in longitude, turned into time, and also subtract the correction. This will again give the required Greenwich time.

The two following examples will apply to all cases falling in Great Britain, other than at Greenwich.

EXAMPLE I.—Find the time of rising of Virgo 14° 24' at Liverpool on August 2nd, 1915.

The sidereal time, when this degree rises, as seen from the table of houses for Liverpool, is less than the sidereal time on August 2nd, showing that the time required is before noon on that date. It is, therefore, more practical to take the sidereal time on August 1st.

The calculation will be as follows :—

	H.	M.	S.
Sid. time, when Virgo, 14° 24′ rises	4	29	10
Add, as before explained	24	0	0
	28	29	10
Sid time on August 1st, 1915 ..	8	36	3
	19	53	7
Liverpool being 3° W., equal to 12 minutes, this amount is to be added		12	0
	20	5	7
Subtract correction for 20h. 5m. 7s.		3	17
Greenwich time required ..	20	1	50

This gives August 1st, 20h. 1m. 50s., or August 2nd, 8h. 1m. 50s. a.m.

EXAMPLE II.—Find the rising of Scorpio 12° 59′ at Lowestoft. Long. 1° 44′ E. Lat. 52° 28′ N., on August 1st, 1915.

	H	M.	S.
Sid. time when degree rises ..	10	8	23
„ „ noon, August 1st ..	8	36	3
	1	32	20
Subtract for E. long. 1° 44′ ..		6	56
	1	25	24
Subtract correction for 1h. 25m. 24s.			14
Greenwich time required ..	1	25	10

This gives August 1st, 1h. 25m. 10s. p.m.

The above rules will apply to all places in any part of the world. After subtracting the two sidereal times, add or subtract the difference in longitude turned into time, and then the correction as shown. The result will be the Greenwich time of the rising or setting.

The following rules will be found of advantage to students in obtaining the sidereal time for the rising or setting of any particular longitude.

Suppose the longitude required in the table of houses for Liverpool is Scorpio 14° 29'. On turning to the table we find the following figures given :

Sidereal Time.	Ascendant.
10h. 12m. 12s.	14° 13'
10h. 16m. 0s.	14° 53'

The procedure is as follows :

(1) Subtract the two sidereal times ; call the result (*a*).
(2) Subtract the two ascendants ; call the result (*b*).
(3) Subtract the lowest ascendant from the ascendant required ; call the result (*c*).
(4) Multiply (*a*) by (*c*) and divide result by (*b*).
(5) Add the result to the lowest sidereal time.

In the example given, the following is obtained :

(1) Difference of sidereal times, 3m. 48s., equal to 228s.
(2) Difference of ascendants, 40s.
(3) Difference of lowest ascendant, and the one required, 16s.
(4) Two hundred and twenty-eight multiplied by 16 and divided by 40 gives 91s., which is equal to 1m. 31s.
(5) Lowest sidereal time, 10h. 12m. 12s., *plus* 1m. 31s., *equals* 10h. 13m. 43s.—the sidereal time at which the required longitude rises.

A further rule will be found of great assistance to students, and will apply to those cases where there is no table of houses for the required latitude.

For example, let it be required to find the sidereal time when Gemini 12° 23' rises in Lat. 52° 48'.

The tables nearest to this are 52° 30' and 53°, in the tables of ascendants at the end of the book.

The rule is as follows :

Find the sidereal time when the required degree rises in the table less than the latitude required, and in the table greater, and place them down against their respective latitudes. In this particular case the following obtains :—

Sidereal Time.	Latitude.
20h. 34m. 28s.	52° 30'
20h. 31m. 51s.	53° 0'

Then proceed as follows :

(1) Subtract the two sidereal times ; call the result (*a*).
(2) Subtract the two latitudes ; call the result (*b*).
(3) Subtract the lowest latitude from the latitude required ; call the result (*c*).
(4) Multiply (*a*) by (*c*) and divide by (*b*).
(5) If the two sidereal times are increasing, add the result of (4) to the first sidereal time. If they are decreasing, as in the above case, subtract the result from the first sidereal time. The answer is the required sidereal time.

In the above example, the following obtains :

(1) Difference of sidereal times, 2m. 37s., equal to 157s.
(2) Difference of latitudes, 30′.
(3) Difference between lowest latitude and that required, 18′.
(4) One hundred and fifty-seven, multiplied by 18, and divided by 30, equals 94, or 1m. 34s.
(5) As sidereal times are decreasing, subtract 1m. 34s. from the first sidereal time, 20h. 34m. 28s., and the result will be the required amount, viz., 20h. 32m. 54s.

All the above rules will be found necessary for the computation of epochs in latitudes within our own country and near foreign countries. Following this will be found a series of tables of ascendants for facilitating this process.

TABLES OF ASCENDANTS

FOR

NORTH LATITUDES.

———

50°	0′	54°	0′
50°	30′	54°	30′
51°	0′	55°	0′
51°	30′	55°	30′
52°	0′	56°	0′
52°	30′	56°	30′
53°	0′	57°	0′
53°	30′	58°	0′

Sidereal Time	50°		50° 30'		51°		51° 30'		52°		52° 30'		53°		53° 30'	
0 0 0	25♋22		25♋46		26♋10		26	35	27♋	0	27♋25		27♋50		28♋16	
0 3 40	26	4	26	27	26	51	27	15	27	39	28	4	28	30	28	55
0 7 20	26	45	27	7	27	31	27	55	28	19	28	44	29	9	29	34
0 11 1	27	26	27	48	28	12	28	35	28	59	29	24	29	48	0♌13	
0 14 41	28	6	28	29	28	52	29	15	29	39	0♌ 3		0♌27		0	52
0 18 21	28	47	29	10	29	32	29	55	0♌19		0	42	1	6	1	31
0 22 2	29	28	29	50	0♌12		0♌35		0	58	1	22	1	45	2	10
0 25 42	0♌ 8		0♌30		0	52	1	15	1	38	2	1	2	24	2	48
0 29 43	0	49	1	11	1	32	1	55	2	17	2	40	3	3	3	27
0 33 4	1	29	1	51	2	12	2	34	2	57	3	19	3	42	4	5
0 36 45	2	10	2	31	2	52	3	14	3	36	3	58	4	21	4	44
0 40 27	2	50	3	11	3	32	3	54	4	15	4	37	5	0	5	22
0 44 8	3	30	3	51	4	12	4	33	4	55	5	16	5	38	6	1
0 47 50	4	11	4	31	4	52	5	13	5	34	5	55	6	17	6	39
0 51 32	4	51	5	11	5	32	5	52	6	13	6	34	6	56	7	17
0 55 15	5	31	5	51	6	11	6	32	6	52	7	13	7	34	7	56
0 58 57	6	12	6	31	6	51	7	11	7	31	7	52	8	13	8	34
1 2 40	6	52	7	11	7	31	7	51	8	11	8	31	8	52	9	13
1 6 24	7	32	7	51	8	11	8	30	8	50	9	10	9	30	9	51
1 10 7	8	13	8	31	8	50	9	10	9	29	9	49	10	9	10	29
1 13 52	8	53	9	11	9	30	9	49	10	9	10	28	10	48	11	8
1 17 36	9	33	9	51	10	10	10	29	10	48	11	7	11	27	11	46
1 21 21	10	14	10	32	10	50	11	8	11	27	11	46	12	5	12	25
1 25 6	10	54	11	12	11	30	11	48	12	6	12	25	12	44	13	3
1 28 52	11	34	11	52	12	10	12	28	12	46	13	4	13	23	13	42
1 32 39	12	15	12	32	12	50	13	8	13	25	13	44	14	2	14	21
1 36 25	12	55	13	13	13	30	13	47	14	5	14	23	14	41	14	59
1 40 13	13	36	13	53	14	10	14	27	14	45	15	2	15	20	15	38
1 44 1	14	17	14	33	14	50	15	7	15	24	15	42	15	59	16	17
1 47 49	14	58	15	14	15	30	15	47	16	4	16	21	16	38	16	56
1 51 38	15	38	15	54	16	11	16	27	16	44	17	1	17	18	17	35
1 55 28	16	19	16	35	16	51	17	7	17	24	17	40	17	57	18	14
1 59 18	16	59	17	16	17	32	17	48	18	4	18	20	18	37	18	53
2 3 8	17	41	17	57	18	12	18	28	18	44	19	0	19	16	19	32
2 7 0	18	23	18	38	18	53	19	8	19	24	19	40	19	56	20	12
2 10 52	19	4	19	19	19	34	19	49	20	4	20	20	20	35	20	51
2 14 44	19	45	20	0	20	15	20	29	20	45	21	0	21	15	21	31
2 18 38	20	27	20	41	20	56	21	10	21	25	21	40	21	55	22	10
2 22 32	21	8	21	22	21	37	21	51	22	6	22	20	22	35	22	50
2 26 26	21	50	22	4	22	18	22	32	22	46	23	1	23	15	23	30
2 30 21	22	32	22	45	22	59	23	13	23	27	23	41	23	56	24	10
2 34 17	23	14	23	27	23	41	23	54	24	8	24	22	24	36	24	50
2 38 14	23	56	24	9	24	22	24	36	24	49	25	3	25	16	25	30
2 42 11	24	38	24	51	25	4	25	17	25	30	25	44	25	57	26	11
2 46 9	25	20	25	33	25	46	25	58	26	11	26	25	26	38	26	51
2 50 8	26	3	26	15	26	28	26	40	26	53	27	6	27	19	27	32

Sidereal Time.	54°		54° 30'		55°		55° 30'		56°		56° 30'		57°		58°	
0 0 0	28♋43		29♋ 9		29♋37		0♌ 4		0♌32		1♌ 1		1♌30		2♌29	
0 3 40	29	21	29	48	0♌15		0	42	1	10	1	38	2	7	3	5
0 7 20	0♌ 0		0♌26		0	53	1	20	1	47	2	15	2	43	3	41
0 11 1	0	39	1	5	1	31	1	57	2	24	2	52	3	20	4	17
0 14 41	1	17	1	43	2	9	2	35	3	2	3	29	3	56	4	53
0 18 21	1	56	2	21	2	46	3	12	3	39	4	5	4	35	5	28
0 22 2	2	34	2	59	3	24	3	50	4	16	4	42	5	9	6	4
0 25 42	3	12	3	37	4	2	4	27	4	53	5	19	5	45	6	39
0 29 43	3	51	4	15	4	39	5	4	5	30	5	55	6	22	7	15
0 33 4	4	29	4	53	5	17	5	42	6	7	6	32	6	58	7	50
0 36 45	5	7	5	31	5	55	6	19	6	44	7	9	7	34	8	26
0 40 27	5	45	6	8	6	32	6	56	7	20	7	45	8	10	9	1
0 44 8	6	23	6	46	7	10	7	33	7	57	8	22	8	46	9	37
0 47 50	7	1	7	24	7	47	8	10	8	34	8	58	9	23	10	12
0 51 32	7	39	8	2	8	25	8	48	9	11	9	35	9	59	10	48
0 55 15	8	18	8	40	9	2	9	25	9	48	10	11	10	35	11	23
0 58 57	8	56	9	17	9	40	10	2	10	25	10	48	11	11	11	59
1 2 40	9	34	9	55	10	17	10	39	11	2	11	24	11	47	12	35
1 6 24	10	12	10	33	10	55	11	16	11	38	12	1	12	24	13	10
1 10 7	10	50	11	11	11	32	11	54	12	15	12	37	13	0	13	46
1 13 52	11	28	11	49	12	10	12	31	12	52	13	14	13	36	14	21
1 17 36	12	6	12	27	12	47	13	8	13	29	13	51	14	13	14	57
1 21 21	12	45	13	5	13	25	13	45	14	6	14	27	14	49	15	33
1 25 6	13	23	13	43	14	3	14	23	14	43	15	4	15	25	16	9
1 28 52	14	1	14	21	14	40	15	0	15	21	15	41	16	2	16	44
1 32 39	14	40	14	59	15	18	15	38	15	58	16	18	16	38	17	20
1 36 25	15	18	15	37	15	56	16	15	16	35	16	55	17	15	17	56
1 40 13	15	57	16	15	16	34	16	53	17	12	17	32	17	52	18	32
1 44 1	16	35	16	53	17	12	17	31	17	50	18	9	18	29	19	8
1 47 49	17	14	17	32	17	50	18	8	18	27	18	46	19	5	19	45
1 51 38	17	52	18	10	18	28	18	46	19	5	19	23	19	42	20	21
1 55 28	18	31	18	49	19	6	19	24	19	42	20	1	20	19	20	57
1 59 18	19	10	19	27	19	45	20	2	20	20	20	38	20	56	21	34
2 3 8	19	49	20	6	20	23	20	40	20	58	21	16	21	34	22	10
2 7 0	20	28	20	45	21	2	21	19	21	36	21	53	22	11	22	47
2 10 52	21	7	21	24	21	40	21	57	22	14	22	31	22	48	23	24
2 14 44	21	47	22	3	22	19	22	35	22	52	23	9	23	26	24	1
2 18 38	22	26	22	42	22	58	23	14	23	30	23	47	24	3	24	37
2 22 32	23	5	23	21	23	37	23	52	24	8	24	25	24	41	25	15
2 26 26	23	45	24	0	24	16	24	31	24	47	25	3	25	19	25	52
2 30 21	24	25	24	40	24	55	25	10	25	25	25	41	25	57	26	29
2 34 17	25	5	25	19	25	34	25	49	26	4	26	19	26	35	27	6
2 38 14	25	45	25	59	26	13	26	28	26	43	26	58	27	13	27	44
2 42 11	26	25	26	39	26	53	27	7	27	22	27	36	27	51	28	22
2 46 9	27	5	27	18	27	32	27	46	28	1	28	15	28	30	28	59
2 50 8	27	45	27	58	28	12	28	26	28	40	28	54	29	8	29	37

Sidereal Time.	50°		50° 30'		51°		51° 30'		52°		52° 30'		53°		53° 30'	
2 50 8	26♌	3	26♌	15	26♌	28	26♌	40	26♌	53	27♌	6	27♌	19	27♌	32
2 54 8	26	45	26	57	27	10	27	22	27	34	27	47	28	0	28	12
2 58 8	27	28	27	40	27	52	28	4	28	16	28	28	28	41	28	53
3 2 9	28	11	28	23	28	34	28	46	28	58	29	10	29	22	29	34
3 6 10	28	54	29	5	29	17	29	28	29	40	29	51	0♍	3	0♍	15
3 10 13	29	37	29	48	29	59	0♍	10	0♍	22	0♍	33	0	45	0	57
3 14 16	0♍	20	0♍	31	0♍	42	0	53	1	4	1	15	1	27	1	38
3 18 20	1	4	1	14	1	25	1	36	1	46	1	57	2	8	2	19
3 22 24	1	47	1	58	2	8	2	18	2	29	2	39	2	50	3	1
3 26 29	2	31	2	41	2	51	3	1	3	11	3	22	3	32	3	43
3 30 35	3	15	3	24	3	34	3	44	3	54	4	4	4	14	4	25
3 34 42	3	59	4	8	4	18	4	27	4	37	4	47	4	57	5	7
3 38 50	4	43	4	52	5	1	5	11	5	20	5	30	5	39	5	49
3 42 58	5	27	5	36	5	45	5	54	6	3	6	12	6	22	6	31
3 47 6	6	11	6	20	6	29	6	38	6	46	6	55	7	5	7	14
3 51 16	6	56	7	4	7	13	7	21	7	30	7	39	7	47	7	56
3 55 26	7	41	7	49	7	57	8	5	8	13	8	22	8	30	8	39
3 59 37	8	25	8	33	8	41	8	49	8	57	9	5	9	14	9	22
4 3 49	9	10	9	18	9	25	9	33	9	41	9	49	9	57	10	5
4 8 1	9	55	10	3	10	10	10	17	10	25	10	32	10	40	10	48
4 12 14	10	40	10	48	10	55	11	2	11	9	11	16	11	24	11	31
4 16 27	11	26	11	33	11	39	11	46	11	53	12	0	12	7	12	14
4 20 41	12	11	12	18	12	24	12	31	12	37	12	44	12	51	12	58
4 24 56	12	57	13	3	13	9	13	16	13	22	13	28	13	35	13	41
4 29 11	13	42	13	48	13	54	14	0	14	6	14	13	14	19	14	25
4 33 26	14	28	14	34	14	40	14	45	14	51	14	57	15	3	15	9
4 37 43	15	14	15	19	15	25	15	30	15	36	15	41	15	47	15	53
4 41 59	16	0	16	5	16	10	16	15	16	21	16	26	16	31	16	37
4 46 17	16	46	16	51	16	56	17	1	17	6	17	11	17	16	17	21
4 50 34	17	32	17	37	17	42	17	46	17	51	17	55	18	0	18	5
4 54 52	18	19	18	23	18	27	18	31	18	36	18	40	18	45	18	49
4 59 11	19	5	19	9	19	13	19	17	19	21	19	25	19	29	19	33
5 3 30	19	51	19	55	19	59	20	3	20	6	20	10	20	14	20	18
5 7 49	20	38	20	41	20	45	20	48	20	52	20	55	20	59	21	2
5 12 9	21	24	21	28	21	31	21	34	21	37	21	40	21	44	21	47
5 16 29	22	11	22	14	22	17	22	20	22	23	22	26	22	29	22	32
5 20 49	22	58	23	0	23	3	23	6	23	8	23	11	23	14	23	16
5 25 10	23	45	23	47	23	49	23	51	23	54	23	56	23	59	24	1
5 29 30	24	31	24	33	24	35	24	37	24	39	24	42	24	44	24	46
5 33 51	25	18	25	20	25	22	25	23	25	25	25	27	25	29	25	31
5 38 13	26	5	26	7	26	8	26	9	26	11	26	12	26	14	26	15
5 42 34	26	52	26	53	26	54	26	56	26	57	26	58	26	59	27	0
5 46 55	27	39	27	40	27	41	27	42	27	43	27	43	27	44	27	45
5 51 17	28	26	28	27	28	27	28	28	28	28	28	29	28	30	28	30
5 55 38	29	13	29	13	29	14	29	14	29	14	29	14	29	15	29	15
6 0 0	30	0	30	0	30	0	30	0	30	0	30	0	30	0	30	0

Sidereal Time.	54°		54° 30′		55°		55° 30′		56°		56° 30′		57°		58°	
2 50 8	27♌45		27♌58		28♌12		28♌26		28♌40		28♌54		29♌	8	29♌37	
2 54 8	28	25	28	39	28	52	29	5	29	19	29	33	29	47	0♍15	
2 58 8	29	6	29	19	29	32	29	45	29	58	0♍12		0♍26		0	53
3 2 9	29	47	29	59	0♍12		0♍25		0♍38		0	51	1	4	1	32
3 6 10	0♍28		0♍40		0	52	1	5	1	18	1	30	1	43	2	10
3 10 13	1	9	1	20	1	33	1	45	1	57	2	10	2	23	2	49
3 14 16	1	50	2	1	2	13	2	25	2	37	2	49	3	2	3	27
3 18 20	2	31	2	42	2	54	3	5	3	17	3	29	3	41	4	6
3 22 24	3	12	3	23	3	34	3	46	3	57	4	9	4	21	4	45
3 26 29	3	54	4	4	4	15	4	26	4	38	4	49	5	1	5	24
3 30 35	4	35	4	46	4	56	5	7	5	18	5	29	5	40	6	3
3 34 42	5	17	5	27	5	38	5	48	5	59	6	9	6	20	6	42
3 38 50	5	59	6	9	6	19	6	29	6	39	6	50	7	0	7	22
3 42 58	6	41	6	51	7	0	7	10	7	20	7	30	7	41	8	1
3 47 6	7	23	7	32	7	42	7	51	8	1	8	11	8	21	8	41
3 51 16	8	5	8	14	8	24	8	33	8	42	8	52	9	1	9	21
3 55 26	8	48	8	56	9	5	9	14	9	23	9	33	9	42	10	1
3 59 37	9	30	9	39	9	47	9	56	10	5	10	14	10	23	10	41
4 3 49	10	13	10	21	10	29	10	38	10	46	10	55	11	4	11	21
4 8 1	10	56	11	4	11	12	11	20	11	28	11	36	11	45	12	2
4 12 14	11	39	11	46	11	54	12	2	12	10	12	17	12	26	12	42
4 16 27	12	22	12	29	12	36	12	44	12	51	12	59	13	7	13	22
4 20 41	13	5	13	12	13	19	13	26	13	33	13	41	13	48	14	3
4 24 56	13	48	13	55	14	2	14	8	14	15	14	22	14	29	14	44
4 29 11	14	31	14	38	14	44	14	51	14	57	15	4	15	11	15	25
4 33 26	15	15	15	21	15	27	15	33	15	40	15	46	15	53	16	6
4 37 43	15	58	16	5	16	10	16	16	16	22	16	28	16	34	16	47
4 41 59	16	42	16	48	16	53	16	59	17	4	17	10	17	16	17	28
4 46 17	17	26	17	31	17	36	17	42	17	47	17	52	17	58	18	9
4 50 34	18	10	18	15	18	20	18	25	18	30	18	35	18	40	18	51
4 54 52	18	54	18	58	19	3	19	8	19	12	19	17	19	22	19	32
4 59 11	19	38	19	42	19	46	19	51	19	55	20	0	20	4	20	13
5 3 30	20	22	20	26	20	30	20	34	20	38	20	42	20	46	20	55
5 7 49	21	6	21	10	21	13	21	17	21	21	21	25	21	29	21	37
5 12 9	21	50	21	54	21	57	22	1	22	4	22	8	22	11	22	18
5 16 29	22	35	22	38	22	41	22	44	22	47	22	50	22	54	23	0
5 20 49	23	19	23	22	23	25	23	27	23	30	23	33	23	36	23	42
5 25 10	24	3	24	6	24	8	24	11	24	13	24	16	24	19	24	24
5 29 30	24	48	24	50	24	52	24	54	24	57	24	59	25	1	25	6
5 33 51	25	32	25	34	25	36	25	38	25	40	25	42	25	44	25	48
5 38 13	26	17	26	18	26	20	26	22	26	23	26	25	26	26	26	30
5 42 34	27	2	27	3	27	4	27	5	27	7	27	8	27	9	27	12
5 46 55	27	46	27	47	27	48	27	49	27	50	27	51	27	52	27	54
5 51 17	28	31	28	31	28	32	28	33	28	33	28	34	28	35	28	36
5 55 38	29	15	29	16	29	16	29	16	29	17	29	17	29	17	29	18
6 0 0	30	0	30	0	30	0	30	0	30	0	30	0	30	0	30	0

Sidereal Time.	50°		50° 30'		51°		51° 30'		52°		52° 30'		53°		53° 30'	
6 0 0	0♎	0	0♎	0	0♎	0	0♎	0	0♎	0	0♎	0	0♎	0	0♎	0
6 4 22	0	47	0	47	0	46	0	46	0	46	0	46	0	45	0	45
6 8 43	1	34	1	33	1	33	1	32	1	32	1	31	1	30	1	30
6 13 5	2	21	2	20	2	19	2	18	2	17	2	17	2	16	2	15
6 17 26	3	8	3	7	3	6	3	4	3	3	3	2	3	1	3	0
6 21 47	3	55	3	53	3	52	3	51	3	49	3	48	3	46	3	45
6 26 9	4	42	4	40	4	38	4	37	4	35	4	33	4	31	4	29
6 30 30	5	29	5	27	5	25	5	23	5	21	5	18	5	16	5	14
6 34 50	6	15	6	13	6	11	6	9	6	6	6	4	6	1	5	59
6 39 11	7	2	7	0	6	57	6	54	6	52	6	49	6	46	6	44
6 43 31	7	49	7	46	7	43	7	40	7	37	7	34	7	31	7	28
6 47 51	8	36	8	32	8	29	8	26	8	23	8	20	8	16	8	13
6 52 11	9	22	9	19	9	15	9	12	9	8	9	5	9	1	8	58
6 56 30	10	9	10	5	10	1	9	57	9	54	9	50	9	46	9	42
7 0 49	10	55	10	51	10	47	10	43	10	39	10	35	10	31	10	27
7 5 8	11	41	11	37	11	33	11	29	11	24	11	20	11	15	11	11
7 9 26	12	28	12	23	12	18	12	14	12	9	12	5	12	0	11	55
7 13 43	13	14	13	9	13	4	12	59	12	54	12	49	12	44	12	39
7 18 1	14	0	13	55	13	50	13	45	13	39	13	34	13	29	13	23
7 22 17	14	46	14	41	14	35	14	30	14	24	14	19	14	13	14	7
7 26 34	15	32	15	26	15	20	15	15	15	9	15	3	14	57	14	51
7 30 49	16	18	16	12	16	6	16	0	15	54	15	47	15	41	15	35
7 35 4	17	3	16	57	16	51	16	44	16	38	16	32	16	25	16	19
7 39 19	17	49	17	42	17	36	17	29	17	23	17	16	17	9	17	2
7 43 31	18	34	18	27	18	21	18	14	18	7	18	0	17	53	17	46
7 47 46	19	20	19	12	19	5	18	58	18	51	18	44	18	36	18	29
7 51 59	20	5	19	57	19	50	19	43	19	35	19	28	19	20	19	12
7 56 11	20	50	20	42	20	35	20	27	20	19	20	11	20	3	19	55
8 0 23	21	35	21	27	21	19	21	11	21	3	20	55	20	46	20	38
8 4 34	22	19	22	11	22	3	21	55	21	47	21	38	21	30	21	21
8 8 44	23	4	22	56	22	47	22	39	22	30	22	21	22	13	22	4
8 12 54	23	49	23	40	23	31	23	22	23	14	23	5	22	55	22	46
8 17 2	24	33	24	24	24	15	24	6	23	57	23	48	23	38	23	29
8 21 10	25	17	25	8	24	59	24	49	24	40	24	30	24	21	24	11
8 25 18	26	1	25	52	25	42	25	33	25	23	25	13	25	3	24	53
8 29 25	26	45	26	36	26	26	26	16	26	6	25	56	25	46	25	35
8 33 31	27	29	27	19	27	9	26	59	26	49	26	38	26	28	26	17
8 37 36	28	13	28	2	27	52	27	42	27	31	27	21	27	10	26	59
8 41 40	28	56	28	46	28	35	28	24	28	14	28	3	27	52	27	41
8 45 44	29	40	29	29	29	18	29	7	28	56	28	45	28	33	28	22
8 49 47	0♍	23	0♍	12	0♍	1	29	50	29	38	29	27	29	15	29	3
8 53 50	1	6	0	55	0	43	0♍	32	0♍	20	0♍	9	29	57	29	45
8 57 51	1	49	1	37	1	26	1	14	1	2	0	50	0♍	38	0♍	26
9 1 52	2	32	2	20	2	8	1	56	1	44	1	32	1	19	1	7
9 5 52	3	15	3	3	2	50	2	38	2	26	2	13	2	0	1	48
9 9 52	3	57	3	45	3	32	3	20	3	7	2	54	2	41	2	28

Sidereal Time	54°		54° 30'		55°		55° 30'		56°		56° 30'		57°		58°	
6 0 0	0♎	0	0♎	0	0♎	0	0♎	0	0♎	0	0♎	0	0♎	0	0♎	0
6 4 22	0	45	0	44	0	44	0	44	0	43	0	43	0	43	0	42
6 8 43	1	29	1	29	1	28	1	27	1	27	1	26	1	25	1	24
6 13 5	2	14	2	13	2	12	2	11	2	10	2	9	2	8	2	6
6 17 26	2	58	2	57	2	56	2	55	2	53	2	52	2	51	2	48
6 21 47	3	43	3	42	3	40	3	38	3	37	3	35	3	34	3	30
6 26 9	4	28	4	26	4	24	4	22	4	20	4	18	4	16	4	12
6 30 30	5	12	5	10	5	8	5	6	5	3	5	1	4	59	4	54
6 34 50	5	57	5	54	5	52	5	49	5	47	5	44	5	41	5	36
6 39 11	6	41	6	38	6	35	6	33	6	30	6	27	6	24	6	18
6 43 31	7	25	7	22	7	19	7	16	7	13	7	10	7	6	7	0
6 47 51	8	10	8	6	8	3	7	59	7	56	7	52	7	49	7	42
6 52 11	8	54	8	50	8	47	8	43	8	39	8	35	8	31	8	23
6 56 30	9	38	9	34	9	30	9	26	9	22	9	18	9	14	9	5
7 0 49	10	22	10	18	10	14	10	9	10	5	10	0	9	56	9	47
7 5 8	11	6	11	2	10	57	10	52	10	48	10	43	10	38	10	28
7 9 26	11	50	11	45	11	40	11	35	11	30	11	25	11	20	11	9
7 13 43	12	34	12	29	12	24	12	18	12	13	12	8	12	2	11	51
7 18 1	13	18	13	12	13	7	13	1	12	56	12	50	12	44	12	32
7 22 17	14	2	13	55	13	50	13	44	13	38	13	32	13	26	13	13
7 26 34	14	45	14	39	14	33	14	27	14	20	14	14	14	7	13	54
7 30 49	15	29	15	22	15	16	15	9	15	3	14	56	14	49	14	35
7 35 4	16	12	16	5	15	58	15	52	15	45	15	38	15	31	15	16
7 39 19	16	55	16	48	16	41	16	34	16	27	16	19	16	12	15	57
7 43 33	17	38	17	31	17	24	17	16	17	9	17	1	16	53	16	38
7 47 46	18	21	18	14	18	6	17	58	17	50	17	43	17	34	17	18
7 51 59	19	4	18	56	18	48	18	40	18	32	18	24	18	15	17	58
7 56 11	19	47	19	39	19	31	19	22	19	14	19	5	18	56	18	39
8 0 23	20	30	20	21	20	13	20	4	19	55	19	46	19	37	19	19
8 4 34	21	12	21	4	20	55	20	46	20	37	20	27	20	18	20	1
8 8 44	21	55	21	46	21	36	21	27	21	18	21	8	20	59	20	39
8 12 54	22	37	22	28	22	18	22	9	21	59	21	49	21	39	21	19
8 17 2	23	19	23	9	23	0	22	50	22	40	22	30	22	19	21	59
8 21 10	24	1	23	51	23	41	23	31	23	21	23	10	23	0	22	38
8 25 18	24	43	24	33	24	22	24	12	24	1	23	51	23	40	23	18
8 29 25	25	25	25	14	25	4	24	53	24	42	24	31	24	20	23	57
8 33 31	26	6	25	56	25	45	25	34	25	22	25	11	24	59	24	36
8 37 36	26	48	26	37	26	26	26	14	26	3	25	51	25	39	25	15
8 41 40	27	29	27	18	27	6	26	55	26	43	26	31	26	19	25	54
8 45 44	28	10	27	59	27	47	27	35	27	23	27	11	26	58	26	33
8 49 47	28	51	28	40	28	27	28	15	28	3	27	50	27	37	27	11
8 53 50	29	32	29	20	29	8	28	55	28	42	28	30	28	17	27	50
8 57 51	0♏	13	0♏	1	29	48	29	35	29	22	29	9	28	56	28	28
9 1 52	0	54	0	41	0♏	28	0♏	15	0♏	2	29	48	29	34	29	7
9 5 52	1	35	1	21	1	8	0	55	0	41	0♏	27	0♏	13	29	45
9 9 52	2	15	2	2	1	48	1	34	1	20	1	6	0	52	0♏	23

Sidereal Time.	50°		50° 30′		51°		51° 30′		52°		52° 30′		53°		53° 30′	
9 9 52	3♍	57	3♍	45	3♍	32	3♍	20	3♍	7	2♍	54	2♍	41	2♍	28
9 13 51	4	40	4	27	4	14	4	2	3	49	3	35	3	22	3	9
9 17 49	5	22	5	9	4	56	4	43	4	30	4	16	4	3	3	49
9 21 46	6	4	5	51	5	38	5	24	5	11	4	57	4	44	4	30
9 25 43	6	46	6	33	6	19	6	6	5	52	5	38	5	24	5	10
9 29 39	7	28	7	15	7	1	6	47	6	33	6	19	6	4	5	50
9 33 34	8	10	7	56	7	42	7	28	7	14	6	59	6	45	6	30
9 37 28	8	52	8	38	8	23	8	9	7	54	7	40	7	25	7	10
9 41 22	9	33	9	19	9	4	8	50	8	35	8	20	8	5	7	50
9 45 16	10	15	10	0	9	45	9	31	9	15	9	0	8	45	8	29
9 49 8	10	56	10	41	10	26	10	11	9	56	9	40	9	25	9	9
9 53 0	11	37	11	22	11	7	10	52	10	36	10	20	10	4	9	48
9 56 52	12	19	12	3	11	48	11	32	11	16	11	0	10	44	10	28
10 0 42	13	1	12	44	12	28	12	12	11	56	11	40	11	23	11	7
10 4 32	13	41	13	25	13	9	12	53	12	36	12	20	12	3	11	46
10 8 22	14	22	14	6	13	49	13	33	13	16	12	59	12	42	12	25
10 12 11	15	2	14	46	14	30	14	13	13	56	13	39	13	22	13	4
10 15 59	15	43	15	27	15	10	14	53	14	36	14	18	14	1	13	43
10 19 47	16	24	16	7	15	50	15	33	15	15	14	58	14	40	14	22
10 23 35	17	5	16	47	16	30	16	13	15	55	15	37	15	19	15	1
10 27 21	17	45	17	28	17	10	16	52	16	35	16	16	15	58	15	39
10 31 8	18	26	18	8	17	50	17	32	17	14	16	56	16	37	16	18
10 34 52	19	6	18	48	18	30	18	12	17	54	17	35	17	16	16	57
10 38 39	19	46	19	28	19	10	18	52	18	33	18	14	17	55	17	35
10 42 24	20	27	20	9	19	50	19	31	19	12	18	53	18	33	18	14
10 46 8	21	7	20	49	20	30	20	11	19	51	19	32	19	12	18	52
10 49 53	21	47	21	29	21	10	20	50	20	31	20	11	19	51	19	31
10 53 26	22	28	22	9	21	49	21	30	21	10	20	50	20	30	20	9
10 57 20	23	8	22	49	22	29	22	9	21	49	21	29	21	8	20	47
11 1 3	23	48	23	29	23	9	22	49	22	29	22	8	21	47	21	26
11 4 45	24	29	24	9	23	49	23	28	23	8	22	47	22	26	22	4
11 8 28	25	9	24	49	24	28	24	8	23	47	23	26	23	4	22	43
11 12 10	25	49	25	29	25	8	24	47	24	26	24	5	23	43	23	21
11 15 52	26	30	26	9	25	48	25	27	25	5	24	44	24	22	23	59
11 19 33	27	10	26	49	26	28	26	6	25	45	25	23	25	0	24	38
11 23 15	27	50	27	29	27	8	26	46	26	24	26	2	25	39	25	16
11 26 56	28	31	28	9	27	48	27	26	27	3	26	41	26	18	25	55
11 30 37	29	11	28	49	28	28	28	5	27	43	27	20	26	57	26	33
11 34 18	29	52	29	30	29	8	28	45	28	22	27	59	27	36	27	12
11 37 58	0♐	32	0♐	10	29	48	29	25	29	2	28	38	28	15	27	50
11 41 39	1	13	0	50	0♐	28	0♐	5	29	41	29	18	28	54	28	29
11 45 19	1	54	1	31	1	8	0	45	0♐	21	29	57	29	33	29	8
11 48 59	2	34	2	12	1	48	1	25	1	1	0♐	36	0♐	12	29	47
11 52 40	3	15	2	53	2	29	2	5	1	41	1	16	0	51	0♐	26
11 56 20	3	56	3	33	3	9	2	45	2	21	1	56	1	30	1	5
12 0 0	4	38	4	14	3	50	3	25	3	0	2	35	2	10	1	44

Sidereal Time.	54°		54° 30'		55°		55° 30'		56°		56° 30'		57°		58°	
9 9 52	2♏	15	2♏	2	1♏	48	1♏	34	1♏	20	1♏	6	0♏	52	0♏	23
9 13 51	2	55	2	42	2	28	2	14	1	59	1	45	1	30	1	1
9 17 49	3	35	3	21	3	7	2	53	2	38	2	24	2	9	1	38
9 21 46	4	15	4	1	3	47	3	32	3	17	3	2	2	47	2	16
9 25 43	4	55	4	41	4	26	4	11	3	56	3	41	3	25	2	54
9 29 39	5	35	5	20	5	5	4	50	4	35	4	19	4	3	3	31
9 33 34	6	15	6	0	5	44	5	29	5	13	4	57	4	41	4	8
9 37 28	6	55	6	39	6	23	6	8	5	52	5	35	5	19	4	45
9 41 22	7	34	7	18	7	2	6	46	6	30	6	13	5	57	5	23
9 45 16	8	13	7	57	7	41	7	25	7	8	6	51	6	34	5	59
9 49 8	8	53	8	36	8	20	8	3	7	46	7	29	7	12	6	36
9 53 0	9	32	9	15	8	58	8	41	8	24	8	7	7	49	7	13
9 56 52	10	11	9	54	9	37	9	20	9	2	8	44	8	26	7	50
10 0 42	10	50	10	33	10	15	9	58	9	40	9	22	9	4	8	26
10 4 32	11	29	11	11	10	54	10	36	10	18	9	59	9	41	9	3
10 8 22	12	8	11	50	11	32	11	14	10	55	10	37	10	18	9	39
10 12 11	12	46	12	28	12	10	11	52	11	33	11	14	10	55	10	15
10 15 59	13	25	13	7	12	48	12	29	12	10	11	51	11	31	10	52
10 19 47	14	3	13	45	13	26	13	7	12	48	12	28	12	8	11	28
10 23 35	14	42	14	23	14	4	13	45	13	25	13	5	12	45	12	4
10 27 21	15	20	15	1	14	42	14	22	14	2	13	42	13	22	12	40
10 31 8	15	59	15	39	15	20	15	0	14	39	14	19	13	58	13	16
10 34 52	16	37	16	17	15	57	15	37	15	17	14	56	14	35	13	51
10 38 39	17	15	16	55	16	35	16	15	15	54	15	33	15	11	14	27
10 42 24	17	54	17	33	17	13	16	52	16	31	16	9	15	47	15	3
10 46 8	18	32	18	11	17	50	17	29	17	8	16	46	16	24	15	39
10 49 53	19	10	18	49	18	28	18	6	17	45	17	23	17	0	16	14
10 53 26	19	48	19	27	19	5	18	44	18	22	17	59	17	36	16	50
10 57 20	20	26	20	5	19	43	19	21	18	58	18	36	18	13	17	25
11 1 3	21	4	20	43	20	20	19	58	19	35	19	12	18	49	18	1
11 4 45	21	42	21	20	20	58	20	35	20	12	19	49	19	25	18	37
11 8 28	22	21	21	58	21	35	21	12	20	49	20	25	20	1	19	12
11 12 10	22	59	22	36	22	13	21	50	21	26	21	2	20	37	19	48
11 15 52	23	37	23	14	22	50	22	27	22	3	21	38	21	14	20	23
11 19 33	24	15	23	52	23	28	23	4	22	40	22	15	21	50	20	59
11 23 15	24	53	24	29	24	5	23	41	23	16	22	51	22	26	21	34
11 26 56	25	31	25	7	24	43	24	18	23	53	23	28	23	2	22	10
11 30 37	26	9	25	45	25	21	24	56	24	30	24	5	23	38	22	45
11 34 18	26	48	26	23	25	58	25	33	25	7	24	41	24	15	23	21
11 37 58	27	26	27	1	26	36	26	10	25	44	25	18	24	51	23	56
11 41 39	28	4	27	39	27	14	26	48	26	21	25	55	25	27	24	32
11 45 19	28	43	28	17	27	51	27	25	26	58	26	31	26	4	25	7
11 48 59	29	21	28	55	28	29	28	3	27	36	27	8	26	40	25	43
11 52 40	0♐	0	29	34	29	7	28	40	28	13	27	45	27	17	26	19
11 56 20	0	39	0♐	12	29	45	29	18	28	50	28	22	27	53	26	55
12 0 0	1	17	0	51	0♐	23	29	56	29	28	28	59	28	30	27	31

Sidereal Time.	50°	50° 30′	51°	51° 30′	52°	52° 30′	53°	53° 30′
12 0 0	4♐38	4♐14	3♐50	3♐25	3♐0	2♐35	2♐10	1♐44
12 3 40	5 19	4 55	4 30	4 6	3 41	3 15	2 49	2 23
12 7 20	6 0	5 36	5 11	4 46	4 21	3 55	3 29	3 2
12 11 1	6 42	6 17	5 52	5 27	5 1	4 35	4 9	3 42
12 14 41	7 24	6 59	6 34	6 8	5 42	5 15	4 49	4 21
12 18 21	8 6	7 40	7 15	6 49	6 23	5 56	5 29	5 1
12 22 2	8 48	8 22	7 56	7 30	7 4	6 37	6 9	5 41
12 25 42	9 30	9 4	8 38	8 12	7 45	7 17	6 49	6 21
12 29 23	10 12	9 46	9 20	8 53	8 26	7 58	7 30	7 1
12 33 4	10 55	10 29	10 2	9 35	9 7	8 39	8 11	7 42
12 36 45	11 38	11 11	10 44	10 17	9 49	9 21	8 52	8 23
12 40 27	12 21	11 54	11 27	10 59	10 31	10 2	9 33	9 4
12 44 8	13 5	12 37	12 10	11 42	11 13	10 44	10 15	9 45
12 47 50	13 48	13 21	12 53	12 24	11 56	11 26	10 56	10 26
12 51 32	14 32	14 4	13 36	13 7	12 38	12 9	11 38	11 8
12 55 15	15 16	14 48	14 20	13 51	13 21	12 51	12 21	11 50
12 58 57	16 1	15 33	15 4	14 34	14 4	13 34	13 3	12 32
13 2 40	16 46	16 17	15 48	15 18	14 48	14 17	13 46	13 14
13 6 24	17 31	17 2	16 32	16 2	15 32	15 1	14 29	13 57
13 10 7	18 17	17 47	17 17	16 47	16 16	15 45	15 13	14 40
13 13 52	19 3	18 33	18 3	17 32	17 1	16 29	15 56	15 23
13 17 36	19 49	19 19	18 48	18 17	17 46	17 13	16 41	16 7
13 21 21	20 36	20 5	19 34	19 3	18 31	17 58	17 25	16 51
13 25 6	21 23	20 52	20 21	19 49	19 17	18 44	18 10	17 36
13 28 52	22 10	21 39	21 8	20 36	20 3	19 29	18 56	18 21
13 32 39	22 58	22 27	21 55	21 22	20 49	20 16	19 41	19 6
13 36 25	23 46	23 15	22 43	22 10	21 36	21 2	20 28	19 52
13 40 13	24 35	24 4	23 31	22 58	22 24	21 50	21 14	20 38
13 44 1	25 25	24 53	24 20	23 46	23 12	22 37	22 2	21 25
13 47 49	26 15	25 42	25 9	24 35	24 1	23 25	22 50	22 13
13 51 38	27 6	26 33	25 59	25 25	24 50	24 14	23 38	23 0
13 55 28	27 57	27 24	26 50	26 15	25 40	25 3	24 27	23 49
13 59 10	28 49	28 15	27 41	27 6	26 30	25 53	25 16	24 38
14 3 8	29 41	29 7	28 32	27 57	27 21	26 44	26 6	25 27
14 7 0	0♑34	0♑0	29 25	28 49	28 12	27 35	26 57	26 18
14 10 52	1 28	0 53	0♑18	29 42	29 5	28 27	27 48	27 9
14 14 44	2 23	1 47	1 12	0♑35	29 58	29 20	28 40	28 0
14 18 38	3 18	2 43	2 6	1 29	0♑52	0♑13	29 33	28 53
14 22 32	4 14	3 38	3 2	2 24	1 46	1 7	0♑27	29 46
14 22 26	5 11	4 35	3 58	3 20	2 42	2 2	1 21	0♑40
14 30 21	6 9	5 32	4 55	4 17	3 38	2 58	2 17	1 35
14 34 17	7 8	6 31	5 53	5 14	4 35	3 54	3 13	2 30
14 38 14	8 7	7 30	6 52	6 13	5 33	4 52	4 10	3 27
14 42 11	9 8	8 30	7 52	7 12	6 32	5 51	5 8	4 25
14 46 9	10 9	9 32	8 53	8 13	7 32	6 50	6 7	5 23
14 50 8	11 12	10 34	9 55	9 15	8 33	7 51	7 7	6 23

Sidereal Time.	54°		54° 30'		55°		55° 30'		56°		56° 30'		57°		58°	
12 0 0	1 ♐17		0 ♐51		0 ♐23		29m 56		29m 27		28m 59		28m 30		27m 31	
12 3 40	1	56	1	29	1	2	0♐34		0♐ 5		29	36	29	7	28	7
12 7 20	2	35	2	8	1	40	1	12	0	43	0♐13		29	44	28	43
12 11 1	3	14	2	47	2	18	1	50	1	20	0	51	0♐21		29	19
12 14 41	3	54	3	26	2	57	2	28	1	58	1	28	0	58	29♐55	
12 18 21	4	33	4	5	3	36	3	6	2	36	2	6	1	35	0♐21	
12 22 2	5	13	4	44	4	15	3	45	3	14	2	44	2	12	1	8
12 25 42	5	52	5	23	4	54	4	23	3	53	3	21	2	50	1	44
12 29 23	6	32	6	3	5	33	5	2	4	31	3	59	3	27	2	21
12 33 4	7	13	6	43	6	12	5	41	5	10	4	38	4	5	2	58
12 36 45	7	53	7	23	6	52	6	20	5	48	5	16	4	43	3	35
12 40 27	8	33	8	3	7	32	7	0	6	27	5	55	5	21	4	12
12 44 8	9	14	8	43	8	12	7	39	7	7	6	33	5	59	4	50
12 47 50	9	55	9	24	8	52	8	19	7	46	7	12	6	38	5	27
12 51 32	10	36	10	5	9	32	8	59	8	26	7	51	7	17	6	5
12 55 15	11	18	10	46	10	13	9	39	9	5	8	31	7	56	6	43
12 58 57	12	0	11	27	10	54	10	20	9	46	9	11	8	35	7	21
13 2 40	12	42	12	9	11	35	11	1	10	26	9	50	9	14	8	0
13 6 24	13	24	12	51	12	17	11	42	11	7	10	31	9	54	8	38
13 10 7	14	7	13	33	12	58	12	23	11	48	11	11	10	34	9	17
13 13 52	14	50	14	16	13	41	13	5	12	29	11	52	11	14	9	57
13 17 36	15	33	14	58	14	23	13	47	13	10	12	33	11	55	10	36
13 21 21	16	17	15	42	15	6	14	30	13	52	13	14	12	36	11	16
13 25 6	17	1	16	26	15	49	15	12	14	35	13	56	13	17	11	56
13 28 52	17	46	17	10	16	33	15	55	15	17	14	38	13	59	12	37
13 32 39	18	31	17	54	17	17	16	39	16	0	15	21	14	40	13	17
13 36 25	19	16	18	39	18	1	17	23	16	44	16	4	15	23	13	59
13 40 13	20	2	19	24	18	46	18	7	17	28	16	47	16	6	14	40
13 44 1	20	48	20	10	19	32	18	52	18	12	17	31	16	49	15	22
13 47 49	21	35	20	57	20	18	19	38	18	57	18	15	17	32	16	4
13 51 38	22	22	21	44	21	4	20	23	19	42	19	0	18	17	16	47
13 55 28	23	10	22	31	21	51	21	10	20	28	19	45	19	1	17	31
13 59 18	23	59	23	19	22	38	21	57	21	14	20	31	19	46	18	14
14 3 8	24	48	24	8	23	26	22	44	22	1	21	17	20	32	18	59
14 7 0	25	38	24	57	24	15	23	32	22	49	22	4	21	18	19	44
14 10 52	26	28	25	47	25	5	24	21	23	37	22	52	22	5	20	29
14 14 44	27	19	26	37	25	55	25	11	24	26	23	40	22	53	21	15
14 18 38	28	11	27	29	26	45	26	1	25	15	24	29	23	41	22	2
14 22 32	29	4	28	21	27	37	26	52	26	5	25	18	24	30	22	49
14 26 26	29	57	29	14	28	29	27	43	26	56	26	8	25	19	23	37
14 30 21	0♑52		0♑ 7		29	22	28	36	27	48	27	0	26	10	24	26
14 34 17	1	47	1	2	0♑16		29	29	28	41	27	52	27	1	25	16
14 38 14	2	43	1	57	1	11	0♑23		29	34	28	44	27	53	26	6
14 42 11	3	40	2	54	2	7	1	19	0♑29		29	38	28	46	26	57
14 46 9	4	38	3	51	3	4	2	15	1	24	0♑33		29	40	27	49
14 50 8	5	37	4	50	4	2	3	12	2	21	1	28	0♑35		28	42

Sidereal Time.	50°	50° 30'	51°	51° 30'	52°	52° 30'	53°	53° 30'
14 50 8	11♑12	10♑34	9♑55	9♑15	8♑33	7♑51	7♑7	6♑23
14 54 8	12 16	11 37	10 58	10 17	9 35	8 53	8 9	7 24
14 58 8	13 21	12 42	12 2	11 21	10 39	9 56	9 11	8 26
15 2 9	14 27	13 48	13 7	12 26	11 44	11 0	10 15	9 29
15 6 10	15 34	14 55	14 14	13 32	12 50	12 5	11 20	10 33
15 10 13	16 43	16 3	15 22	14 40	13 57	13 12	12 26	11 39
15 14 16	17 53	17 13	16 32	15 49	15 5	14 20	13 34	12 46
15 18 20	19 4	18 24	17 43	17 0	16 16	15 30	14 43	13 55
15 22 24	20 17	19 37	18 55	18 12	17 27	16 41	15 54	15 5
15 26 29	21 32	20 51	20 9	19 25	18 40	17 54	17 7	16 17
15 30 35	22 48	22 7	21 24	20 41	19 55	19 9	18 21	17 31
15 34 42	24 6	23 24	22 42	21 58	21 12	20 25	19 37	18 46
15 38 50	25 25	24 43	24 1	23 16	22 31	21 43	20 55	20 4
15 42 58	26 46	26 5	25 22	24 37	22 51	23 3	22 14	21 23
15 47 6	28 9	27 28	26 44	26 0	24 13	24 26	23 36	22 44
15 51 16	29 34	28 52	28 9	27 24	26 38	25 50	25 0	24 8
15 55 26	1≈1	0≈19	29 36	28 51	28 5	27 16	26 26	25 34
15 59 37	2 30	1 48	1≈5	0≈20	29 34	28 45	27 55	27 2
16 3 49	4 1	3 20	2 36	1 51	1≈5	0≈16	29 26	28 33
16 8 1	5 35	5 53	4 10	3 25	2 39	1 50	0≈59	0≈7
16 12 14	7 10	7 29	5 46	5 1	4 15	3 26	2 36	1 43
16 16 27	8 48	8 7	7 25	6 40	5 54	5 5	4 15	3 22
16 20 41	10 29	9 48	9 6	8 21	7 35	6 47	5 57	5 4
16 24 56	12 11	11 31	10 49	10 6	9 20	8 32	7 42	6 50
16 29 11	13 57	13 17	12 36	11 52	11 7	10 20	9 30	8 38
16 33 26	15 45	15 6	14 25	13 42	12 58	12 11	11 22	10 30
16 37 43	17 33	16 57	16 17	15 35	14 51	14 5	13 16	12 25
16 41 59	19 28	18 51	18 12	17 31	16 48	16 2	15 14	14 24
16 46 17	21 24	20 48	20 10	19 29	18 47	18 3	17 16	16 27
16 50 34	23 23	22 47	22 10	21 31	20 50	20 7	19 21	18 33
16 54 52	25 24	24 50	24 14	23 36	22 57	22 15	21 30	20 43
16 59 11	27 28	26 55	26 20	25 44	25 6	24 26	23 43	22 57
17 3 30	29 34	29 3	28 30	27 55	27 19	26 40	25 59	25 15
17 7 49	1⨯43	1⨯13	0⨯42	0⨯9	29 35	28 58	28 19	27 37
17 12 9	3 54	3 27	2 57	2 27	1⨯54	1⨯19	0⨯42	0⨯3
17 16 29	6 8	5 42	5 15	4 46	4 16	3 43	3 9	2 32
17 20 49	8 24	8 1	7 36	7 9	6 41	6 11	5 39	5 5
17 25 10	10 42	10 21	9 58	9 34	9 9	8 41	8 12	7 41
17 29 30	13 2	12 43	12 23	12 1	11 39	11 15	10 49	10 21
17 33 51	15 24	15 8	14 50	14 32	14 12	13 50	13 28	13 3
17 38 13	17 48	17 34	17 19	17 3	16 46	16 28	16 9	15 49
17 42 34	20 13	20 1	19 49	19 37	19 23	19 8	18 53	18 36
17 46 55	22 39	22 30	22 21	22 11	22 1	21 50	21 38	21 25
17 51 17	25 5	24 59	24 53	24 47	24 40	24 33	24 25	24 16
17 55 38	27 32	27 29	27 26	27 23	27 20	27 16	27 12	27 8
18 0 0	30 0	30 0	30 0	30 0	30 0	30 0	30 0	30 0

Sidereal Time.	54°		54° 30'		55°		55° 30'		56°		56° 30'		57°		58°	
14 50 8	5♑37		4♑50		4♑2		3♑12		2♑21		1♑28		0♑35		28♐42	
14 54 8	6	37	5	50	5	1	4	10	3	18	2	25	1	30	29	36
14 58 8	7	39	6	50	6	1	5	10	4	17	3	23	2	27	0♑32	
15 2 9	8	41	7	52	7	2	6	10	5	17	4	22	3	26	1	28
15 6 10	9	45	8	56	8	5	7	12	6	18	5	22	4	25	2	25
15 10 13	10	50	10	0	9	9	8	15	7	21	6	24	5	26	3	24
15 14 16	11	57	11	6	10	14	9	20	8	24	7	27	6	28	4	24
15 18 20	13	5	12	14	11	21	10	26	9	30	8	32	7	32	5	26
15 22 24	14	15	13	23	12	29	11	34	10	37	9	38	8	37	6	29
15 26 29	15	26	14	34	13	39	12	43	11	45	10	45	9	44	7	33
15 30 35	16	39	15	46	14	51	13	55	12	56	11	55	10	52	8	40
15 34 42	17	54	17	1	16	5	15	8	14	8	13	6	12	2	9	48
15 38 50	19	11	18	17	17	21	16	22	15	22	14	20	13	15	10	58
15 42 58	20	30	19	35	18	38	17	40	16	38	15	35	14	29	12	10
15 47 6	21	51	20	56	19	58	18	59	17	57	16	53	15	46	13	24
15 51 16	23	14	22	19	21	21	20	20	19	18	18	13	17	5	14	41
15 55 26	24	40	23	44	22	45	21	44	20	41	19	35	18	26	16	0
15 59 37	26	8	25	11	24	12	23	11	22	7	21	0	19	50	17	22
16 3 49	27	39	26	42	25	42	24	40	23	35	22	28	21	18	18	47
16 8 1	29	12	28	15	27	15	26	12	25	7	23	59	22	48	20	15
16 12 14	0≈48		29	50	28	50	27	47	26	42	25	33	24	21	21	46
16 16 27	2	27	1≈29		0≈29		29	26	28	20	27	10	25	58	23	21
16 20 41	4	9	3	12	2	11	1≈8		0≈1		28	51	27	38	25	0
16 24 56	5	55	4	57	3	57	2	53	1	46	0≈36		29	22	26	42
16 29 11	7	43	6	46	5	46	4	42	3	35	2	25	1≈10		28	29
16 33 26	9	36	8	39	7	39	6	35	5	28	4	18	3	3	0≈21	
16 37 43	11	32	10	35	9	35	8	32	7	26	6	15	5	0	2	17
16 41 59	13	31	12	35	11	36	10	34	9	27	8	17	7	3	4	19
16 46 17	15	35	14	40	13	41	12	40	11	34	10	24	9	10	6	27
16 50 34	17	42	16	48	15	51	14	50	13	45	12	36	11	23	8	40
16 54 52	19	54	19	1	18	5	17	5	16	2	14	54	13	41	11	0
16 59 11	22	9	21	18	20	24	19	26	18	24	17	17	16	6	13	30
17 3 30	24	29	23	40	22	47	21	51	20	51	19	46	18	36	16	1
17 7 49	26	53	26	6	25	15	24	21	23	23	22	21	21	13	18	42
17 12 9	29	21	28	36	27	48	26	56	26	1	25	1	23	57	21	30
17 16 29	1×53		1×11		0×25		29	37	28	44	27	48	26	46	24	27
17 20 49	4	29	3	50	3	8	2×22		1×33		0×40		29	43	27	31
17 25 10	7	8	6	32	5	54	5	12	4	27	3	38	2×45		0×43	
17 29 30	9	51	9	19	8	44	8	7	7	26	6	42	6	54	4	2
17 33 51	12	37	12	9	11	39	11	6	10	30	9	51	9	8	7	29
17 38 13	15	26	15	3	14	37	14	9	13	38	13	5	12	28	11	3
17 42 34	18	18	17	59	17	38	17	15	16	50	16	22	15	52	14	42
17 46 55	21	12	20	57	20	41	20	23	20	4	19	44	19	21	18	27
17 51 17	24	7	23	57	23	46	23	34	23	22	23	7	22	52	22	16
17 55 38	27	3	26	58	26	53	26	47	26	40	26	33	26	26	26	7
18 0 0	30	0	30	0	30	0	30	0	30	0	30	0	30	0	30	0

Sidereal Time.	50°	50° 30'	51°	51° 30'	52°	52° 30'	53°	53° 30'
18 0 0	0♈0	0♈0	0♈0	0♈0	0♈0	0♈0	0♈0	0♈0
18 4 22	2 28	2 31	2 34	2 37	2 40	2 44	2 48	2 52
18 8 43	4 55	5 1	5 7	5 13	5 20	5 27	5 35	5 44
18 13 5	7 21	7 30	7 39	7 49	7 59	8 10	8 22	8 35
18 17 26	9 47	9 59	10 11	10 23	10 37	10 52	11 7	11 24
18 21 47	12 12	12 26	12 41	12 57	13 14	13 32	13 51	14 11
18 26 9	14 36	14 52	15 10	15 28	15 48	16 10	16 32	16 57
18 30 30	16 58	17 17	17 37	17 59	18 21	18 45	19 11	19 39
18 34 50	19 18	19 39	20 2	20 26	20 51	21 19	21 48	22 19
18 39 11	21 36	21 59	22 24	22 51	23 19	23 49	24 21	24 55
18 43 31	23 52	24 18	24 45	25 14	25 44	26 17	26 51	27 28
18 47 51	26 6	26 33	27 3	27 33	28 6	28 41	29 18	29 57
18 52 11	28 17	28 47	29 18	29 51	0♉25	1♉2	1♉41	2♉23
18 56 30	0♉26	0♉57	1♉30	2♉5	2 41	3 20	4 1	4 45
19 0 49	2 32	3 5	3 40	4 16	4 54	5 34	6 17	7 3
19 5 8	4 36	5 10	5 46	6 24	7 3	7 45	8 30	9 17
19 9 26	6 37	7 13	7 50	8 29	9 10	9 53	10 39	11 27
19 13 43	8 36	9 12	9 50	10 31	11 13	11 56	12 44	13 33
19 18 1	10 32	11 9	11 48	12 29	13 12	13 58	14 46	15 36
19 22 17	12 25	13 3	13 43	14 25	15 9	15 55	16 44	17 35
19 26 34	14 15	14 54	15 35	16 18	17 2	17 49	18 38	19 30
19 30 49	16 3	16 43	17 24	18 8	18 53	19 40	20 30	21 22
19 35 4	17 49	18 29	19 11	19 54	20 40	21 28	22 18	23 10
19 39 19	19 31	20 12	20 54	21 39	22 25	23 13	24 3	24 56
19 43 33	21 12	21 53	22 35	23 20	24 6	24 55	25 45	26 38
19 47 46	22 50	23 31	24 14	24 59	25 45	26 34	27 24	28 17
19 51 59	24 25	25 7	25 50	26 35	27 21	28 10	29 1	29 53
19 56 11	25 59	26 40	27 24	28 19	28 55	29 44	0♊34	1♊27
20 0 23	27 30	28 12	28 55	29 40	0♊26	1♊15	2 5	2 58
20 4 34	28 59	29 41	0♊24	1♊9	1 55	2 34	3 34	4 26
20 8 44	0♊26	1♊8	1 51	2 36	3 22	4 10	5 0	5 52
20 12 54	1 51	2 32	3 16	4 0	4 47	5 34	6 24	7 16
20 17 2	3 14	3 55	4 38	5 23	6 9	6 57	7 46	8 37
20 21 10	4 35	5 17	5 59	6 44	7 29	8 17	9 5	9 56
20 25 18	5 54	6 36	7 18	8 2	8 48	9 35	10 23	11 14
20 29 25	7 12	7 53	8 36	9 19	10 5	10 51	11 39	12 29
20 33 31	8 28	9 9	9 51	10 35	11 20	12 6	12 53	13 43
20 37 36	9 43	10 23	11 5	11 48	12 33	13 19	14 6	14 55
20 41 40	10 56	11 36	12 17	13 0	13 44	14 30	15 17	16 5
20 45 44	12 7	12 47	13 28	14 11	14 55	15 40	16 26	17 14
20 49 47	13 17	13 57	14 38	15 20	16 3	16 48	17 34	18 21
20 53 50	14 26	15 5	15 46	16 28	17 10	17 53	18 40	19 27
20 57 51	15 33	16 12	16 53	17 34	18 16	19 0	19 45	20 31
20 1 52	16 39	17 18	17 58	18 39	19 21	20 4	20 49	21 34
20 5 52	17 44	18 23	19 2	19 43	20 25	21 7	21 51	22 36
20 9 52	18 48	19 26	20 5	20 45	21 27	22 9	22 53	23 37

Sidereal Time	54°	54° 30'	55°	55° 30'	56°	56° 30'	57°	58°
18 0 0	0♈ 0	0♈ 0	0♈ 0	0♈ 0	0♈ 0	0♈ 0	0♈ 0	0♈ 0
18 4 22	2 57	3 2	3 7	3 13	3 20	3 27	3 34	3 53
18 8 43	5 53	6 3	6 14	6 26	7 38	6 53	7 8	7 44
18 13 5	8 48	9 3	9 19	9 37	9 56	10 16	10 39	11 33
18 17 26	11 42	12 1	12 22	12 45	13 10	13 38	14 8	15 18
18 21 47	14 34	14 57	15 23	15 51	16 22	16 55	17 32	18 57
18 26 9	17 23	17 51	18 21	18 54	19 30	20 9	20 52	22 31
18 30 30	20 9	20 41	21 16	21 53	22 34	23 18	23 6	25 58
18 34 50	22 52	23 28	24 6	24 48	25 33	26 22	27 15	29 17
18 39 11	25 31	26 10	26 52	27 38	28 27	29 20	0♉17	2♉29
18 43 31	28 7	28 49	29 35	0♉23	1♉16	2♉12	3 14	5 33
18 47 51	0♉39	1♉24	2♉12	3 4	3 59	4 59	6 3	8 30
18 52 11	3 7	3 54	4 45	5 39	6 37	7 39	8 47	11 18
18 56 30	5 31	6 20	7 13	8 9	9 9	10 14	11 24	13 59
19 0 49	7 51	8 42	9 36	10 34	11 36	12 43	13 54	16 30
19 5 8	10 6	10 59	11 55	12 55	13 58	15 6	16 19	19 0
19 9 26	12 18	13 12	14 9	15 10	16 15	17 24	18 37	21 20
19 13 43	14 25	15 20	16 19	17 20	18 26	19 36	20 50	23 33
19 18 1	16 29	17 25	18 24	19 26	20 33	21 43	22 57	25 41
19 22 17	18 28	19 25	20 25	21 28	22 34	23 45	25 0	27 43
19 26 34	20 24	21 21	22 21	23 25	24 32	25 42	26 57	29 39
19 30 49	22 17	23 14	24 14	25 18	26 25	27 35	28 50	1♊31
19 35 4	24 5	25 3	26 3	27 7	28 14	29 24	0♊38	3 18
19 39 19	25 51	26 48	27 49	28 52	29 59	1♊9	2 22	5 0
19 43 33	27 33	28 31	29 31	0♊34	1♊40	2 50	4 2	6 39
19 47 46	29 12	0♊10	1♊10	2 13	3 18	4 27	5 39	8 14
19 51 59	0♊48	1 45	2 45	3 48	4 53	6 1	7 12	9 45
19 56 11	2 21	3 18	3 18	5 20	6 25	7 32	8 42	11 13
20 0 23	3 52	4 49	5 48	6 49	7 53	9 0	10 10	12 38
20 4 34	5 20	6 16	7 15	8 16	9 19	10 25	11 34	14 0
20 8 44	6 46	7 41	8 39	9 40	10 42	11 47	12 55	15 19
20 12 54	8 9	9 4	10 2	11 1	12 3	13 7	14 14	16 36
20 17 2	9 30	10 25	11 22	12 20	13 22	14 25	15 31	17 50
20 21 10	10 49	11 43	12 39	13 38	14 38	15 40	16 45	19 2
20 25 18	12 6	12 59	13 55	14 52	15 52	16 54	17 58	20 12
20 29 25	13 21	14 14	15 9	16 5	17 4	18 5	19 2	21 20
20 33 31	14 34	15 26	16 21	17 17	18 15	19 15	20 16	22 27
20 37 36	15 45	16 37	17 31	18 26	19 23	20 22	21 23	23 31
20 41 40	16 55	17 46	18 39	19 34	20 30	21 28	22 28	24 34
20 45 44	18 3	18 54	19 46	20 40	21 36	22 33	23 32	25 36
20 49 47	19 10	20 0	20 51	21 45	22 39	23 36	24 34	26 36
20 53 50	20 15	21 4	21 55	22 48	23 42	24 38	25 35	27 35
20 57 51	21 19	22 8	22 58	23 50	24 43	25 38	26 34	28 32
21 1 52	22 21	23 10	23 59	24 50	25 43	26 37	27 33	29 28
21 5 52	23 23	24 10	24 59	25 50	26 42	27 35	28 30	0♋24
21 9 52	24 23	25 10	25 58	26 48	27 39	28 32	29 25	1 18

238   THE PRENATAL EPOCH.

Sidereal Time.	50°	50° 30′	51°	51° 30′	52°	52° 30′	53°	53° 30′
21 9 52	18♊48	19♊26	20♊5	20♊45	21♊27	22♊9	22♊53	23♊37
21 13 51	19 51	20 28	21 7	21 47	22 28	23 10	23 53	24 37
21 17 49	20 52	21 30	22 8	22 48	23 28	24 9	24 52	25 35
21 21 46	21 53	22 30	23 8	23 47	24 27	25 8	25 50	26 33
21 25 43	22 52	23 29	24 7	24 46	25 25	26 6	26 47	27 30
21 29 39	23 51	24 28	25 5	25 43	26 22	27 2	27 43	28 25
21 33 34	24 49	25 25	26 2	26 40	27 18	27 58	28 39	29 20
21 37 28	25 46	26 22	26 58	27 36	28 14	28 53	29 33	0♋14
21 41 22	26 42	27 17	27 54	28 31	29 8	29 47	0♋27	1 7
21 45 16	27 37	28 13	28 48	29 25	0♋2	0♋40	1 20	2 0
21 49 8	28 32	29 7	29 42	0♋18	0 55	1 33	2 12	2 51
21 53 0	29 26	0♋0	0♋35	1 11	1 48	2 25	3 3	3 42
21 56 52	0♋19	0 53	1 28	2 3	2 39	3 16	3 54	4 33
22 0 42	1 11	1 45	2 19	2 54	3 30	4 7	4 44	5 22
24 4 32	2 3	2 36	3 10	3 45	4 20	4 57	5 33	6 11
22 8 22	2 54	3 27	4 1	4 35	5 10	5 46	6 22	7 0
22 12 11	3 45	4 18	4 51	5 25	6 9	6 35	7 10	7 47
22 15 59	4 35	5 7	5 40	6 14	6 48	7 23	7 58	8 35
22 19 47	5 25	5 56	6 29	7 2	7 36	8 10	8 46	9 22
22 23 35	6 14	6 45	7 17	7 50	8 24	8 58	9 32	10 8
22 27 21	7 2	7 33	8 5	8 38	9 11	9 44	10 19	10 54
22 31 8	7 50	8 21	8 52	9 24	9 57	10 31	11 4	11 39
22 34 54	8 37	9 8	9 39	10 11	10 43	11 16	11 50	12 24
22 38 39	9 24	9 55	10 26	10 57	11 29	12 2	12 35	13 9
22 42 24	10 11	10 41	11 12	11 43	12 14	12 47	13 19	13 53
22 46 8	10 57	11 27	11 57	12 28	12 59	13 31	14 4	14 37
22 49 53	11 43	12 13	12 43	13 13	13 13	14 15	14 47	15 20
22 53 36	12 29	12 58	13 28	13 58	14 28	14 59	15 31	16 3
22 57 20	13 14	13 43	14 12	14 42	15 12	15 43	16 14	16 46
23 1 3	13 59	14 27	14 56	15 26	15 56	16 26	16 57	17 28
23 4 45	14 44	15 12	15 40	16 9	16 39	17 9	17 39	18 10
23 8 28	15 28	15 56	16 24	16 53	17 22	17 51	18 22	18 52
23 12 10	16 12	16 39	17 7	17 36	18 4	18 34	19 4	19 34
23 15 52	16 55	17 23	17 50	18 18	18 47	19 16	19 45	20 15
23 19 33	17 39	18 6	18 33	19 1	19 29	19 58	20 27	20 56
23 23 15	18 22	18 49	19 16	19 43	20 11	20 39	21 8	21 37
23 26 56	19 5	19 31	19 58	20 25	20 53	21 21	21 49	22 18
23 30 37	19 48	20 14	20 40	21 7	21 34	22 2	22 30	22 59
23 34 18	20 30	20 56	21 22	21 48	22 15	22 43	23 11	23 39
23 37 58	21 12	21 38	22 4	22 30	22 56	23 23	23 51	24 19
23 41 39	21 54	22 20	22 45	23 11	23 37	24 4	24 31	24 59
23 45 19	22 36	23 1	23 26	23 52	24 18	24 45	25 11	25 39
23 48 59	23 18	23 43	24 8	24 33	24 59	25 25	25 51	26 18
23 52 40	24 0	24 24	24 49	25 14	25 39	26 5	26 31	26 58
23 56 20	24 41	25 5	25 30	25 54	26 19	26 45	27 11	27 37
24 0 0	25 22	25 46	26 10	26 35	27 0	27 25	27 50	28 16

Sidereal Time.	54°		54° 30′		55°		55° 30′		56°		56° 30′		57°		58°	
21 9 52	24♊23		25♊10		25♊58		26♊48		27♊39		28♊32		29♊25		1♋18	
21 13 52	25	22	26	9	26	56	27	45	28	36	29	27	0♋20		2	11
21 17 49	26	20	27	6	27	53	28	41	29	31	0♋22		1	14	3	3
21 21 46	27	17	28	3	28	49	29	37	0♋26		1	16	2	7	3	54
21 25 43	28	13	28	58	29	44	0♋31		1	19	2	8	2	59	4	44
21 29 39	29	8	29	53	0♋38		1	24	2	12	3	0	3	50	5	34
21 33 34	0♋3		0♋46		1	31	2	17	3	4	3	52	4	41	6	23
21 37 28	0	56	1	39	2	23	3	8	3	55	4	42	5	30	7	11
21 41 22	1	49	2	31	3	15	3	59	4	45	5	31	6	19	7	58
21 45 16	2	41	3	23	4	5	4	49	5	34	6	20	7	7	8	45
21 49 8	3	32	4	13	4	55	5	39	6	23	7	8	7	55	9	31
21 53 0	4	22	5	3	5	45	6	28	7	11	7	56	8	42	10	16
21 56 52	5	12	5	52	6	34	7	16	7	59	8	43	9	28	11	1
22 0 42	6	1	6	41	7	22	8	13	8	46	9	29	10	14	11	46
22 4 32	6	50	7	29	8	9	8	50	9	32	10	15	10	59	12	29
22 8 22	7	38	8	16	8	56	9	37	10	18	11	0	11	43	13	13
22 12 11	8	25	9	3	9	42	10	22	11	3	11	45	12	28	13	56
22 15 59	9	12	9	50	10	28	11	8	11	48	12	29	13	11	14	38
22 19 47	9	58	10	36	11	14	11	53	12	32	13	13	13	54	15	20
22 23 35	10	44	11	21	11	59	12	37	13	16	13	56	14	37	16	1
22 27 21	11	29	12	6	12	43	13	21	14	0	14	39	15	20	16	43
22 31 8	12	14	12	50	13	27	14	5	14	43	15	22	16	1	17	23
22 34 54	12	59	13	34	14	11	14	48	15	25	16	4	16	43	18	4
22 38 39	13	43	14	18	14	54	15	30	16	8	16	56	17	24	18	44
22 42 24	14	27	15	2	15	37	16	13	16	50	17	27	18	5	19	24
22 46 8	15	10	15	44	16	19	16	55	17	31	18	8	18	46	20	3
22 49 53	15	53	16	27	17	2	17	37	18	12	18	49	19	26	20	43
22 53 36	16	36	17	9	17	43	18	18	18	53	19	29	20	6	21	22
22 57 20	17	18	17	51	18	25	18	59	19	34	20	10	20	46	22	0
23 1 3	18	0	18	33	19	6	19	30	20	14	20	49	21	25	22	39
23 4 45	18	42	19	14	19	47	20	21	20	55	21	29	22	4	23	17
23 8 28	19	24	19	55	20	28	21	1	21	34	22	9	22	43	23	55
23 12 10	20	5	20	36	21	8	21	41	22	14	22	48	23	22	24	33
23 15 52	20	46	21	17	21	48	22	21	22	53	23	27	24	1	25	10
23 19 33	21	27	22	7	22	28	23	0	23	33	24	5	24	39	25	48
23 23 15	22	7	22	37	23	8	23	40	24	12	24	44	25	17	26	25
23 26 56	22	47	23	17	23	48	24	19	24	50	25	22	25	55	27	2
23 30 37	23	28	23	57	24	27	24	58	25	29	26	1	26	33	27	39
23 34 18	24	8	24	37	25	6	25	37	26	7	26	39	27	10	28	16
23 37 58	24	47	25	16	25	45	26	15	26	46	27	16	27	48	28	52
23 41 39	25	27	25	55	26	24	26	54	27	24	27	54	28	25	29	39
23 45 19	26	6	26	34	27	3	27	32	28	2	28	32	29	2	0♌5	
23 48 59	26	46	27	13	27	42	28	10	28	40	29	9	29	39	0	41
23 52 40	27	25	27	52	28	20	28	48	29	17	29	47	0♌16		1	17
23 56 20	28	4	28	31	28	58	29	26	29	55	0♌24		0	53	1	53
24 0 0	28	43	29	9	29	37	0♌4		0♌33		1	1	1	30	2	29

Better books make better astrologers.
Here are some of our other titles:

AstroAmerica's Daily Ephemeris, 2000-2010
AstroAmerica's Daily Ephemeris, 2010-2020
AstroAmerica's Daily Ephemeris, 2000-2020
   - *all for Midnight. Compiled & formatted by David R. Roell*

Al Biruni
The Book of Instructions in the Elements of the Art of
   Astrology, *1029 AD, translated by R. Ramsay Wright*

Derek Appleby
Horary Astrology: The Art of Astrological Divination

C.E.O. Carter
An Encyclopaedia of Psychological Astrology

Charubel & Sepharial
Degrees of the Zodiac Symbolized, *1898*

H.L. Cornell, M.D.
Encyclopaedia of Medical Astrology
   958 pages, hardcover, the ultimate astro-medical reference

Nicholas Culpeper
Astrological Judgement of Diseases from the Decumbiture
   of the Sick, *1655, and,* **Urinalia**, *1658*

Dorotheus of Sidon
Carmen Astrologicum, *c. 50 AD, translated by David Pingree*

Nicholas deVore
Encyclopedia of Astrology

Firmicus Maternus
Ancient Astrology Theory & Practice: Matheseos Libri VIII,
c. 350 AD, translated by Jean Rhys Bram

William Lilly
Christian Astrology, books 1 & 2, *1647*
   The Introduction to Astrology, Resolution of all manner of questions
Christian Astrology, book 3, *1647*
   Easie and plaine method teaching how to judge upon nativities

Alan Leo
The Progressed Horoscope, *1905*

Claudius Ptolemy
Tetrabiblos, *c. 140 AD, translated by J.M. Ashmand*
  The great book, in the classic translation.

Vivian Robson
Astrology and Sex
Electional Astrology
Fixed Stars & Constellations in Astrology

Richard Saunders
The Astrological Judgement and Practice of Physick, *1677*
  By the Richard who inspired Ben Franklin's famous Almanac

Sepharial
Primary Directions, a definitive study
  A complete, detailed guide

Sepharial On Money. *For the first time in one volume, complete texts:*
  • **Law of Values**
  • **Silver Key**
  • **Arcana, or Stock and Share Key**

James Wilson, Esq.
Dictionary of Astrology
  From 1820. Quirky, opinionated, a fascinating read

H.S. Green, Raphael & C.E.O. Carter
Mundane Astrology: *3 Books*
  Comprehensive guide to the mundane

If not available from your local bookseller, order directly from:
The Astrology Center of America
207 Victory Lane
Bel Air, MD 21014

on the web at:
http://www.astroamerica.com

CPSIA information can be obtained at www.ICGtesting.com
Printed in the USA
LVOW06s1821220913

353570LV00001B/258/A

9 781933 303246